All Quiet in Vikaspuri

Sarnath Banerjee is the author of the graphic novels *Corridor*, *The Barn Owl's Wondrous Capers* and *The Harappa Files*. He currently runs an advertising agency that campaigns for out-of-fashion political ideas, outdated celebrities and out-of-favour social trends.

All
QUIET in
SARNATH
BANERJEE
VIKASPURI

HarperCollins *Publishers* India

First published in hardback in India in 2015 by
HarperCollins *Publishers* India

Copyright © Sarnath Banerjee 2015

P-ISBN: 978-93-5177-574-4
E-ISBN: 978-93-5177-575-1

2 4 6 8 10 9 7 5 3 1

Sarnath Banerjee asserts the moral right to be identified
as the author of this work.

HarperCollins *Publishers*
A-75, Sector 57, Noida, Uttar Pradesh 201301, India
1 London Bridge Street, London, SE1 9GF, United Kingdom
Hazelton Lanes, 55 Avenue Road, Suite 2900, Toronto, Ontario M5R 3L2
and 1995 Markham Road, Scarborough, Ontario M1B 5M8, Canada
25 Ryde Road, Pymble, Sydney, NSW 2073, Australia
195 Broadway, New York, NY 10007, USA

Typeset in Garamond, Regular, 12 pt. & Sarnath TT, Regular, 12 pt.

Printed and bound at
Replika Press Pvt. Ltd.

For
Mir Ali Banerjee

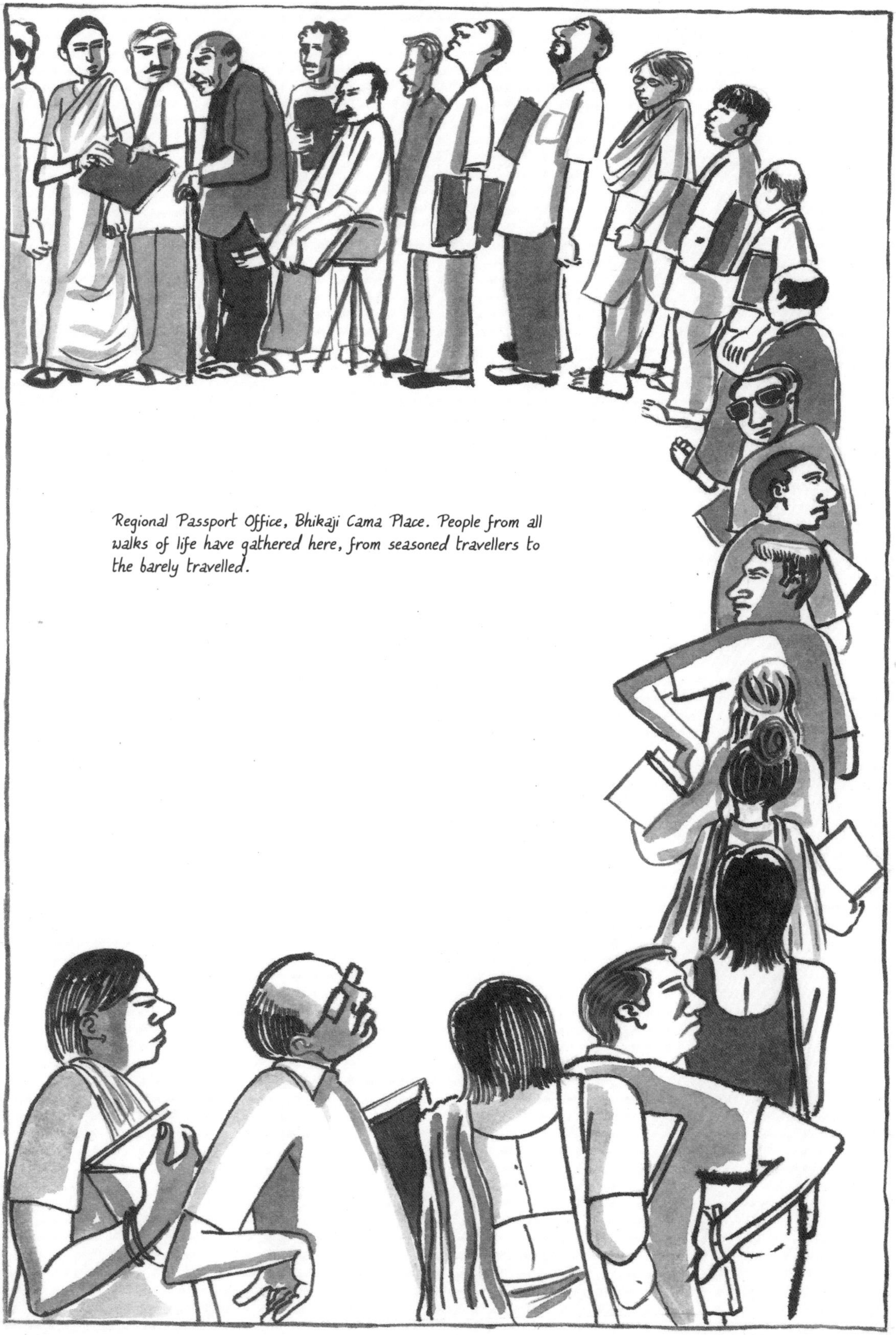
Regional Passport Office, Bhikaji Cama Place. People from all walks of life have gathered here, from seasoned travellers to the barely travelled.

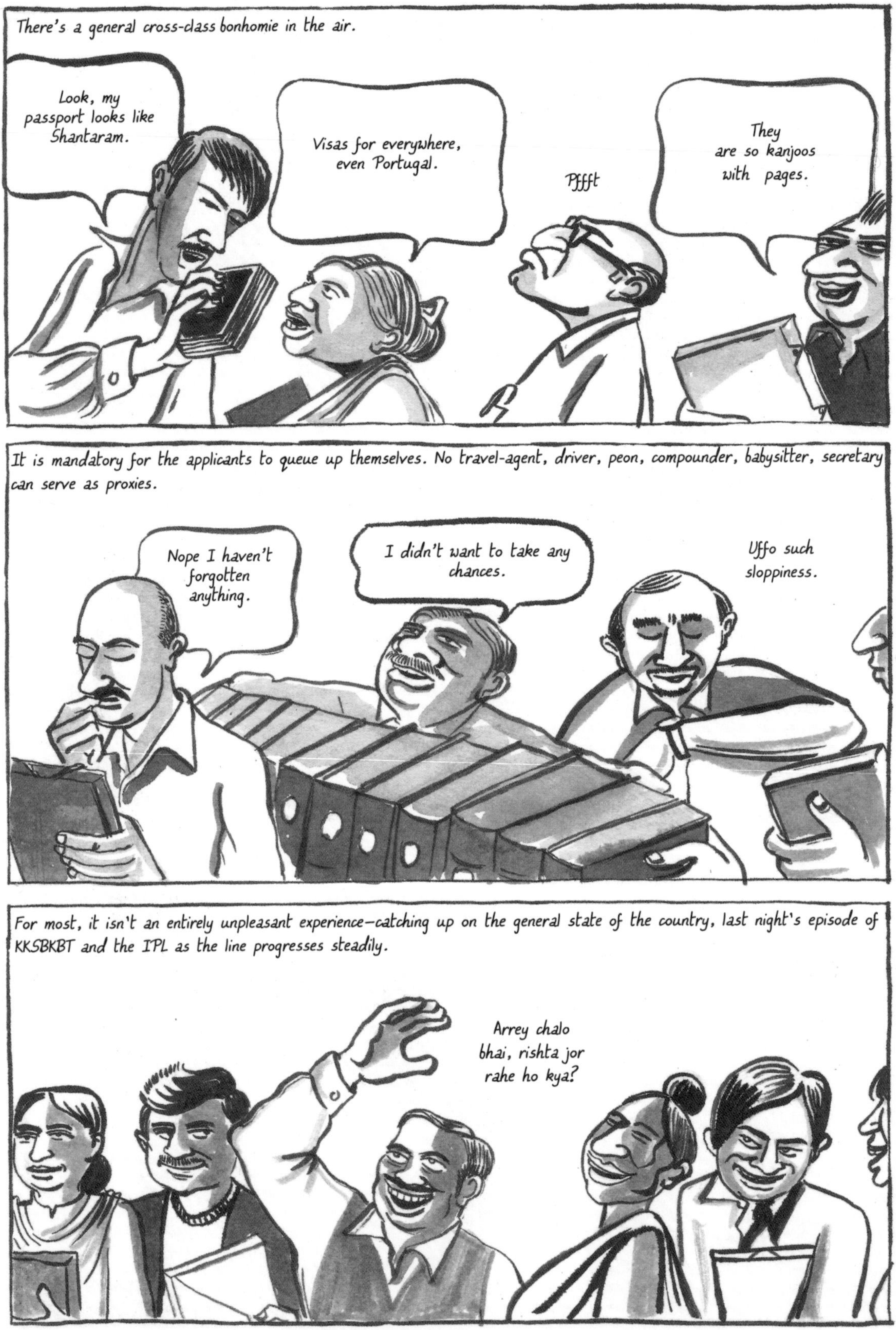
There's a general cross-class bonhomie in the air.
Look, my passport looks like Shantaram.
Visas for everywhere, even Portugal.
Pffft
They are so kanjoos with pages.
It is mandatory for the applicants to queue up themselves. No travel-agent, driver, peon, compounder, babysitter, secretary can serve as proxies.
Nope I haven't forgotten anything.
I didn't want to take any chances.
Uffo such sloppiness.
For most, it isn't an entirely unpleasant experience—catching up on the general state of the country, last night's episode of KKSBKBT and the IPL as the line progresses steadily.
Arrey chalo bhai, rishta jor rahe ho kya?

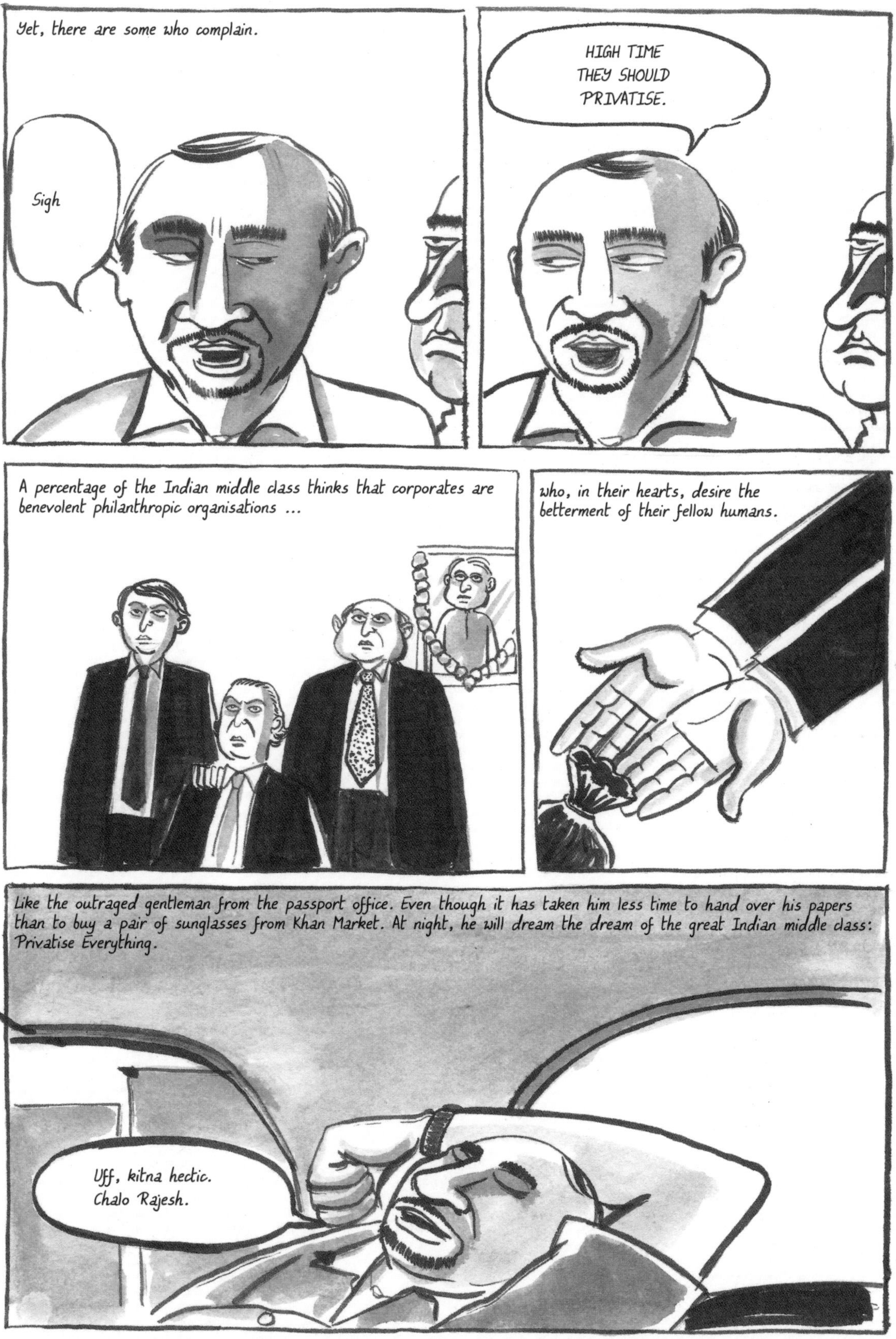
Yet, there are some who complain.
Sigh
HIGH TIME THEY SHOULD PRIVATISE.
A percentage of the Indian middle class thinks that corporates are benevolent philanthropic organisations ...
who, in their hearts, desire the betterment of their fellow humans.
Like the outraged gentleman from the passport office. Even though it has taken him less time to hand over his papers than to buy a pair of sunglasses from Khan Market. At night, he will dream the dream of the great Indian middle class: Privatise Everything.
Uff, kitna hectic. Chalo Rajesh.

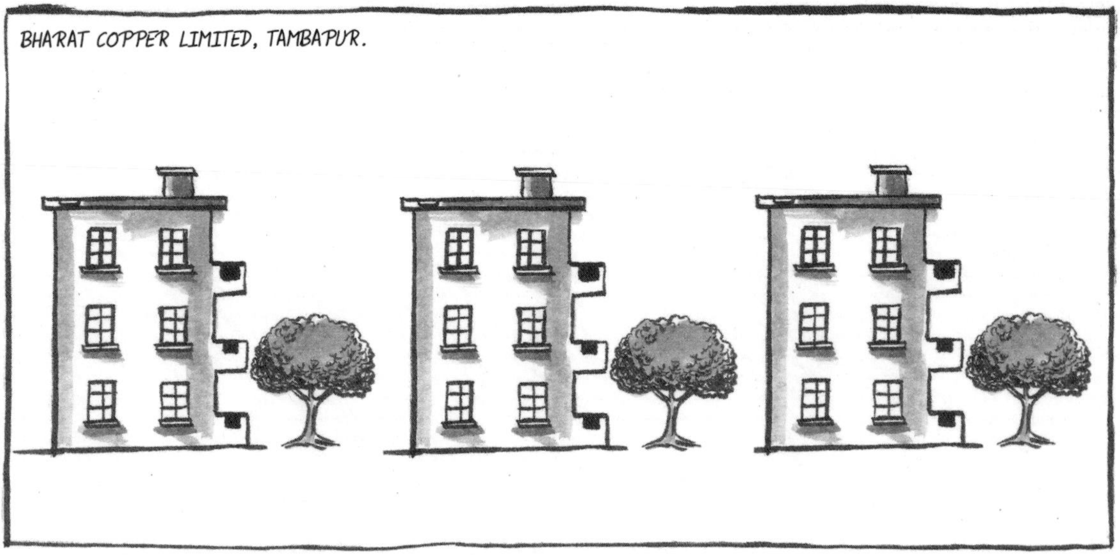
BHARAT COPPER LIMITED, TAMBAPUR.

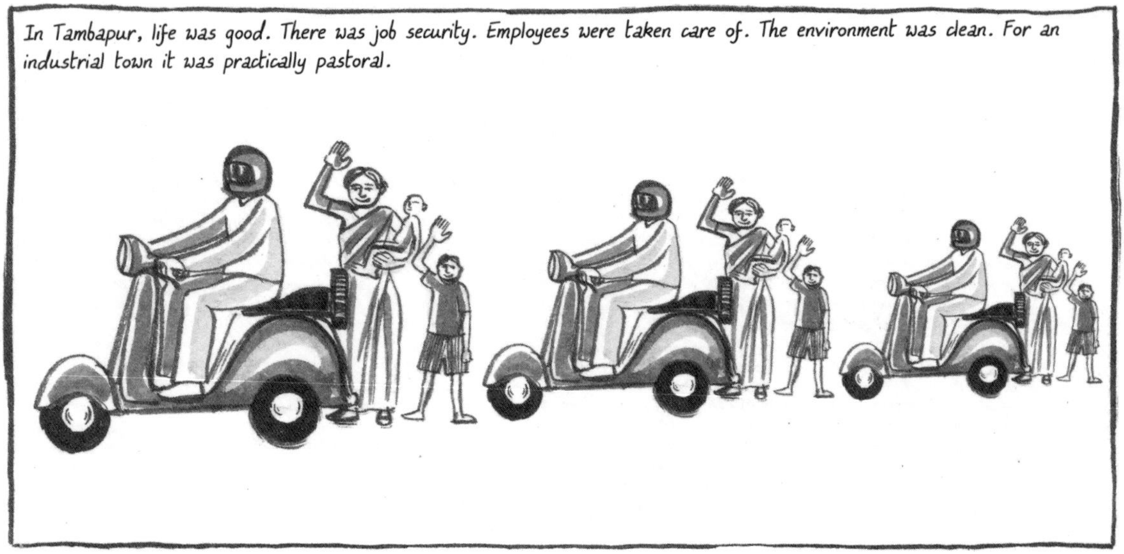
In Tambapur, life was good. There was job security. Employees were taken care of. The environment was clean. For an industrial town it was practically pastoral.

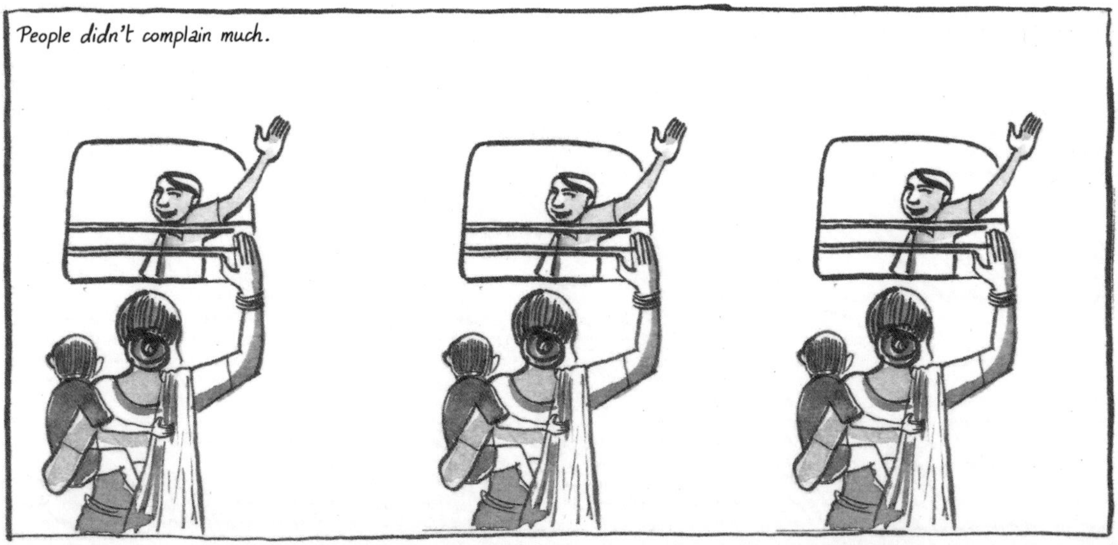
People didn't complain much.

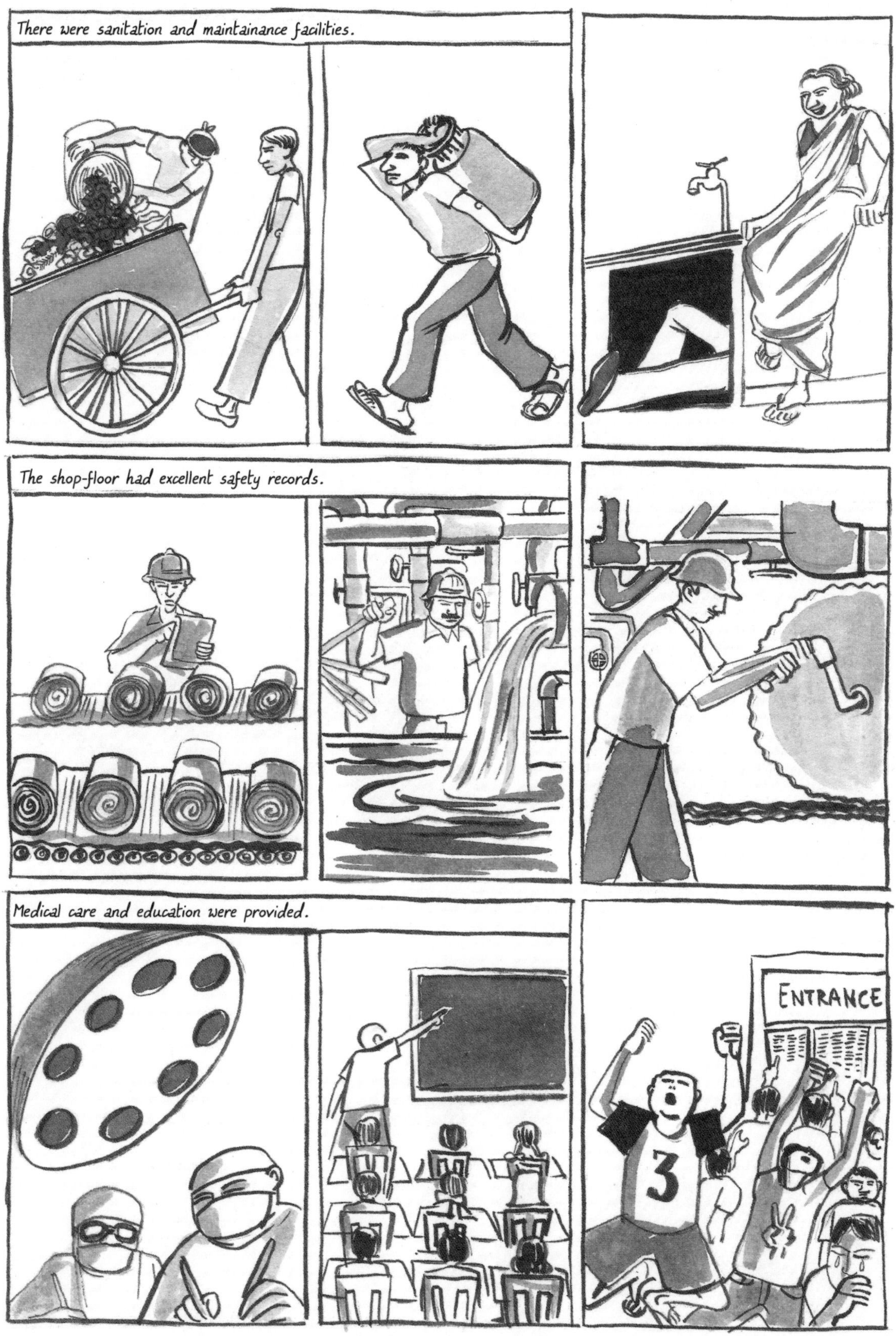
There were sanitation and maintainance facilities.
The shop-floor had excellent safety records.
Medical care and education were provided.
ENTRANCE
3

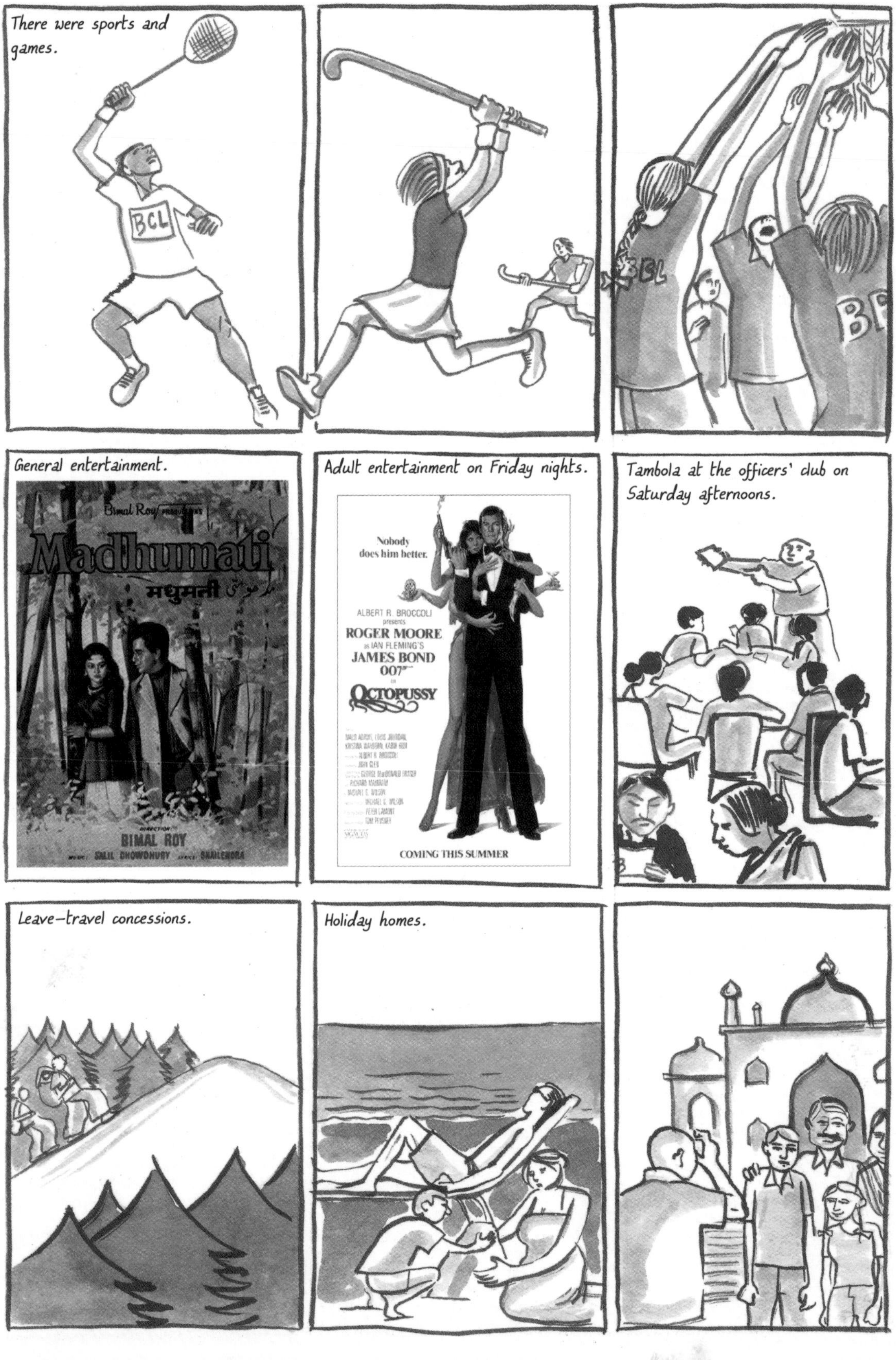
There were sports and games.
BCL
General entertainment.
Bimal Roy productions
Madhumati
मधुमती
BIMAL ROY
SALIL CHOWDHURY
SHAILENDRA
Adult entertainment on Friday nights.
Nobody does him better.
ALBERT R. BROCCOLI presents
ROGER MOORE
as IAN FLEMING'S
JAMES BOND 007
OCTOPUSSY
COMING THIS SUMMER
Tambola at the officers' club on Saturday afternoons.
Leave-travel concessions.
Holiday homes.

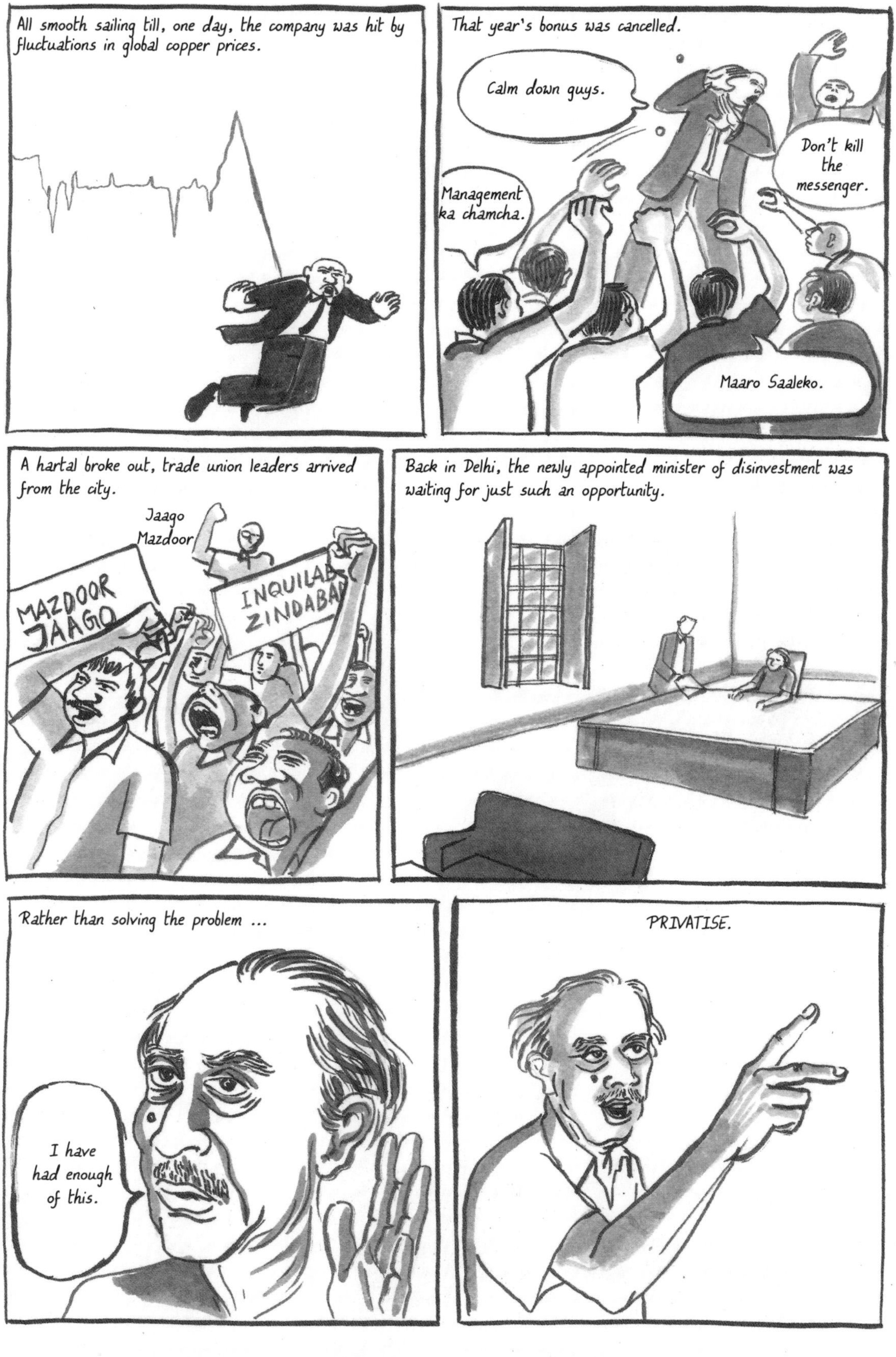
All smooth sailing till, one day, the company was hit by fluctuations in global copper prices.
That year's bonus was cancelled.
Calm down guys.
Management ka chamcha.
Don't kill the messenger.
Maaro Saaleko.
A hartal broke out, trade union leaders arrived from the city.
Jaago Mazdoor
MAZDOOR JAAGO
INQUILAB ZINDABA
Back in Delhi, the newly appointed minister of disinvestment was waiting for just such an opportunity.
Rather than solving the problem ...
I have had enough of this.
PRIVATISE.

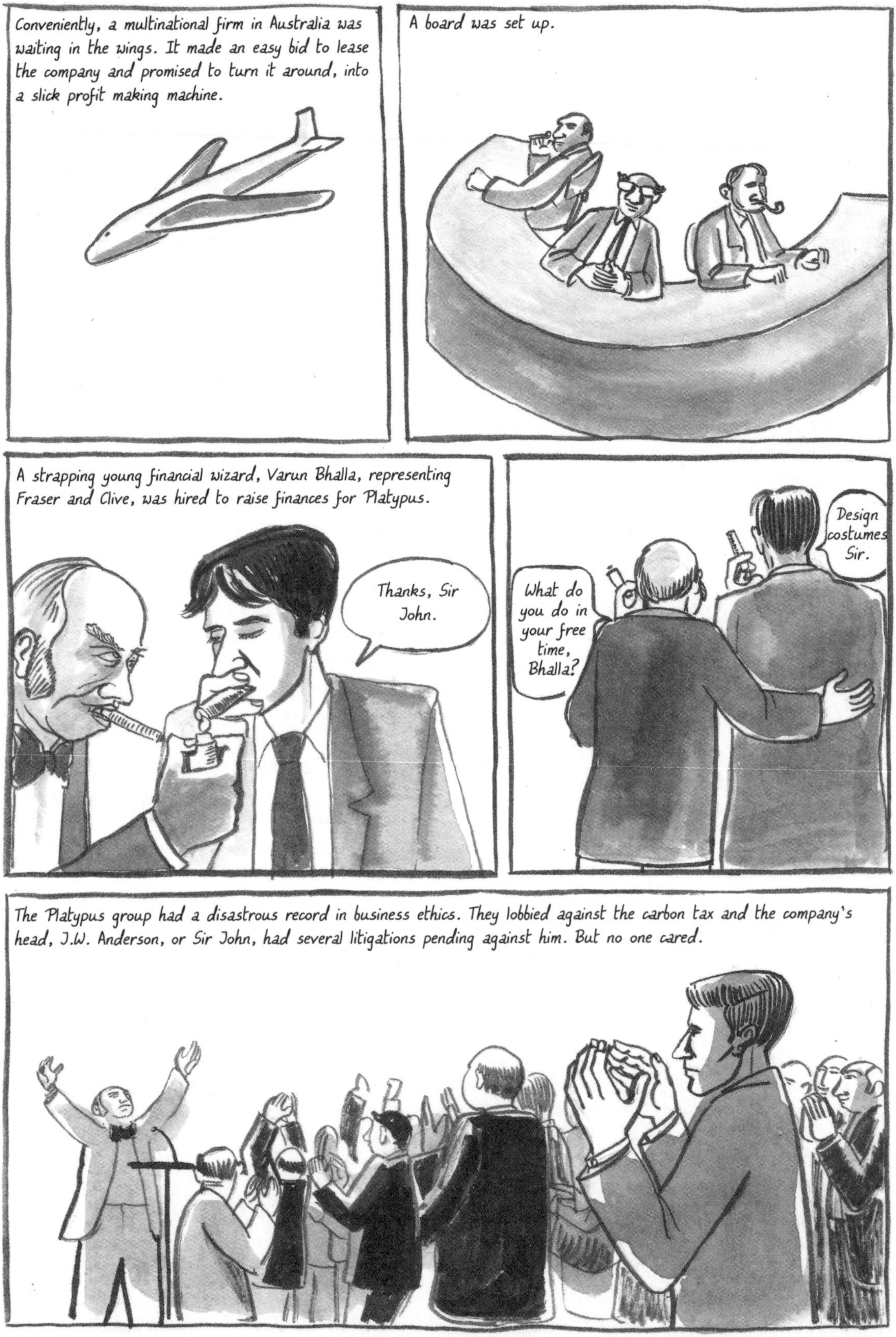
Conveniently, a multinational firm in Australia was waiting in the wings. It made an easy bid to lease the company and promised to turn it around, into a slick profit making machine.
A board was set up.
A strapping young financial wizard, Varun Bhalla, representing Fraser and Clive, was hired to raise finances for Platypus.
Thanks, Sir John.
What do you do in your free time, Bhalla?
Design costumes Sir.
The Platypus group had a disastrous record in business ethics. They lobbied against the carbon tax and the company's head, J.W. Anderson, or Sir John, had several litigations pending against him. But no one cared.

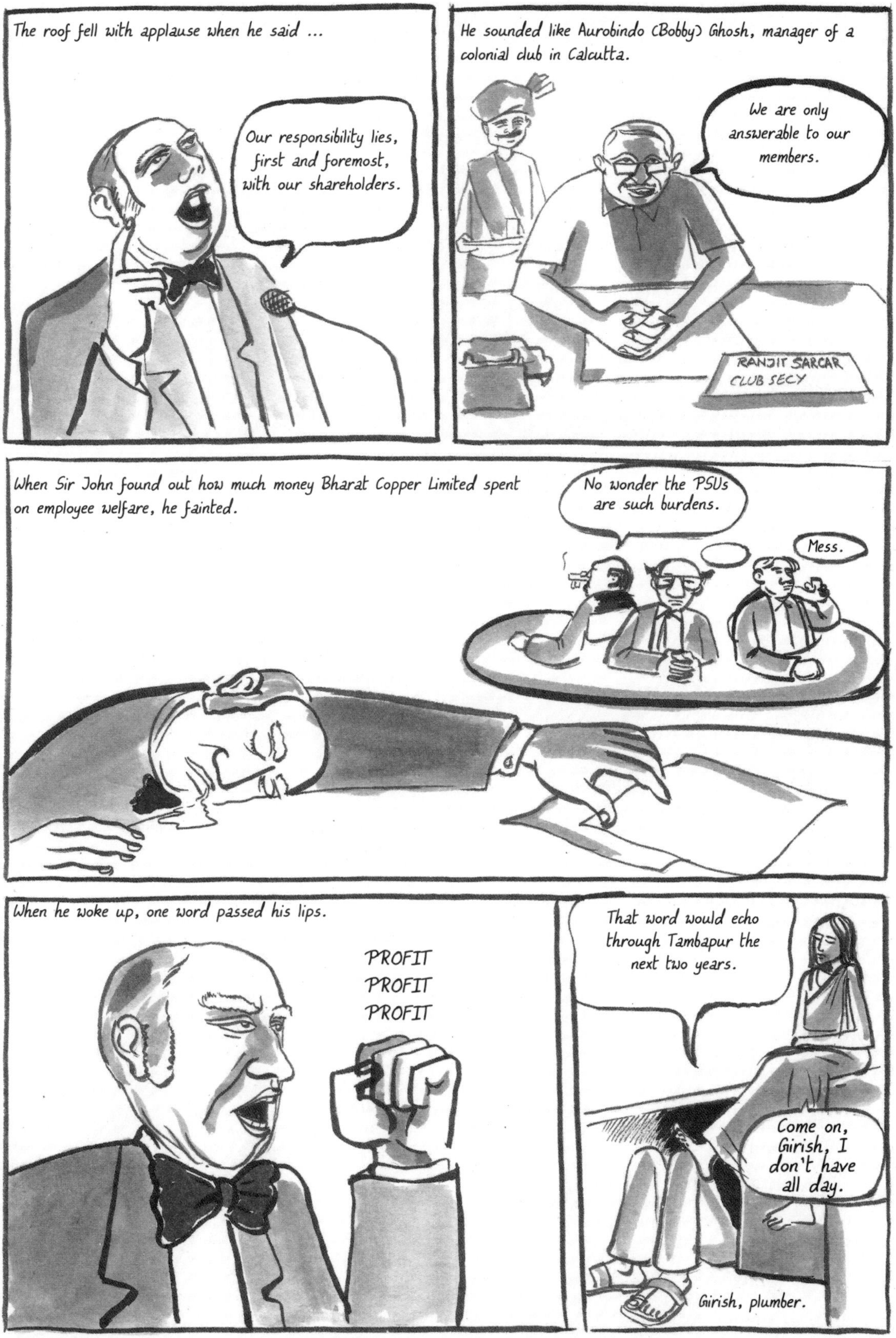

The roof fell with applause when he said ...
Our responsibility lies, first and foremost, with our shareholders.
He sounded like Aurobindo (Bobby) Ghosh, manager of a colonial club in Calcutta.
We are only answerable to our members.
RANJIT SARCAR CLUB SECY
When Sir John found out how much money Bharat Copper Limited spent on employee welfare, he fainted.
No wonder the PSUs are such burdens.
Mess.
When he woke up, one word passed his lips.
PROFIT
PROFIT
PROFIT
That word would echo through Tambapur the next two years.
Come on, Girish, I don't have all day.
Girish, plumber.

Then began the disintegration of the township.

Salaries were halved.

Schools were closed for lack of teachers.

Industrial accidents became common. The hospital became overcrowded and unusable. A local newspaper called it 'a festering cesspit of the vilest germs'.

10

The water filtration plant was abandoned.

The water had become toxic, leading to terrible diseases.

Mining is a thirsty business. The water table fell drastically,
slimy ponds emerged everywhere.

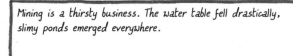

In desperation, the workers rose in protest even though
strikes were forbidden. No trade unionists came from
the city, neither did angels from the sky.

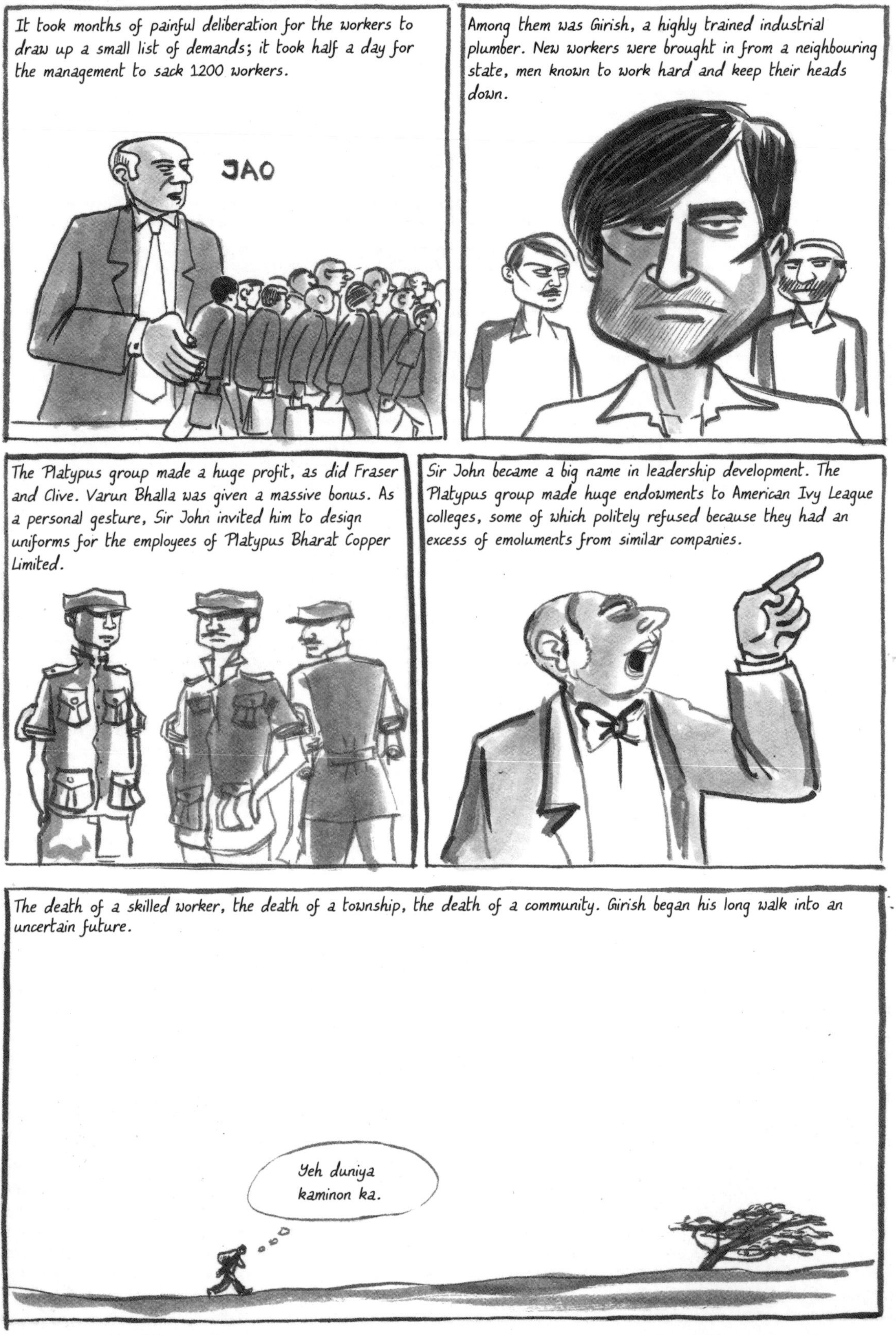
It took months of painful deliberation for the workers to draw up a small list of demands; it took half a day for the management to sack 1200 workers.
JAO
Among them was Girish, a highly trained industrial plumber. New workers were brought in from a neighbouring state, men known to work hard and keep their heads down.
The Platypus group made a huge profit, as did Fraser and Clive. Varun Bhalla was given a massive bonus. As a personal gesture, Sir John invited him to design uniforms for the employees of Platypus Bharat Copper Limited.
Sir John became a big name in leadership development. The Platypus group made huge endowments to American Ivy League colleges, some of which politely refused because they had an excess of emoluments from similar companies.
The death of a skilled worker, the death of a township, the death of a community. Girish began his long walk into an uncertain future.
Yeh duniya kaminon ka.

THE WATER WARS OF DELHI

BRRRRR
SSSSSSSSSSSSSsss
grrrrrrrrrrr
PPPFFFFFFTT
phisssssssshhhh

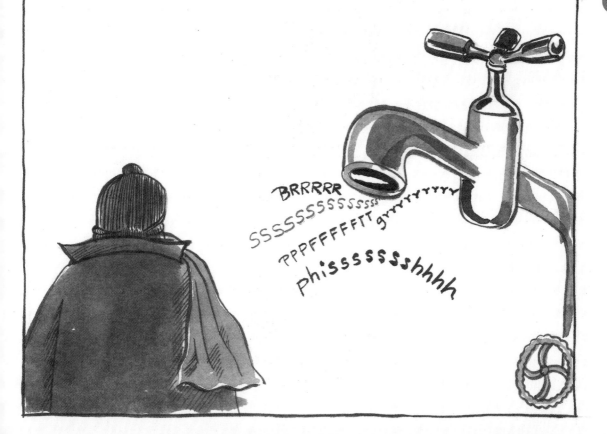

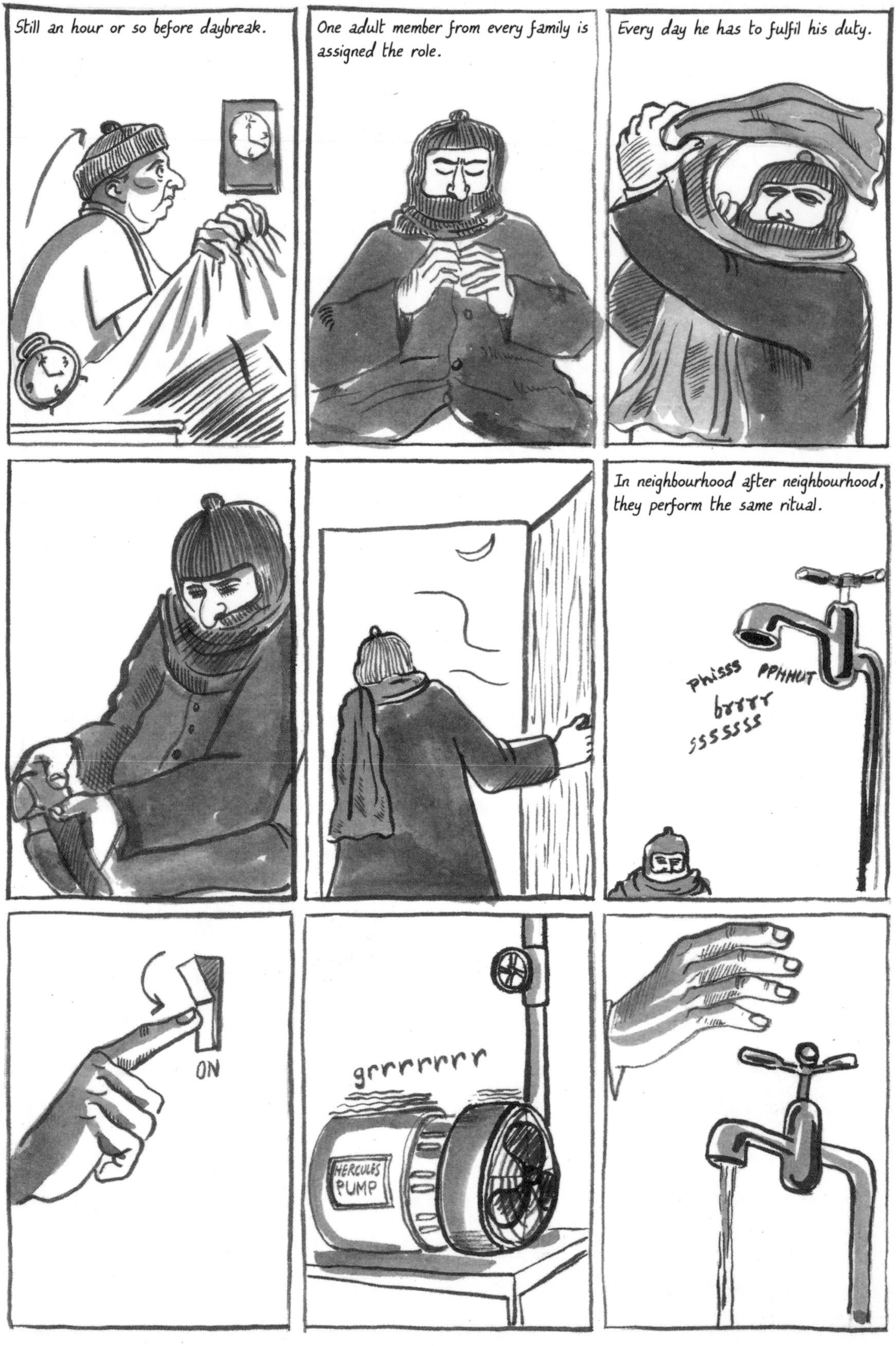
Still an hour or so before daybreak.
One adult member from every family is assigned the role.
Every day he has to fulfil his duty.
In neighbourhood after neighbourhood, they perform the same ritual.
PHISSS PPHHUT
brrrr
SSSSSSS
ON
grrrrrrr
HERCULES PUMP

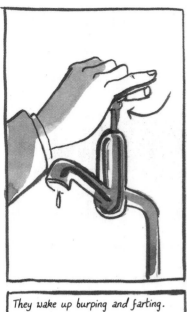

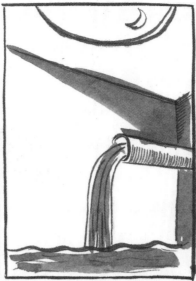

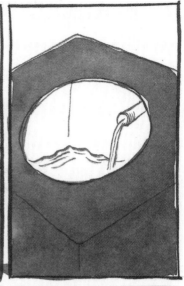

They wake up burping and farting.

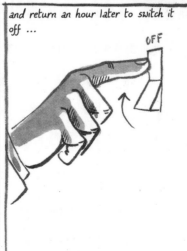

Muttering foul words in Punjabi.

They put on their overcoats and step out into the cold morning air.

15

With shivering hands they switch on the booster pump ...

and return an hour later to switch it off ...

OFF

Before returning to bed.

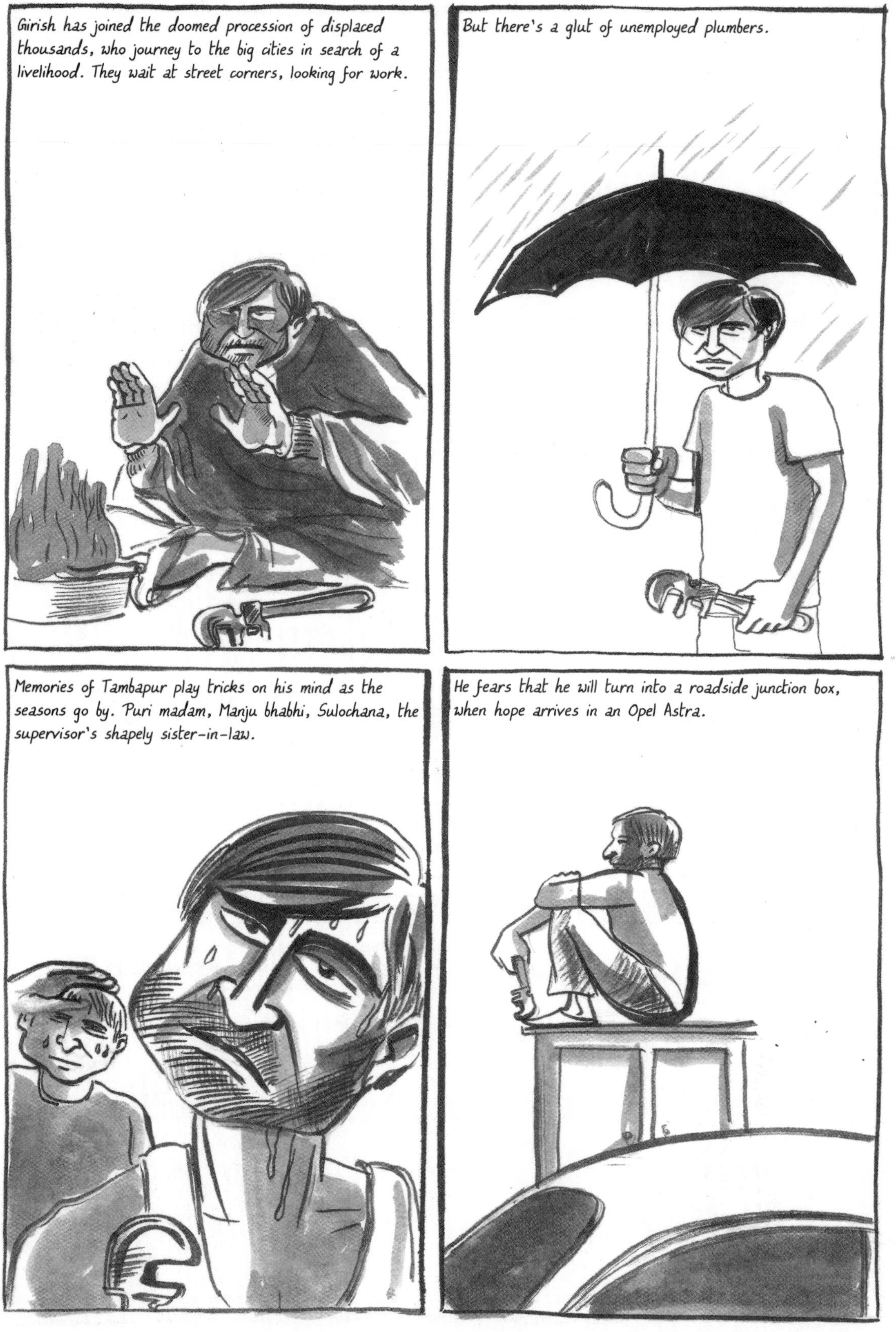
Girish has joined the doomed procession of displaced thousands, who journey to the big cities in search of a livelihood. They wait at street corners, looking for work.
But there's a glut of unemployed plumbers.
Memories of Tambapur play tricks on his mind as the seasons go by. Puri madam, Manju bhabhi, Sulochana, the supervisor's shapely sister-in-law.
He fears that he will turn into a roadside junction box, when hope arrives in an Opel Astra.

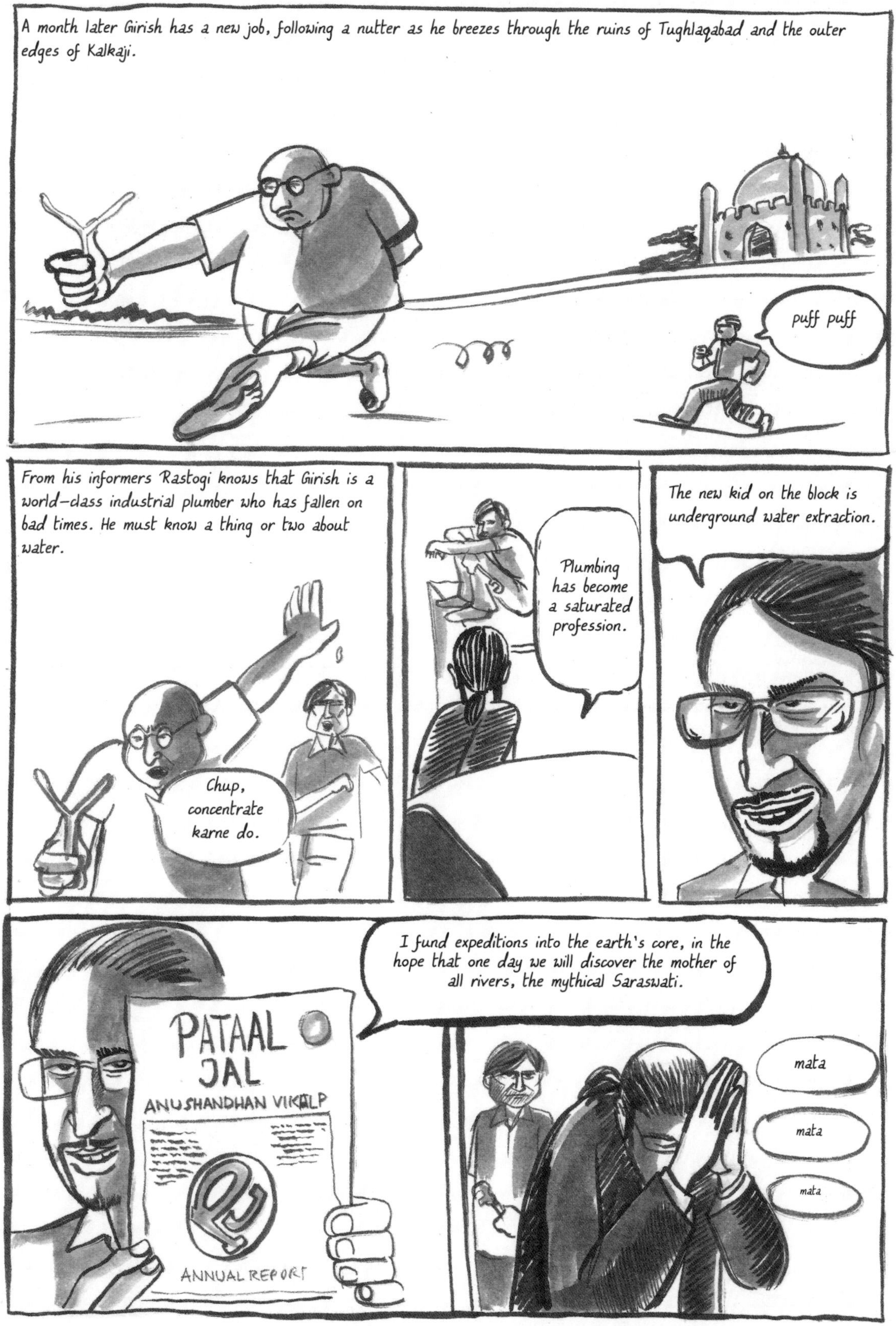
A month later Girish has a new job, following a nutter as he breezes through the ruins of Tughlaqabad and the outer edges of Kalkaji.
puff puff
From his informers Rastogi knows that Girish is a world-class industrial plumber who has fallen on bad times. He must know a thing or two about water.
Chup, concentrate karne do.
Plumbing has become a saturated profession.
The new kid on the block is underground water extraction.
I fund expeditions into the earth's core, in the hope that one day we will discover the mother of all rivers, the mythical Saraswati.
PATAAL JAL
ANUSHANDHAN VIKALP
ANNUAL REPORT
mata
mata
mata

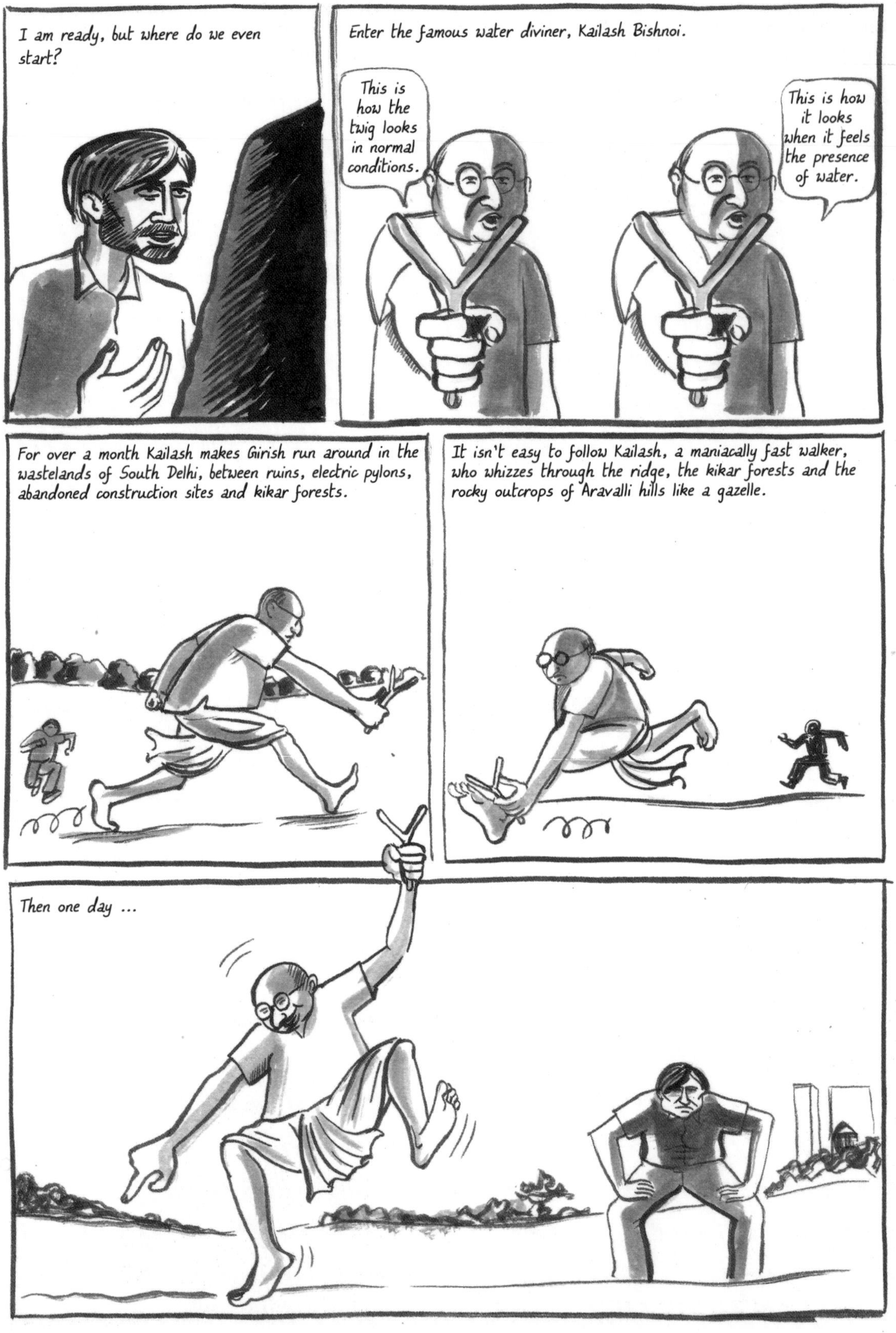
I am ready, but where do we even start?
Enter the famous water diviner, Kailash Bishnoi.
This is how the twig looks in normal conditions.
This is how it looks when it feels the presence of water.
For over a month Kailash makes Girish run around in the wastelands of South Delhi, between ruins, electric pylons, abandoned construction sites and kikar forests.
It isn't easy to follow Kailash, a maniacally fast walker, who whizzes through the ridge, the kikar forests and the rocky outcrops of Aravalli hills like a gazelle.
Then one day ...

With some scepticism, Girish starts drilling. He has been given the most advanced drilling machine that man has ever held.

The portable and light-weight GABOR—HKV22x.

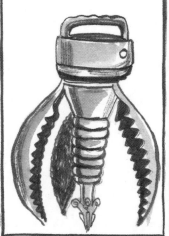

He takes great care in preparing for the journey.

Body and Mind.

With the patience and rigour of Arctic explorer Roald Amundsen.

Then, after putting together a year's ration of litti, jaggery and beedi, he sets out for the great voyage.

19

The first few days are hard. He can only drill for a few hours before coming up, gasping for air.

But with time he gets accustomed to the restricted workspace.

He even finds the depth and darkness comforting.

After dinner he smokes a beedi and goes to sleep.

He dreams of Tambapur and Sulochana, the supervisor's sister-in-law.

Night and day become one. Time becomes a river on which he swims, occasionally resting on the banks.

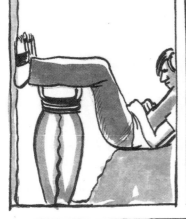

A worker by temperament, he finds comfort in labour. He enjoys this cycle of work and rest.

He digs not just vertically but horizontally as well. There is still no sign of water.

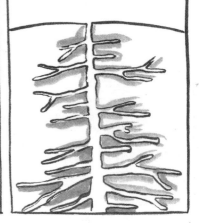

One night, while preparing to go to sleep, Girish hears music. 'Is this the first sign of madness?' he wonders.

He follows the sound. It comes from a rock. On closer inspection, it isn't a rock but the mouth of a hidden tunnel.

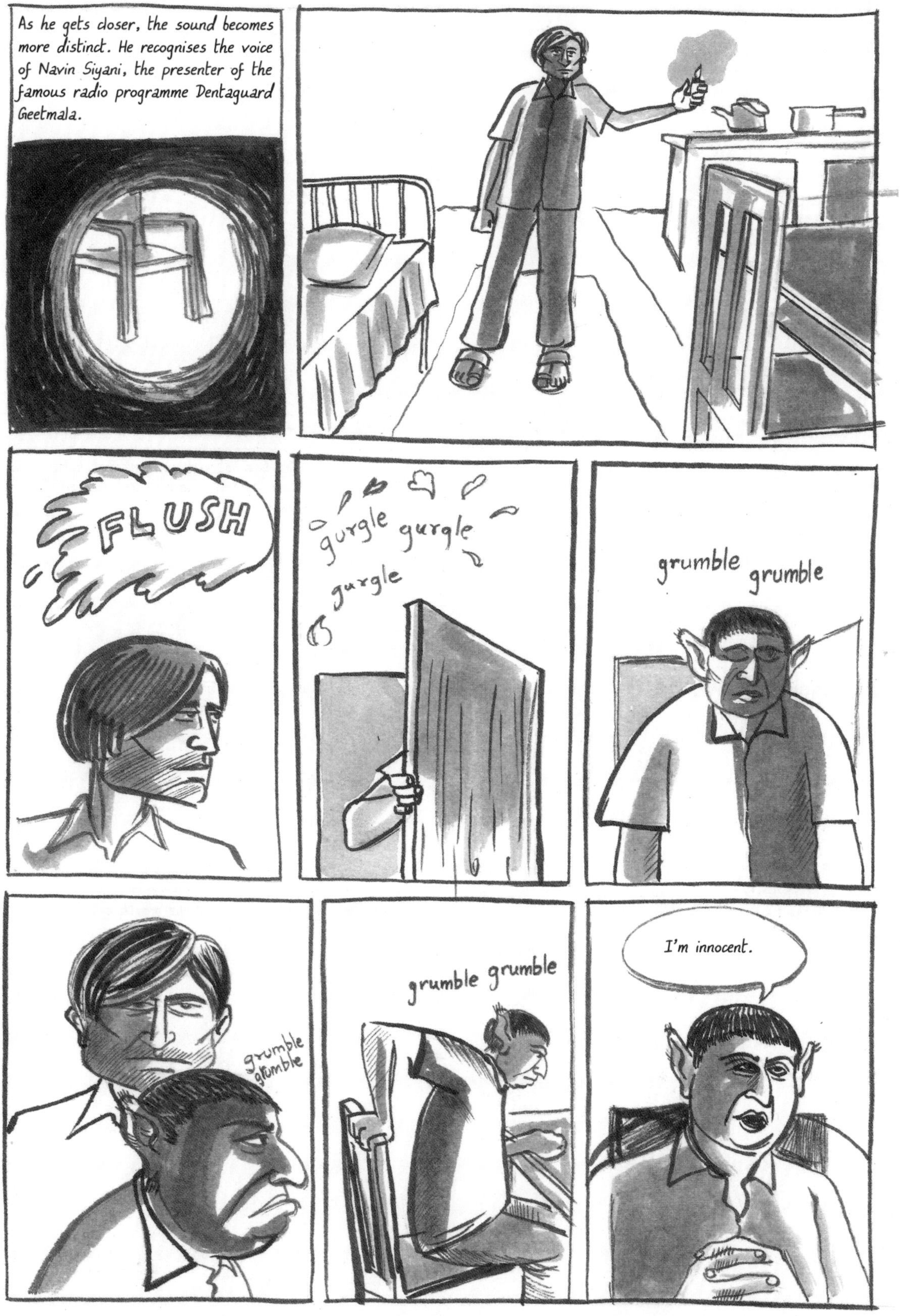
As he gets closer, the sound becomes more distinct. He recognises the voice of Navin Siyani, the presenter of the famous radio programme Dentaguard Geetmala.
FLUSH
gurgle gurgle
gurgle
grumble grumble
grumble grumble
grumble grumble
I'm innocent.

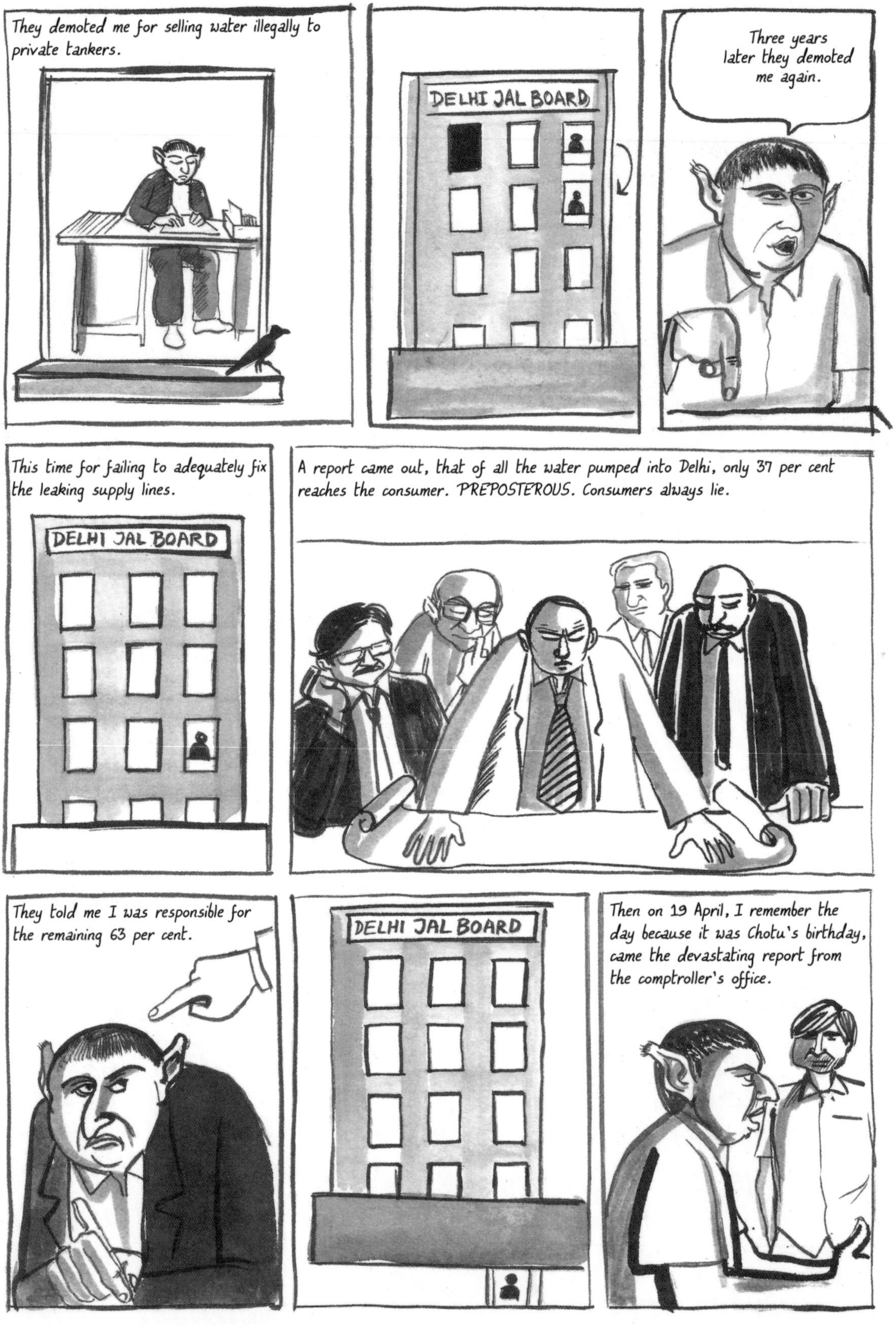
They demoted me for selling water illegally to private tankers.
DELHI JAL BOARD
Three years later they demoted me again.
This time for failing to adequately fix the leaking supply lines.
DELHI JAL BOARD
A report came out, that of all the water pumped into Delhi, only 37 per cent reaches the consumer. PREPOSTEROUS. Consumers always lie.
They told me I was responsible for the remaining 63 per cent.
DELHI JAL BOARD
Then on 19 April, I remember the day because it was Chotu's birthday, came the devastating report from the comptroller's office.

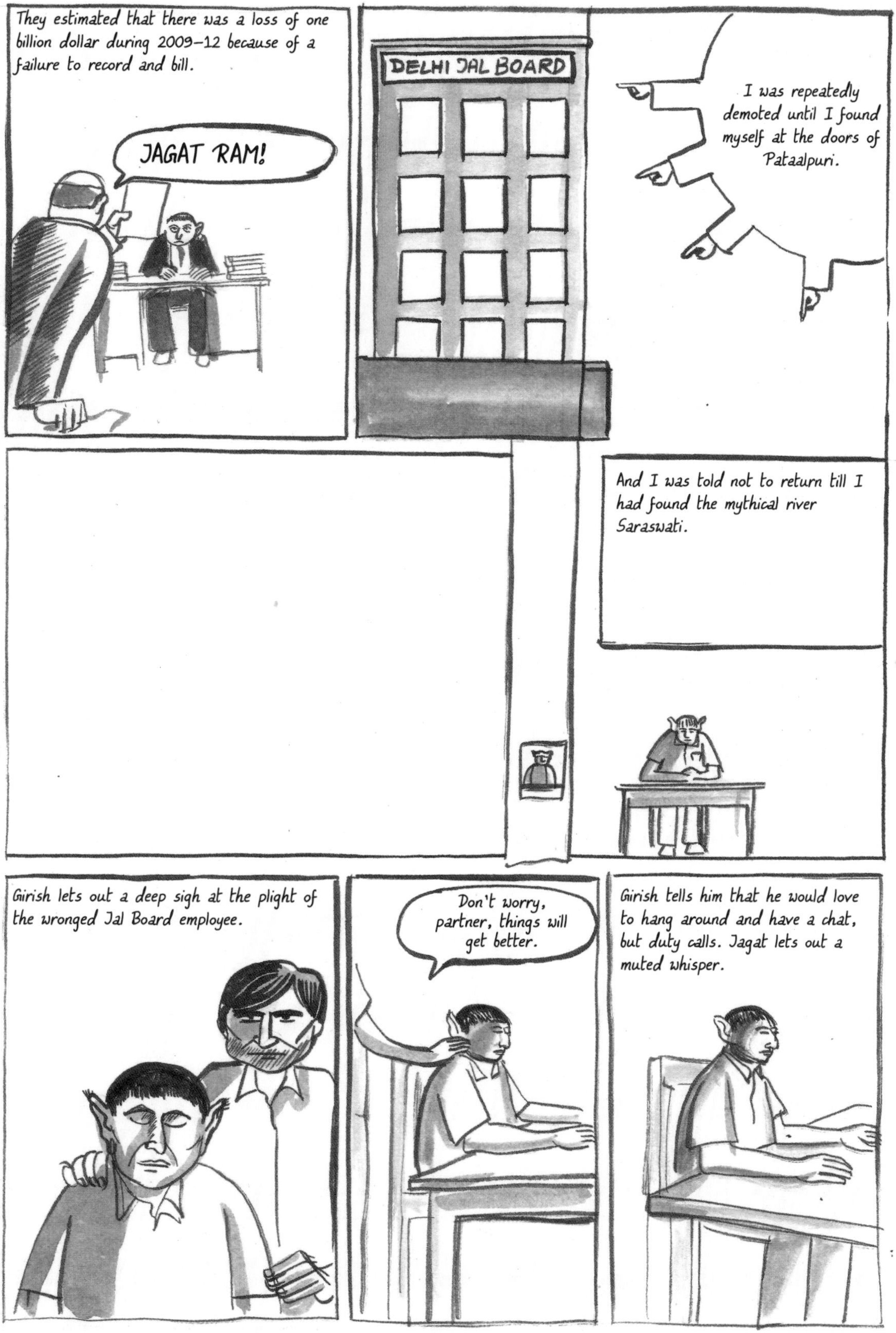

They estimated that there was a loss of one billion dollar during 2009–12 because of a failure to record and bill.
JAGAT RAM!
DELHI JAL BOARD
I was repeatedly demoted until I found myself at the doors of Pataalpuri.
And I was told not to return till I had found the mythical river Saraswati.
Girish lets out a deep sigh at the plight of the wronged Jal Board employee.
Don't worry, partner, things will get better.
Girish tells him that he would love to hang around and have a chat, but duty calls. Jagat lets out a muted whisper.

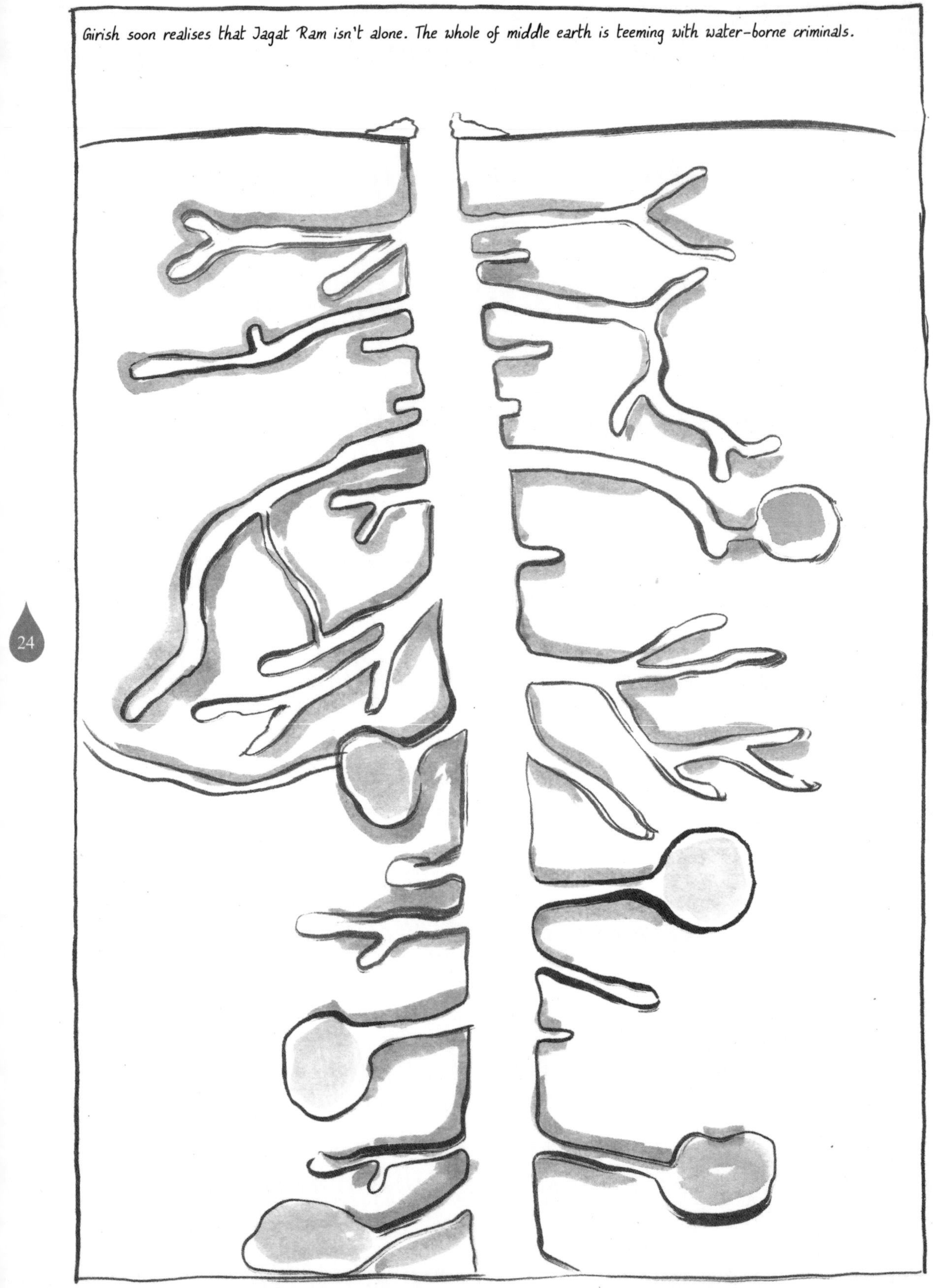
Girish soon realises that Jagat Ram isn't alone. The whole of middle earth is teeming with water-borne criminals.

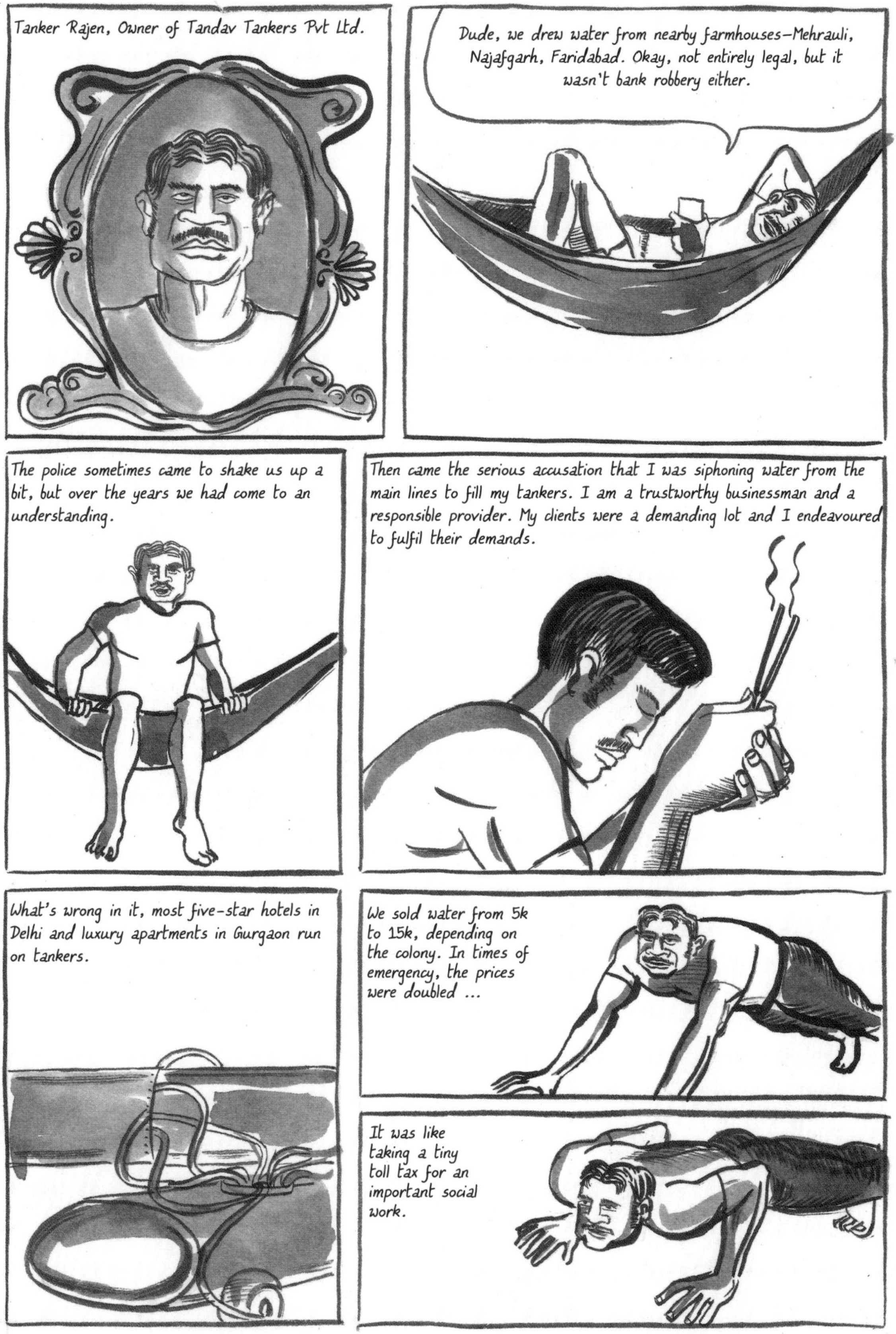
Tanker Rajen, Owner of Tandav Tankers Pvt Ltd.
Dude, we drew water from nearby farmhouses—Mehrauli, Najafgarh, Faridabad. Okay, not entirely legal, but it wasn't bank robbery either.
The police sometimes came to shake us up a bit, but over the years we had come to an understanding.
Then came the serious accusation that I was siphoning water from the main lines to fill my tankers. I am a trustworthy businessman and a responsible provider. My clients were a demanding lot and I endeavoured to fulfil their demands.
What's wrong in it, most five-star hotels in Delhi and luxury apartments in Gurgaon run on tankers.
We sold water from 5k to 15k, depending on the colony. In times of emergency, the prices were doubled ...
It was like taking a tiny toll tax for an important social work.

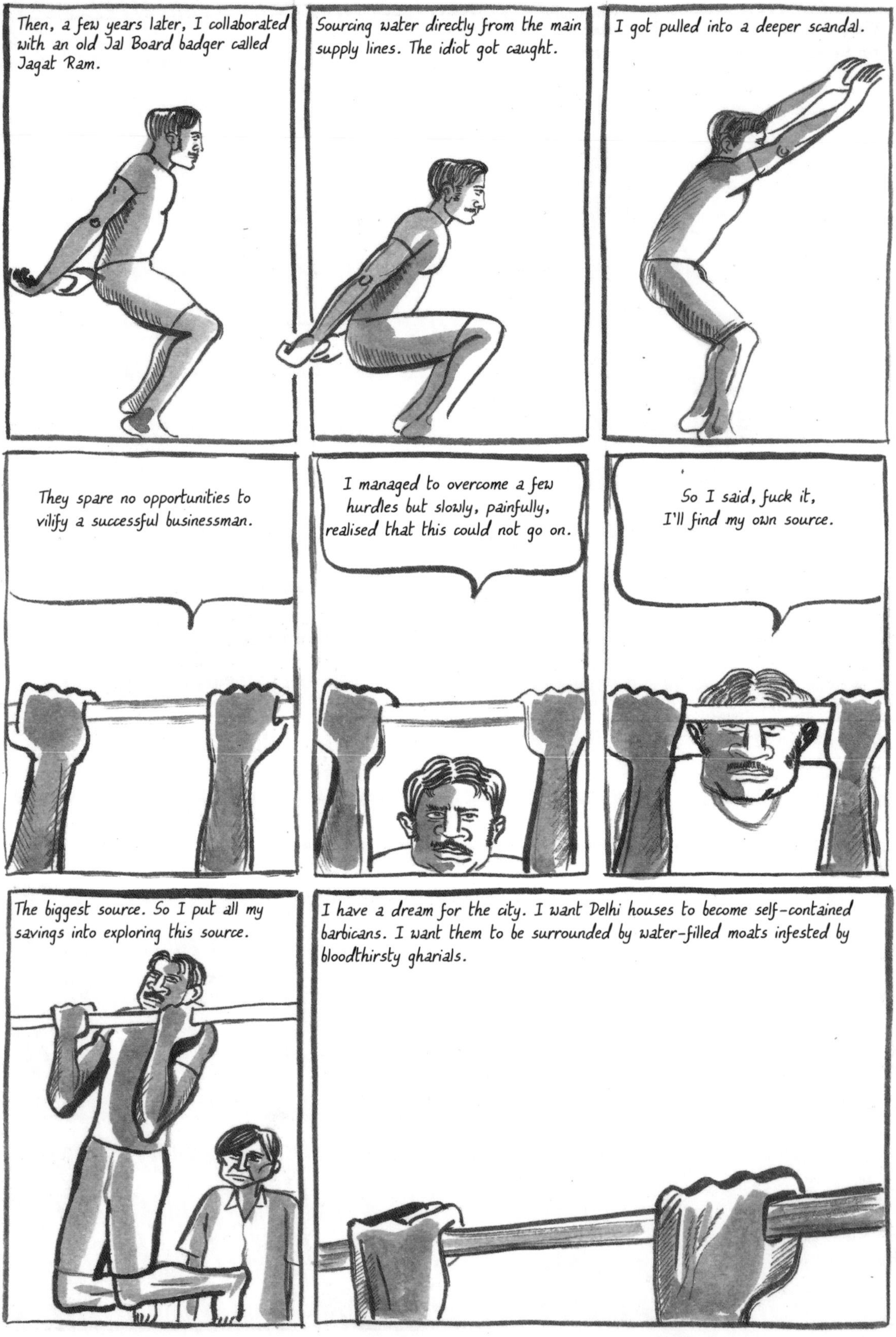
Then, a few years later, I collaborated with an old Jal Board badger called Jagat Ram.
Sourcing water directly from the main supply lines. The idiot got caught.
I got pulled into a deeper scandal.
They spare no opportunities to vilify a successful businessman.
I managed to overcome a few hurdles but slowly, painfully, realised that this could not go on.
So I said, fuck it, I'll find my own source.
The biggest source. So I put all my savings into exploring this source.
I have a dream for the city. I want Delhi houses to become self-contained barbicans. I want them to be surrounded by water-filled moats infested by bloodthirsty gharials.

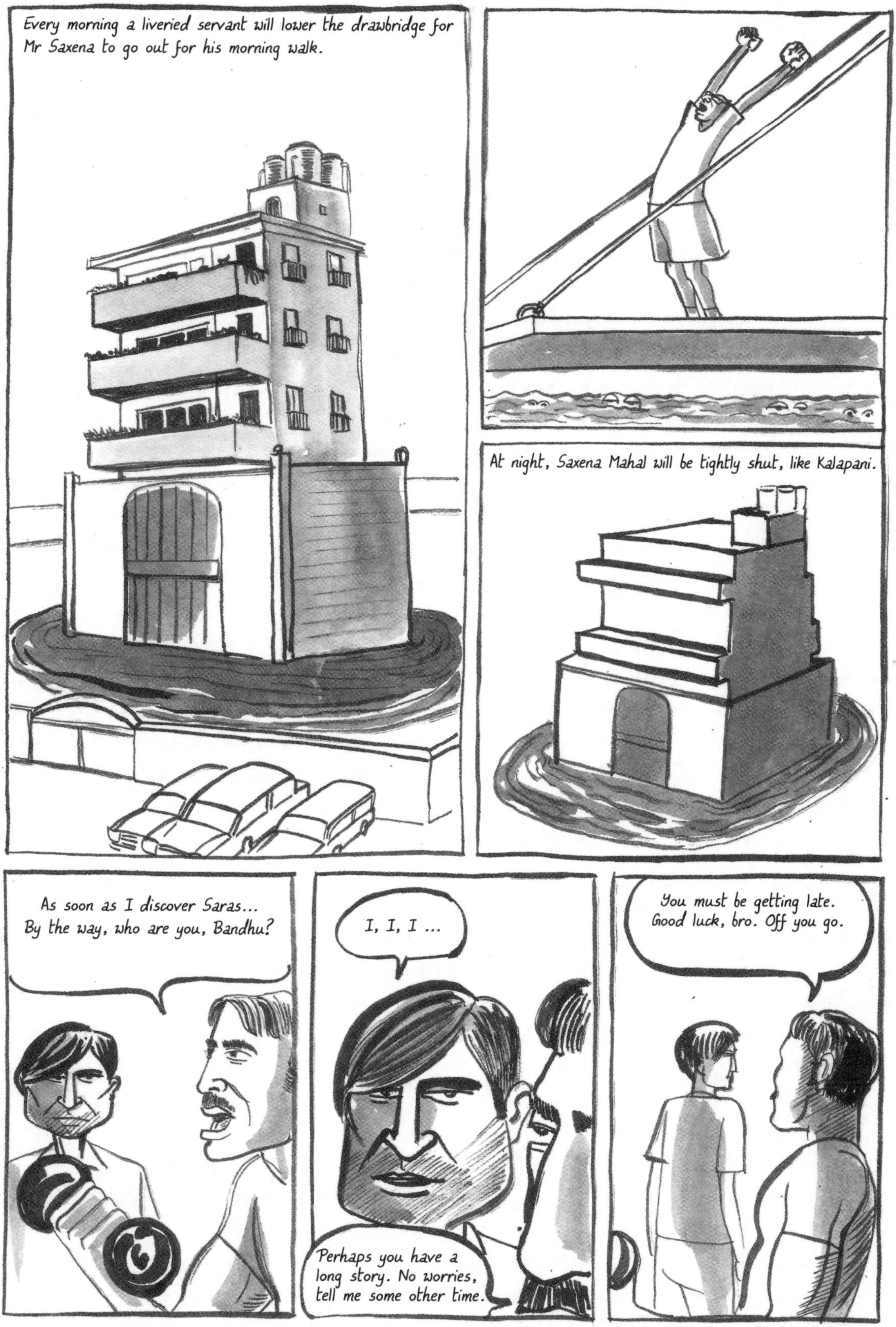
Every morning a liveried servant will lower the drawbridge for Mr Saxena to go out for his morning walk.
At night, Saxena Mahal will be tightly shut, like Kalapani.
As soon as I discover Saras... By the way, who are you, Bandhu?
I, I, I ...
Perhaps you have a long story. No worries, tell me some other time.
You must be getting late. Good luck, bro. Off you go.

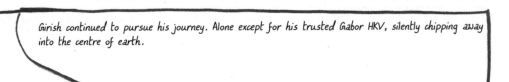

Girish continued to pursue his journey. Alone except for his trusted Gabor HKV, silently chipping away into the centre of earth.

The next person he met was Lt Col. B.K. Gambhir, who, in the right circumstances, could have got a *Param Vir Chakra*. Though, personally, he would have preferred to be a martyr.

I am a fallen soldier. My story began a few years ago. I committed a crime which, although minor in scale, brought me into disgrace.

I had my eye on my neighbour's house ...

... it grew into an obsession.

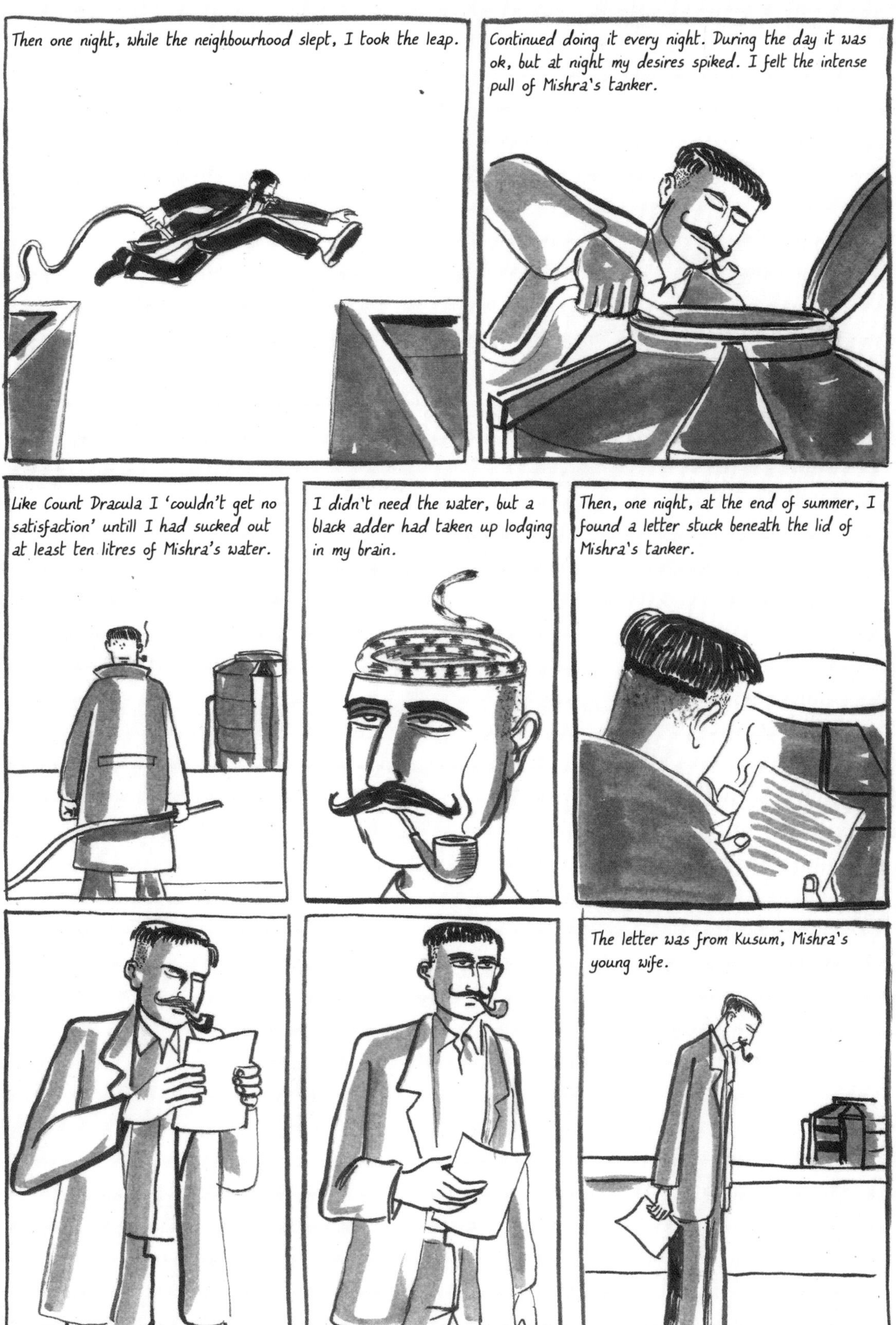
Then one night, while the neighbourhood slept, I took the leap.
Continued doing it every night. During the day it was ok, but at night my desires spiked. I felt the intense pull of Mishra's tanker.
Like Count Dracula I 'couldn't get no satisfaction' untill I had sucked out at least ten litres of Mishra's water.
I didn't need the water, but a black adder had taken up lodging in my brain.
Then, one night, at the end of summer, I found a letter stuck beneath the lid of Mishra's tanker.
The letter was from Kusum, Mishra's young wife.

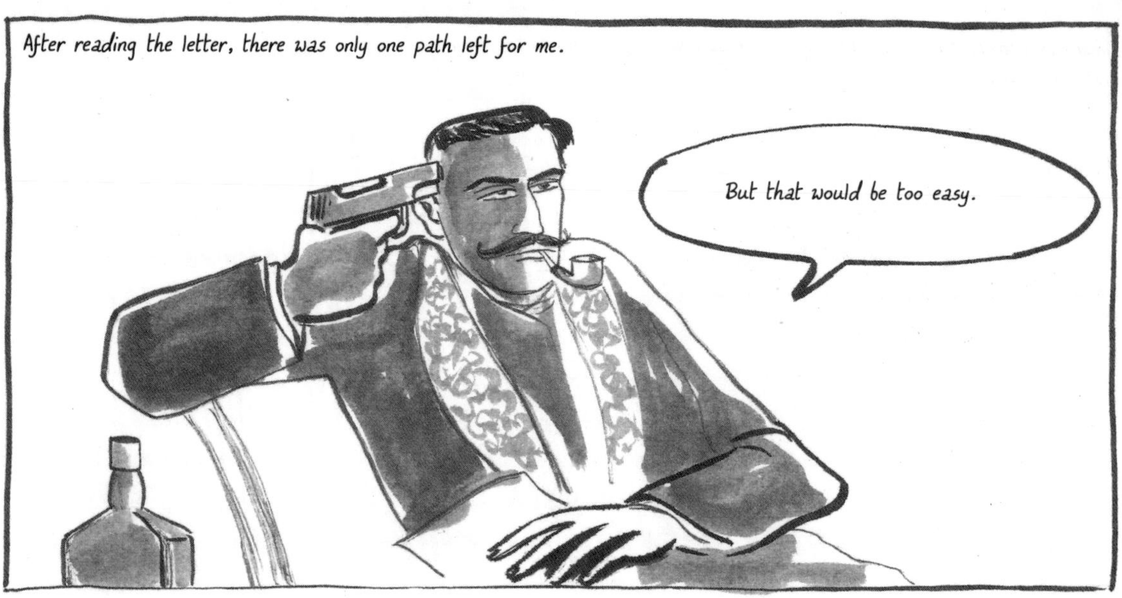
After reading the letter, there was only one path left for me.
But that would be too easy.

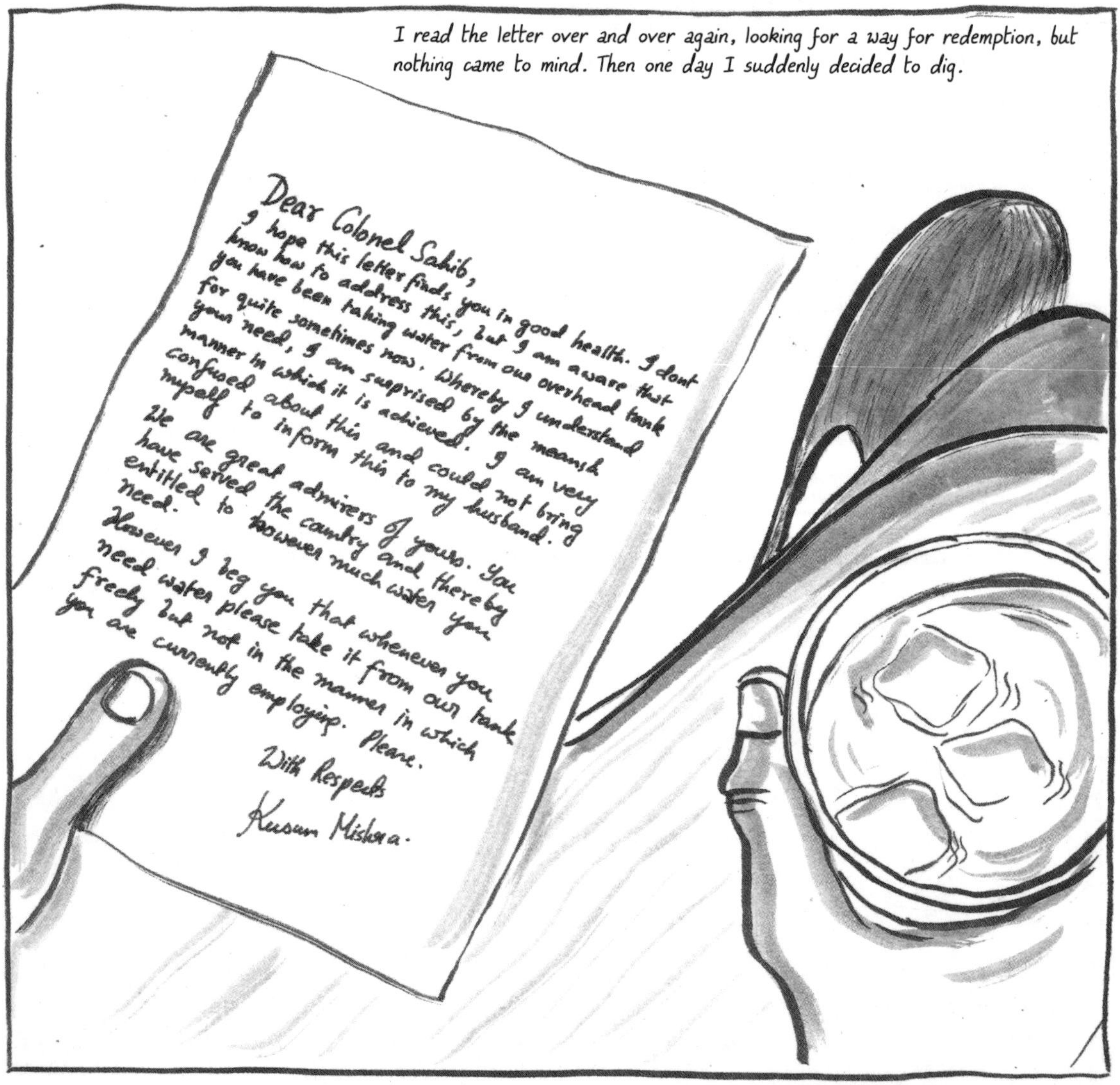
I read the letter over and over again, looking for a way for redemption, but nothing came to mind. Then one day I suddenly decided to dig.
Dear Colonel Sahib,
I hope this letter finds you in good health. I dont know how to address this, but I am aware that you have been taking water from our overhead tank for quite sometimes now. Whereby I understand your need, I am suprised by the meansh manner in which it is achieved. I am very confused about this and could not bring myself to inform this to my husband.
We are great admirers of yours. You have served the country and thereby entitled to however much water you need.
However I beg you that whenever you need water please take it from our tank freely but not in the manner in which you are currently employing. Please.
With Respects
Kusum Mishra.

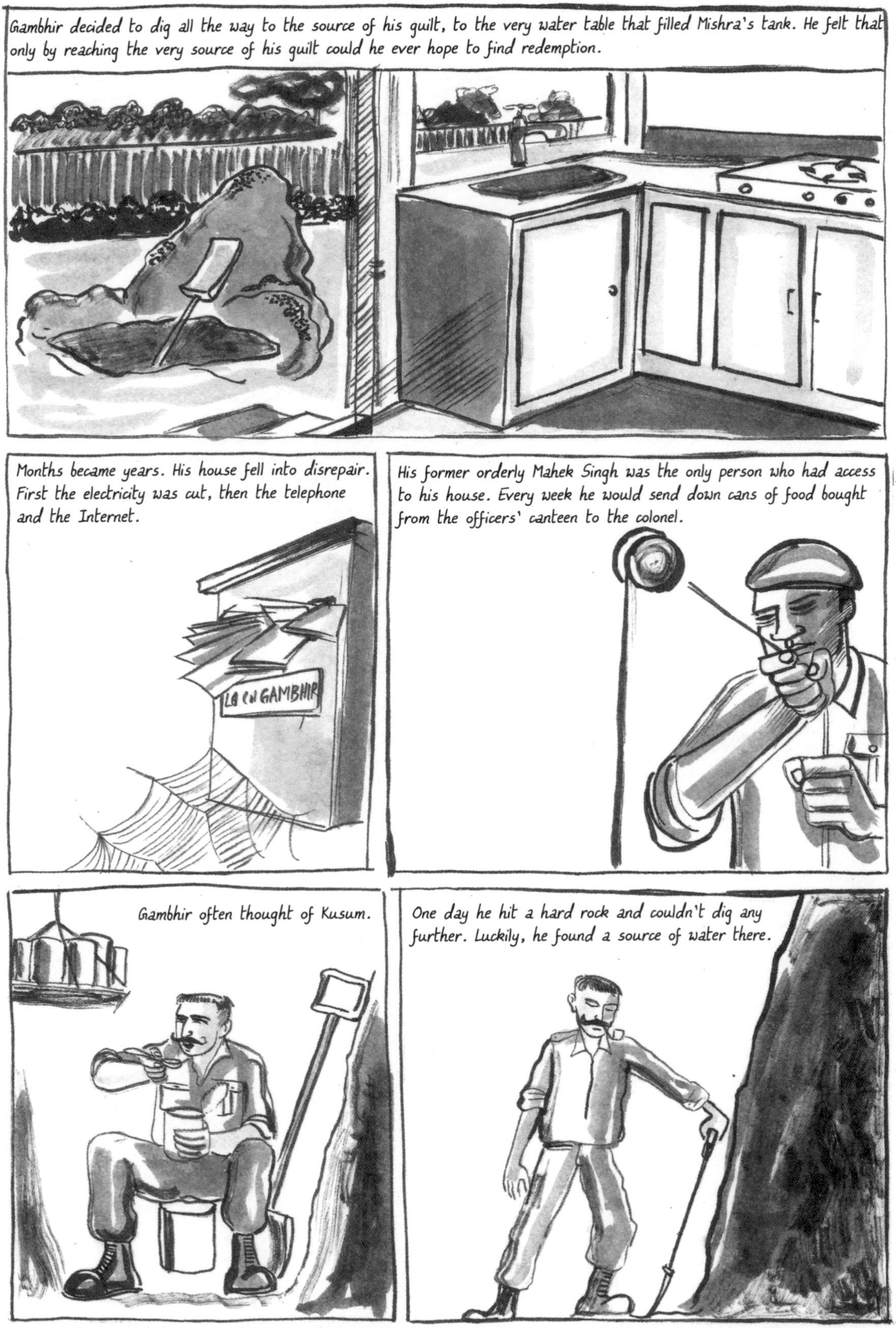
Gambhir decided to dig all the way to the source of his guilt, to the very water table that filled Mishra's tank. He felt that only by reaching the very source of his guilt could he ever hope to find redemption.
Months became years. His house fell into disrepair. First the electricity was cut, then the telephone and the Internet.
His former orderly Mahek Singh was the only person who had access to his house. Every week he would send down cans of food bought from the officers' canteen to the colonel.
Gambhir often thought of Kusum.
One day he hit a hard rock and couldn't dig any further. Luckily, he found a source of water there.

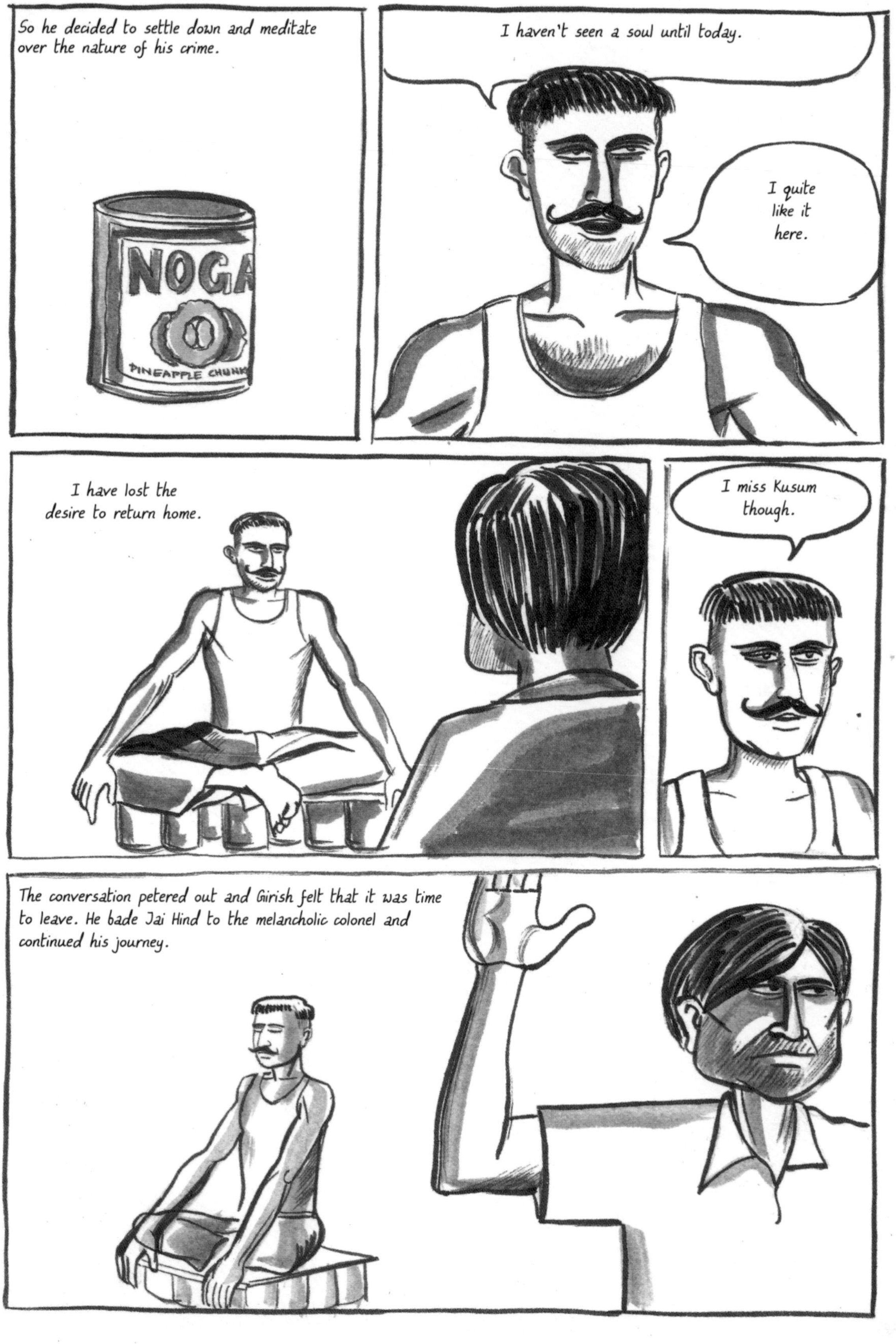
So he decided to settle down and meditate over the nature of his crime.
NOGA
PINEAPPLE CHUNKS
I haven't seen a soul until today.
I quite like it here.
I have lost the desire to return home.
I miss Kusum though.
The conversation petered out and Girish felt that it was time to leave. He bade Jai Hind to the melancholic colonel and continued his journey.

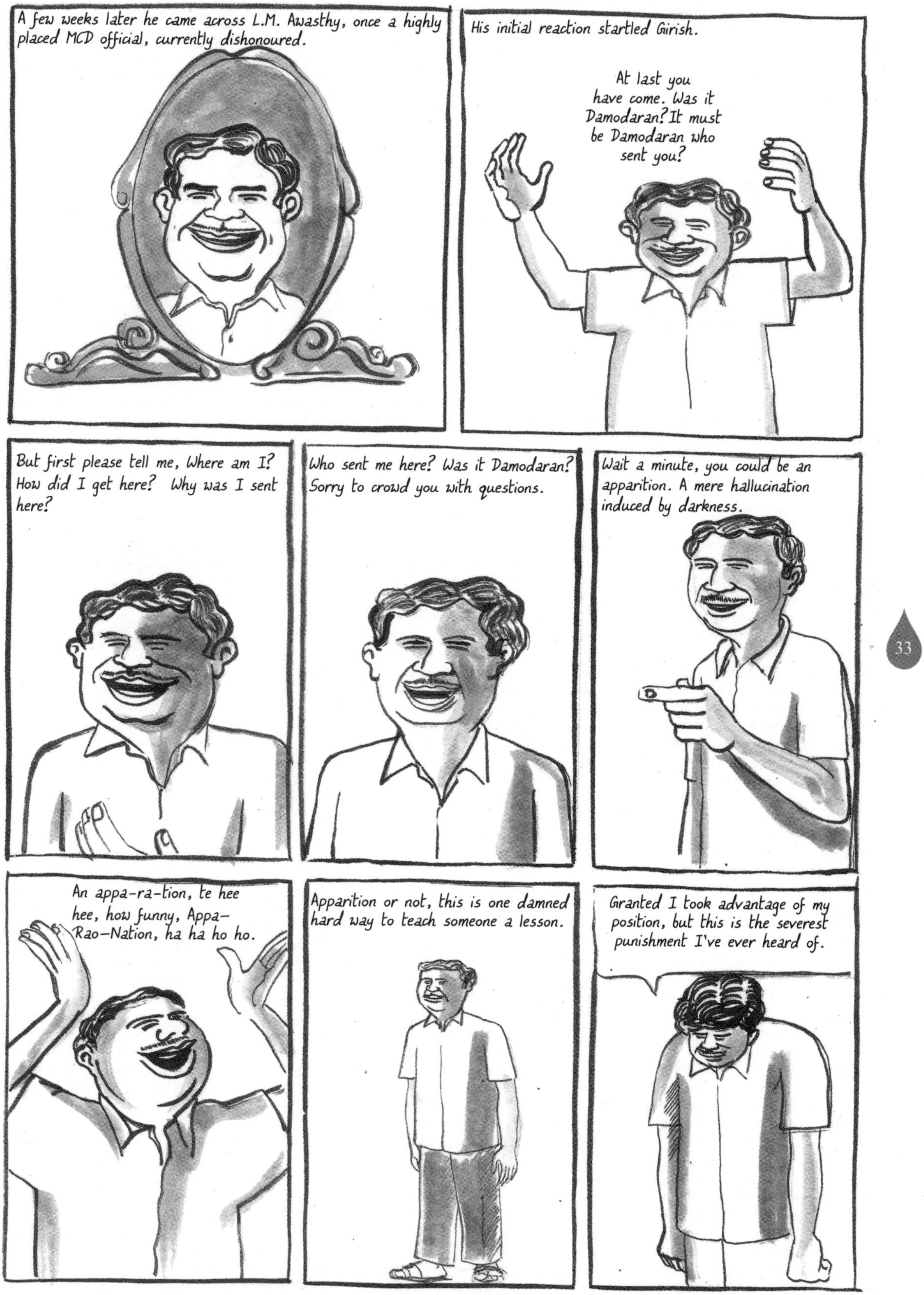
A few weeks later he came across L.M. Awasthy, once a highly placed MCD official, currently dishonoured.
His initial reaction startled Girish.
At last you have come. Was it Damodaran? It must be Damodaran who sent you?
But first please tell me, Where am I? How did I get here? Why was I sent here?
Who sent me here? Was it Damodaran? Sorry to crowd you with questions.
Wait a minute, you could be an apparition. A mere hallucination induced by darkness.
An appa-ra-tion, te hee hee, how funny, Appa-Rao-Nation, ha ha ho ho.
Apparition or not, this is one damned hard way to teach someone a lesson.
Granted I took advantage of my position, but this is the severest punishment I've ever heard of.

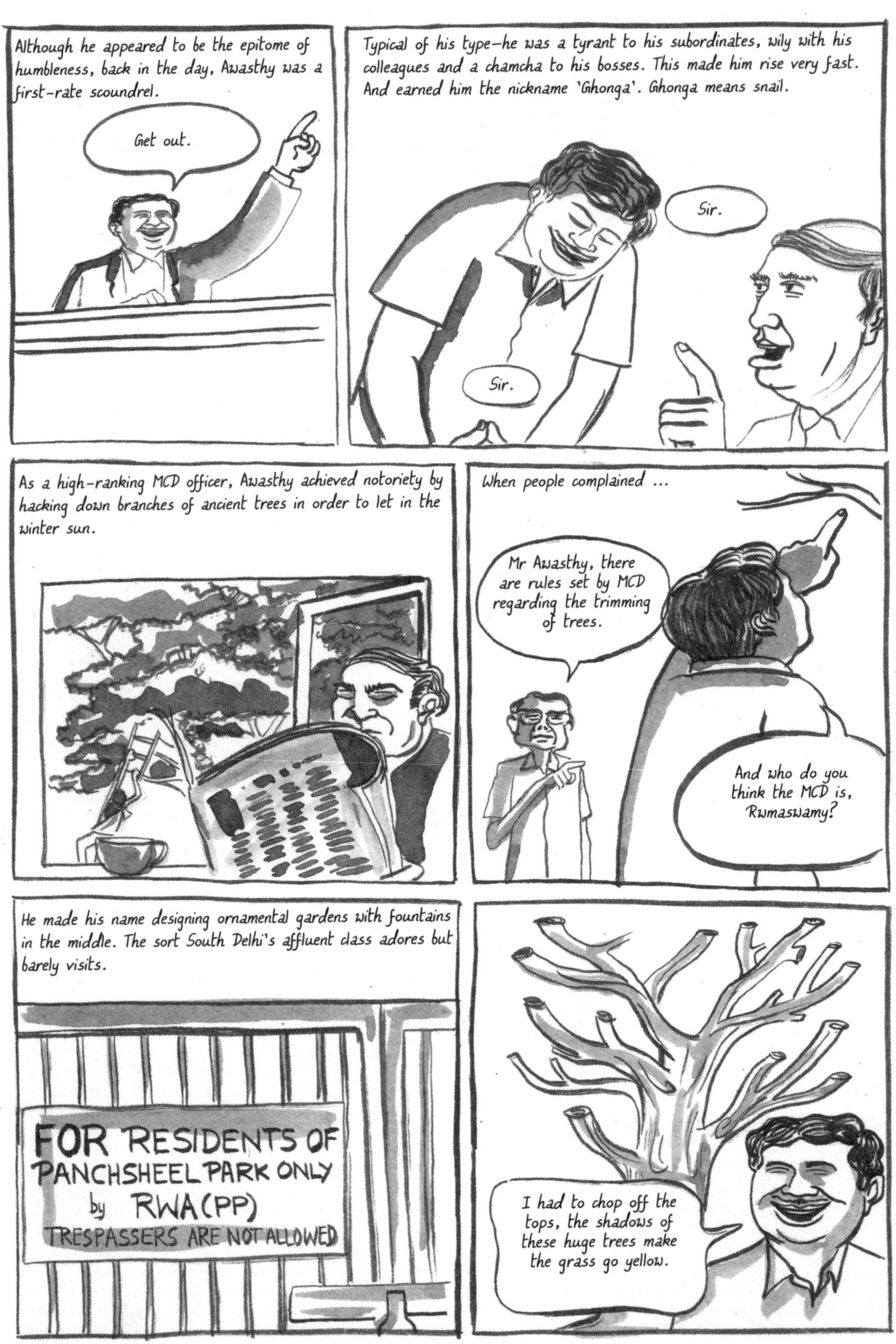
Although he appeared to be the epitome of humbleness, back in the day, Awasthy was a first-rate scoundrel.
Get out.
Typical of his type—he was a tyrant to his subordinates, wily with his colleagues and a chamcha to his bosses. This made him rise very fast. And earned him the nickname 'Ghonga'. Ghonga means snail.
Sir.
Sir.
As a high-ranking MCD officer, Awasthy achieved notoriety by hacking down branches of ancient trees in order to let in the winter sun.
When people complained ...
Mr Awasthy, there are rules set by MCD regarding the trimming of trees.
And who do you think the MCD is, Rwmaswamy?
He made his name designing ornamental gardens with fountains in the middle. The sort South Delhi's affluent class adores but barely visits.
FOR RESIDENTS OF PANCHSHEEL PARK ONLY
by RWA(PP)
TRESPASSERS ARE NOT ALLOWED
I had to chop off the tops, the shadows of these huge trees make the grass go yellow.

Because of the constant overflow from his tank, the area around his house and the rest of the neighbourhood looked like a mangrove forest.

But sins were piling up, he knew it in his guts. All night he tossed and turned, tortured by terrible dreams.

In one recurring dream, he saw himself falling into a very dark abyss.

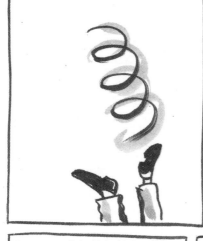

Then, one night, he woke up in the middle of the dream. It was so dark he couldn't even see his hand, but he knew intuitively that he was not in his room.

GASP

For a moment he thought he was dead or had gone blind. He groped about desperately and found a matchbox. Next to it sat an old-style lantern.

He found himself in a small room, quite self-contained, with pots, pans, oil, salt, grains, veggies, and a copy of Manusmriti.

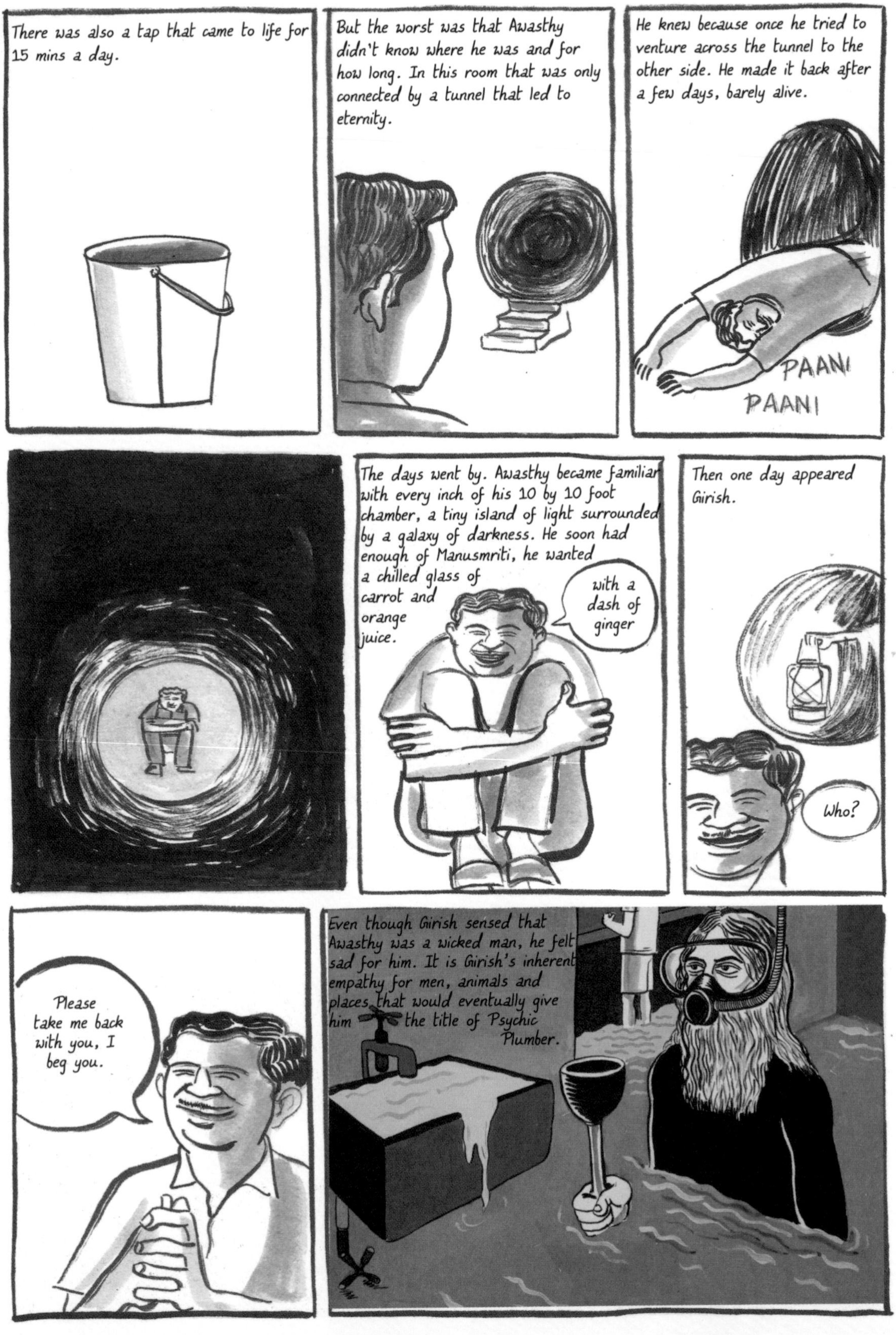
There was also a tap that came to life for 15 mins a day.
But the worst was that Awasthy didn't know where he was and for how long. In this room that was only connected by a tunnel that led to eternity.
He knew because once he tried to venture across the tunnel to the other side. He made it back after a few days, barely alive.
PAANI
PAANI
The days went by. Awasthy became familiar with every inch of his 10 by 10 foot chamber, a tiny island of light surrounded by a galaxy of darkness. He soon had enough of Manusmriti, he wanted a chilled glass of carrot and orange juice.
with a dash of ginger
Then one day appeared Girish.
Who?
Please take me back with you, I beg you.
Even though Girish sensed that Awasthy was a wicked man, he felt sad for him. It is Girish's inherent empathy for men, animals and places that would eventually give him the title of Psychic Plumber.

I will never throw my weight around. I will never waste water. I like the sound of the breeze blowing through leaves, it reminds me of Gulzar.

I will protect trees with my life, please take me home.

I am touched by your candidness in confiding in me. Many brave men cannot do that. You will see better days soon. But now I must leave.

Oh, thank you, thank you. The moment you walked in, I knew that you are a man of noble birth.

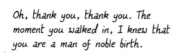

Perhaps even an incarnation of Lord Vishnu.

Bye.

Next, Girish met Philippa Carrey Jones, the wife of the ambassador of a hitherto unnameable country which considers India as a punishment posting.

BOMBAY SAPPHIRE

81 TIPS TO SURVIVE INDIA

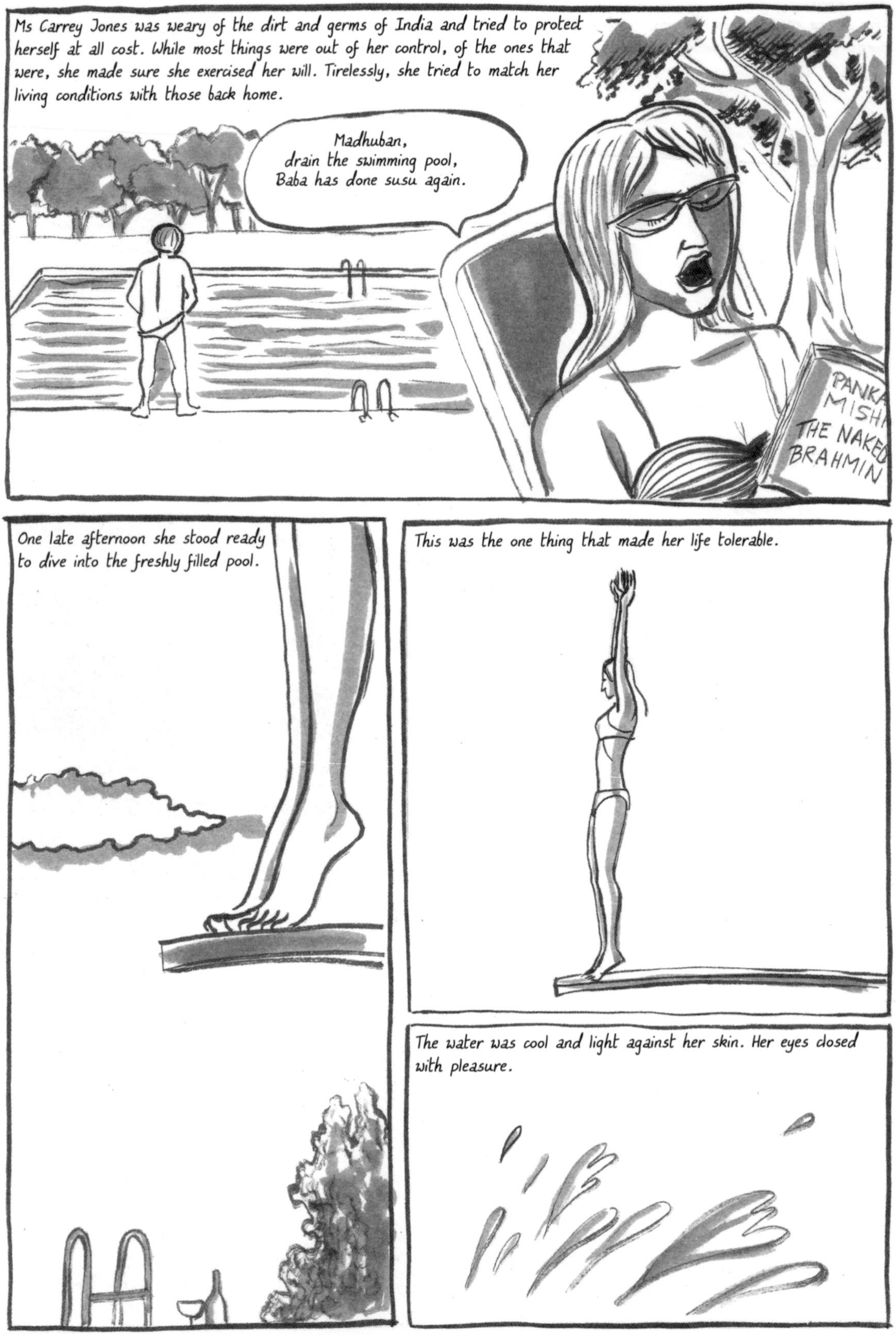
Ms Carrey Jones was weary of the dirt and germs of India and tried to protect herself at all cost. While most things were out of her control, of the ones that were, she made sure she exercised her will. Tirelessly, she tried to match her living conditions with those back home.
Madhuban, drain the swimming pool, Baba has done susu again.
PANKA MISH THE NAKED BRAHMIN
One late afternoon she stood ready to dive into the freshly filled pool.
This was the one thing that made her life tolerable.
The water was cool and light against her skin. Her eyes closed with pleasure.

With strong easy strokes she went towards the deep end. It was dark and cool there, shaded by a jamun tree. She went deeper into the pool, seeking more darkness.

She lingered at the bottom, to check whether the chipped floor tiles had been replaced, but where were the tiles?

The floor looked rough. Instead of tiles, there were pebbles and dirt. It felt very dark. She swam up.

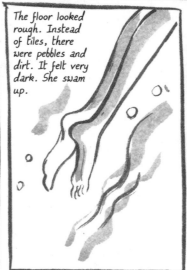

When she reached the surface, it was entirely dark. Night had fallen.

She could hardly see anything, but she realised that the pool had shrunk considerably.

Although there is nothing to prove that something happened between Philippa and Girish, after meeting her, he starts digging with renewed vigour.

For many months he doesn't bump into anyone.

In between digs, he feels nostalgic about the early days of his excavation.

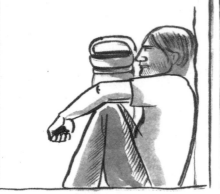

One day an entire wall of loose stones comes tumbling down from a small knock of the Gabor—HKV22X. A path sloped downward.

Who could have made steps here? And what is this smell, and what is this that I hear?

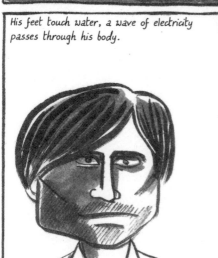

His feet touch water, a wave of electricity passes through his body.

He bends down to check. Not only is there water, there is plenty of it, and the current is strong.

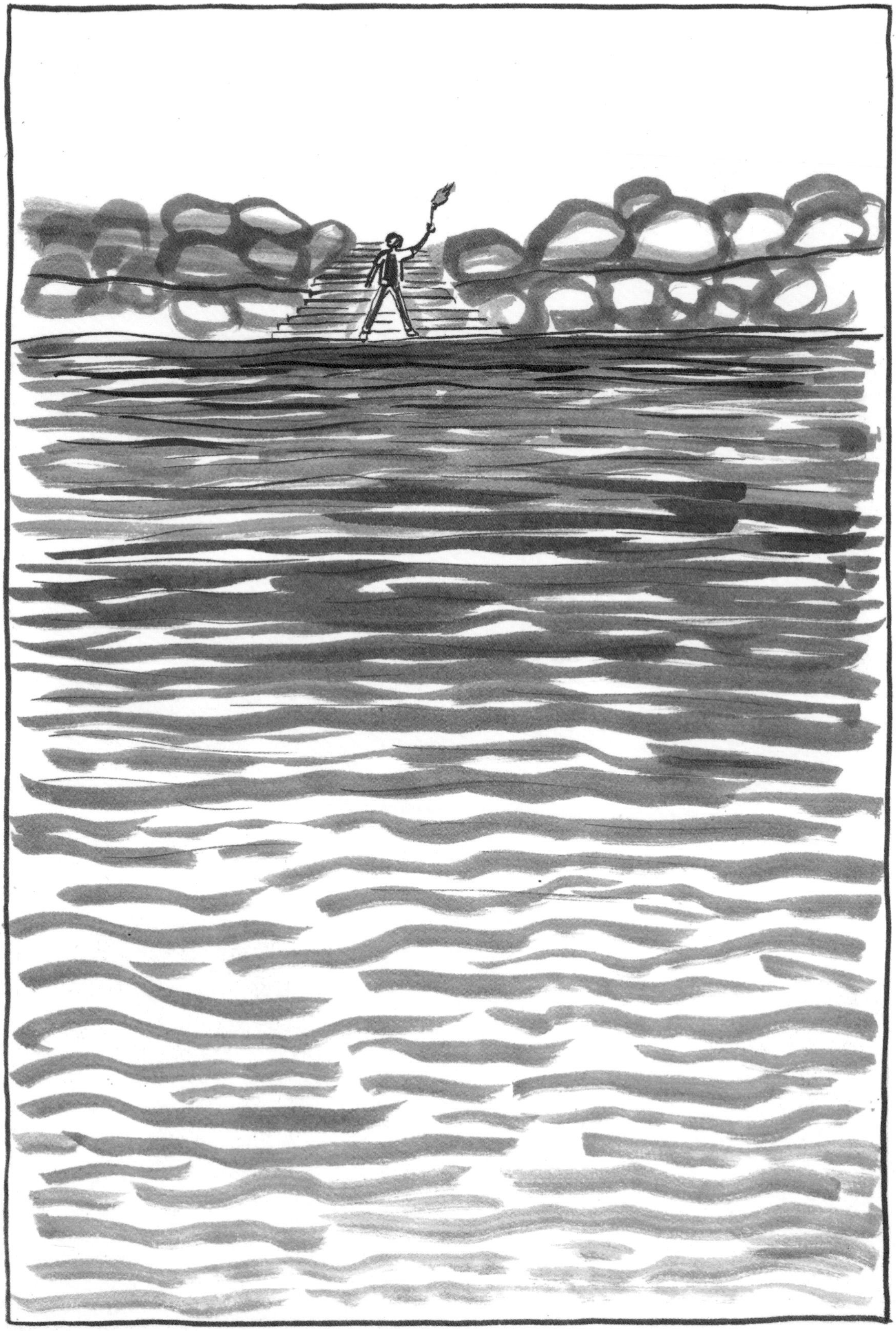

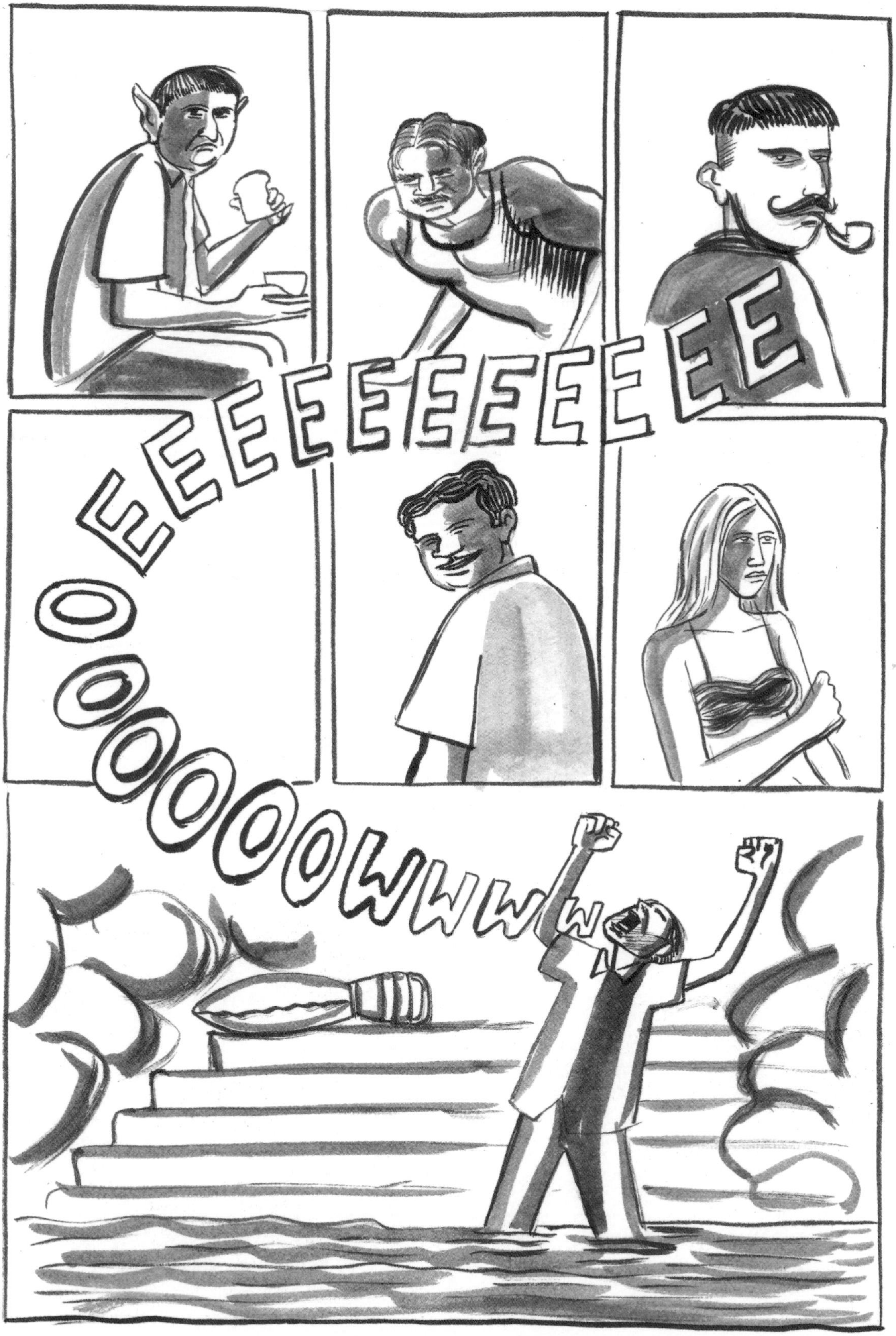
EEEEEEEEEEEEE
OOOOOOWWWWW

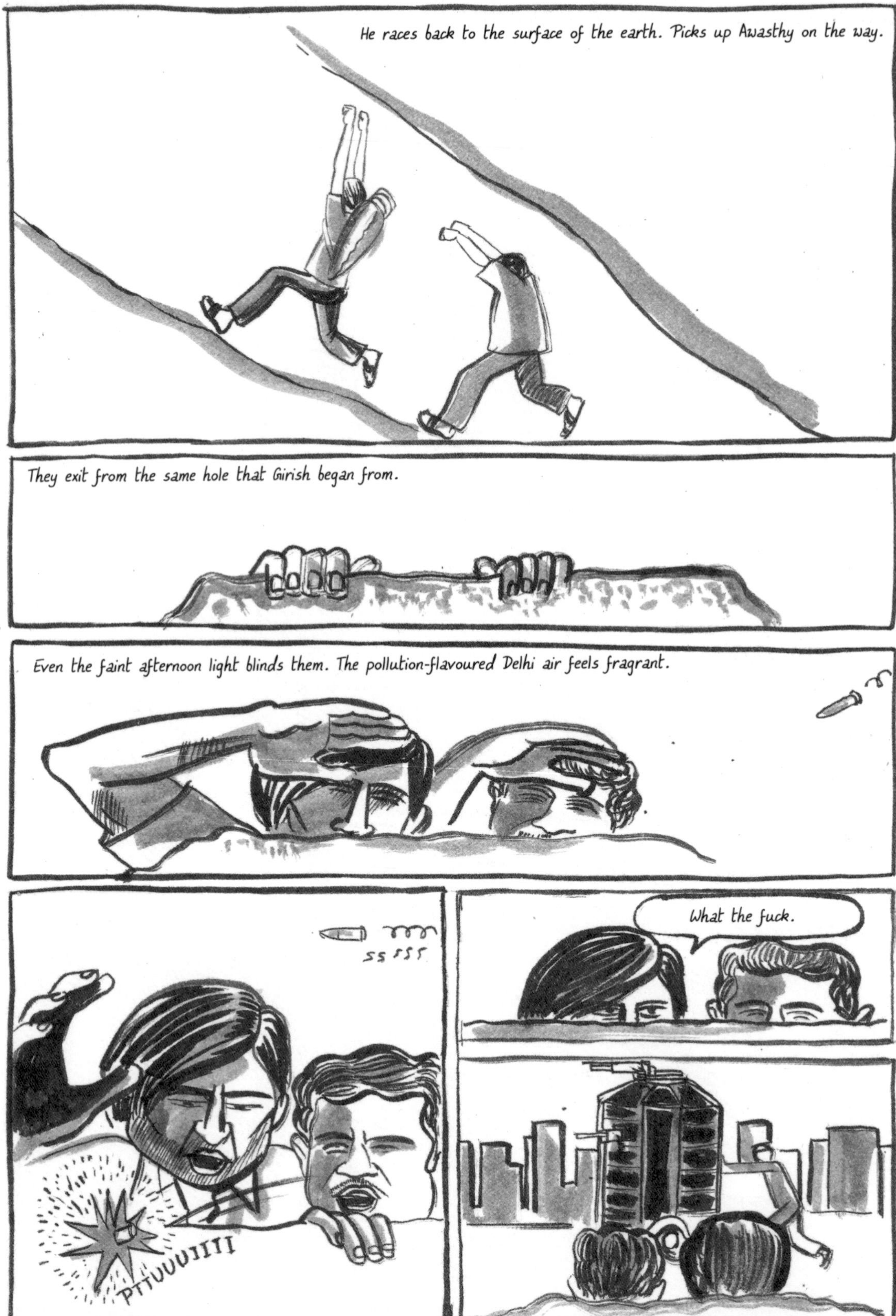
He races back to the surface of the earth. Picks up Awasthy on the way.
They exit from the same hole that Girish began from.
Even the faint afternoon light blinds them. The pollution-flavoured Delhi air feels fragrant.
PTTUUUIIIII
What the fuck.

While Girish was away, the Battle of Kalkaji had commenced.

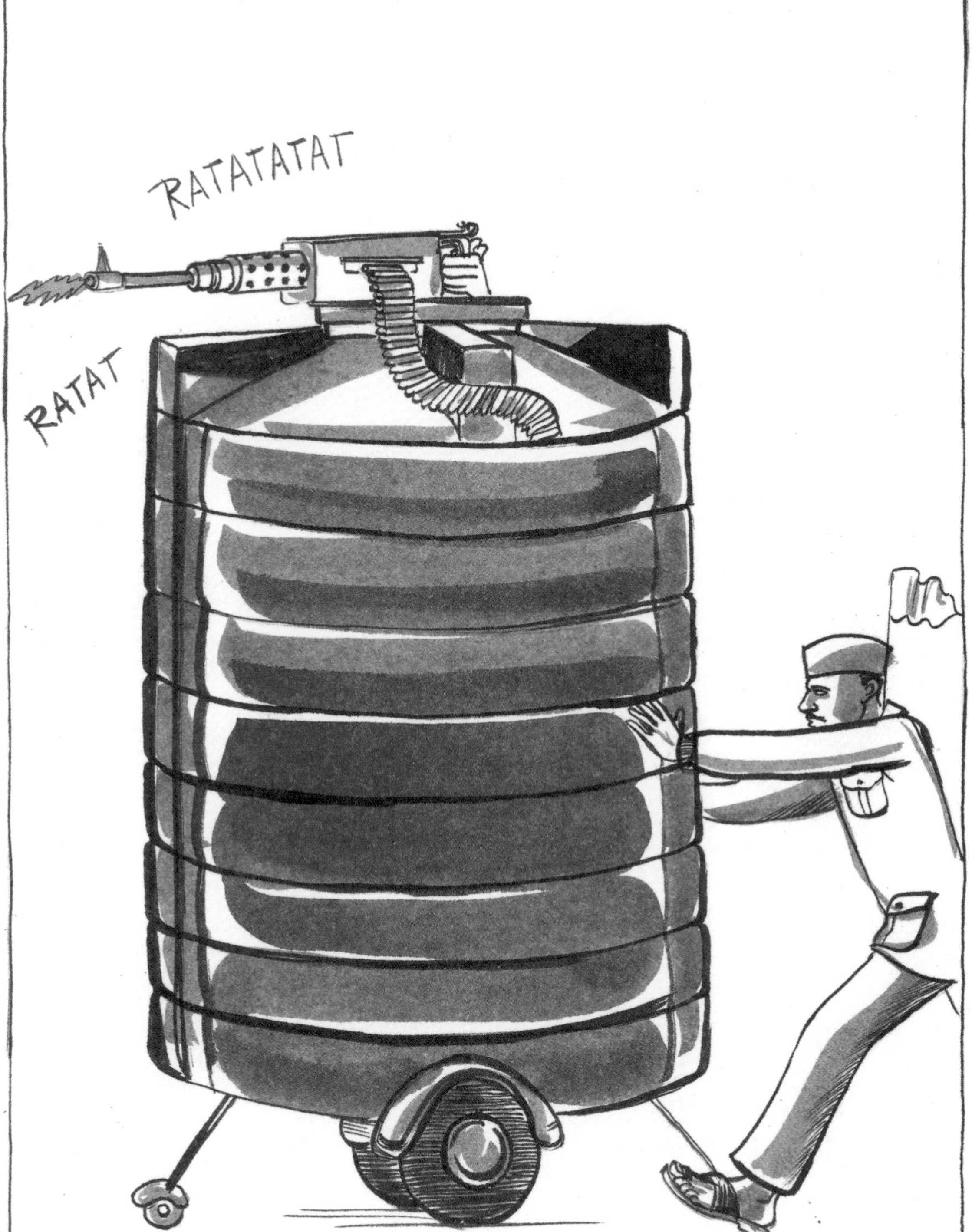
RATATATAT
RATAT

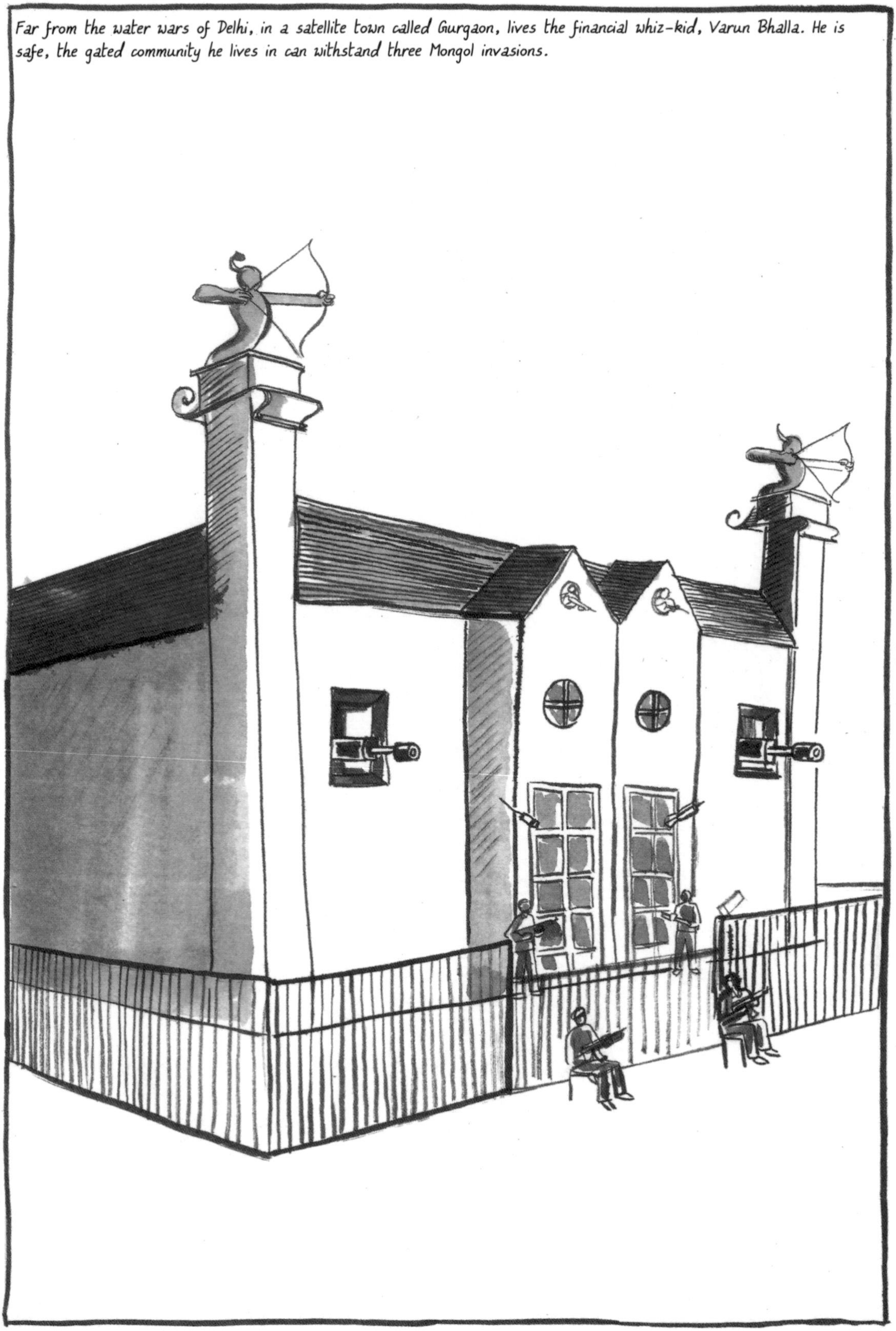
Far from the water wars of Delhi, in a satellite town called Gurgaon, lives the financial whiz-kid, Varun Bhalla. He is safe, the gated community he lives in can withstand three Mongol invasions.

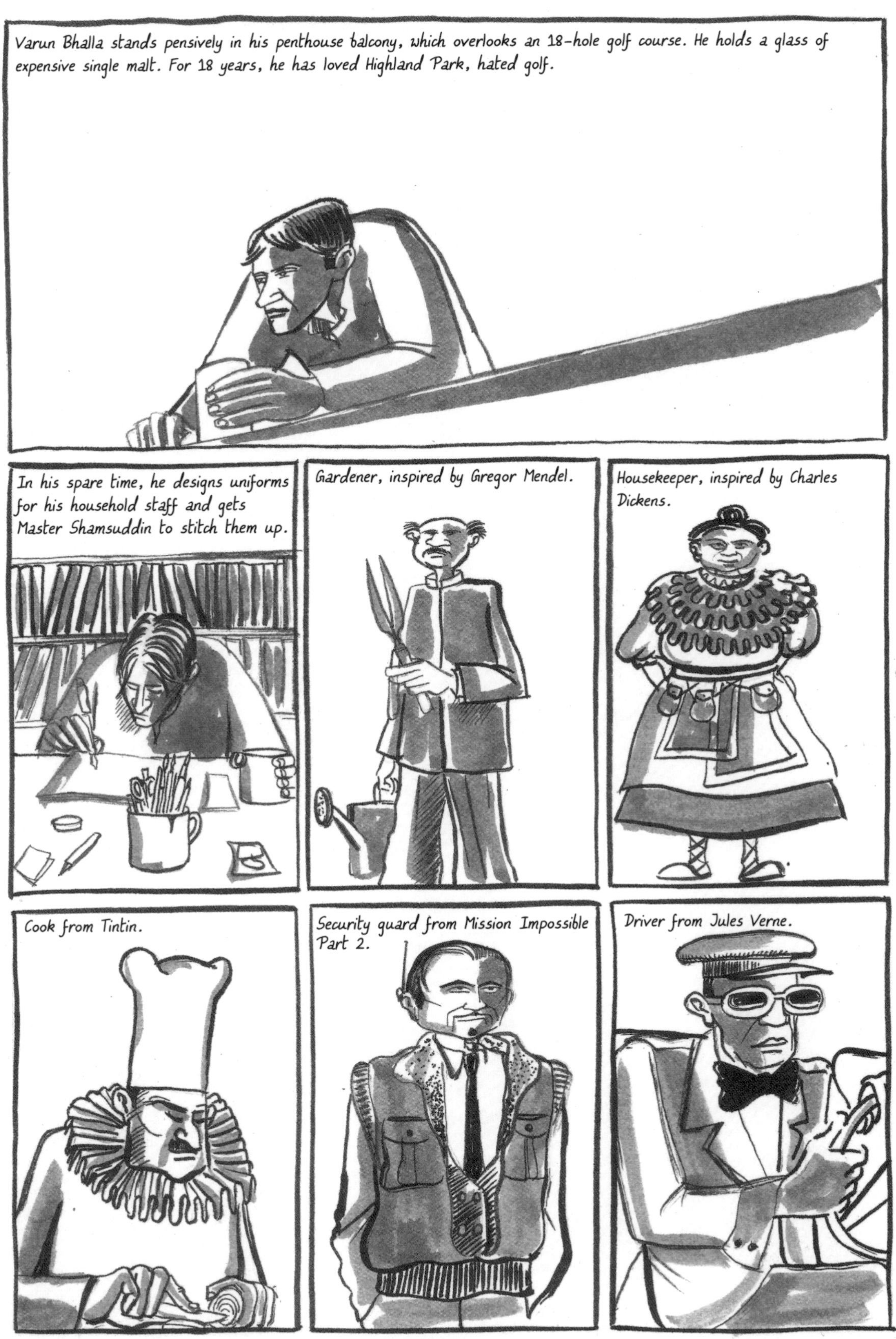
Varun Bhalla stands pensively in his penthouse balcony, which overlooks an 18-hole golf course. He holds a glass of expensive single malt. For 18 years, he has loved Highland Park, hated golf.
In his spare time, he designs uniforms for his household staff and gets Master Shamsuddin to stitch them up.
Gardener, inspired by Gregor Mendel.
Housekeeper, inspired by Charles Dickens.
Cook from Tintin.
Security guard from Mission Impossible Part 2.
Driver from Jules Verne.

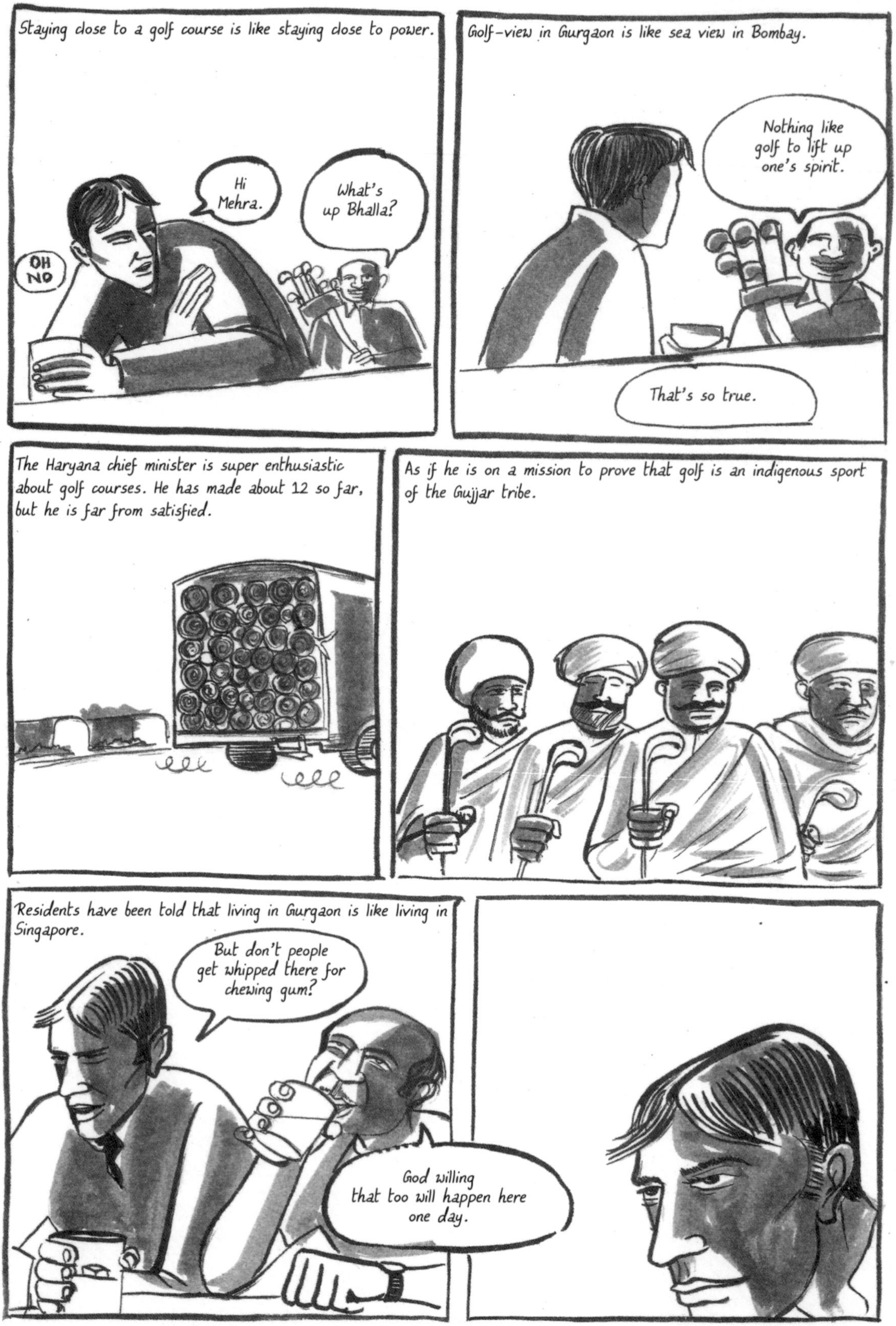
Staying close to a golf course is like staying close to power.
Hi Mehra.
What's up Bhalla?
OH NO
Golf-view in Gurgaon is like sea view in Bombay.
Nothing like golf to lift up one's spirit.
That's so true.
The Haryana chief minister is super enthusiastic about golf courses. He has made about 12 so far, but he is far from satisfied.
As if he is on a mission to prove that golf is an indigenous sport of the Gujjar tribe.
Residents have been told that living in Gurgaon is like living in Singapore.
But don't people get whipped there for chewing gum?
God willing that too will happen here one day.

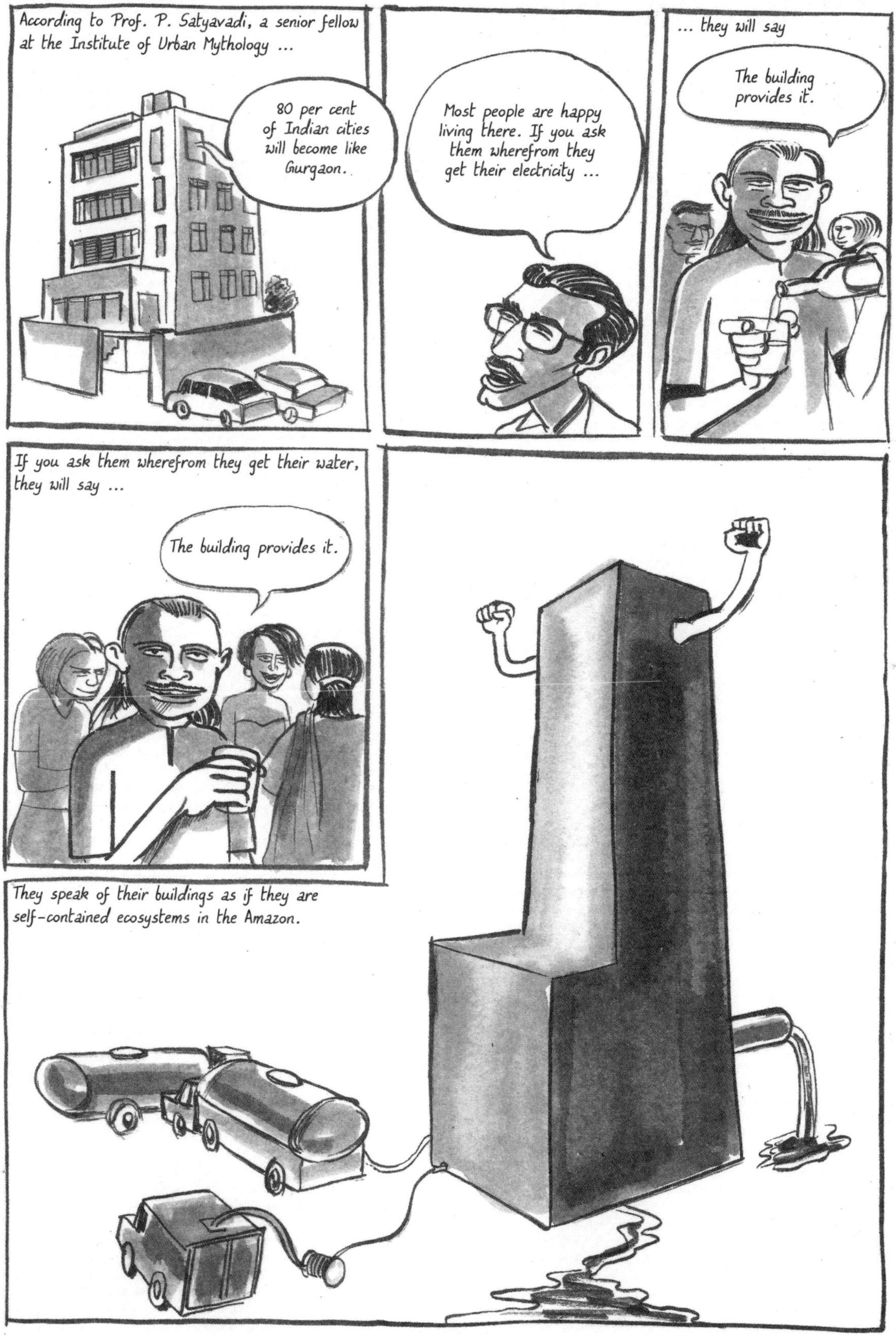
According to Prof. P. Satyavadi, a senior fellow at the Institute of Urban Mythology ...
80 per cent of Indian cities will become like Gurgaon.
Most people are happy living there. If you ask them wherefrom they get their electricity ...
... they will say
The building provides it.
If you ask them wherefrom they get their water, they will say ...
The building provides it.
They speak of their buildings as if they are self-contained ecosystems in the Amazon.

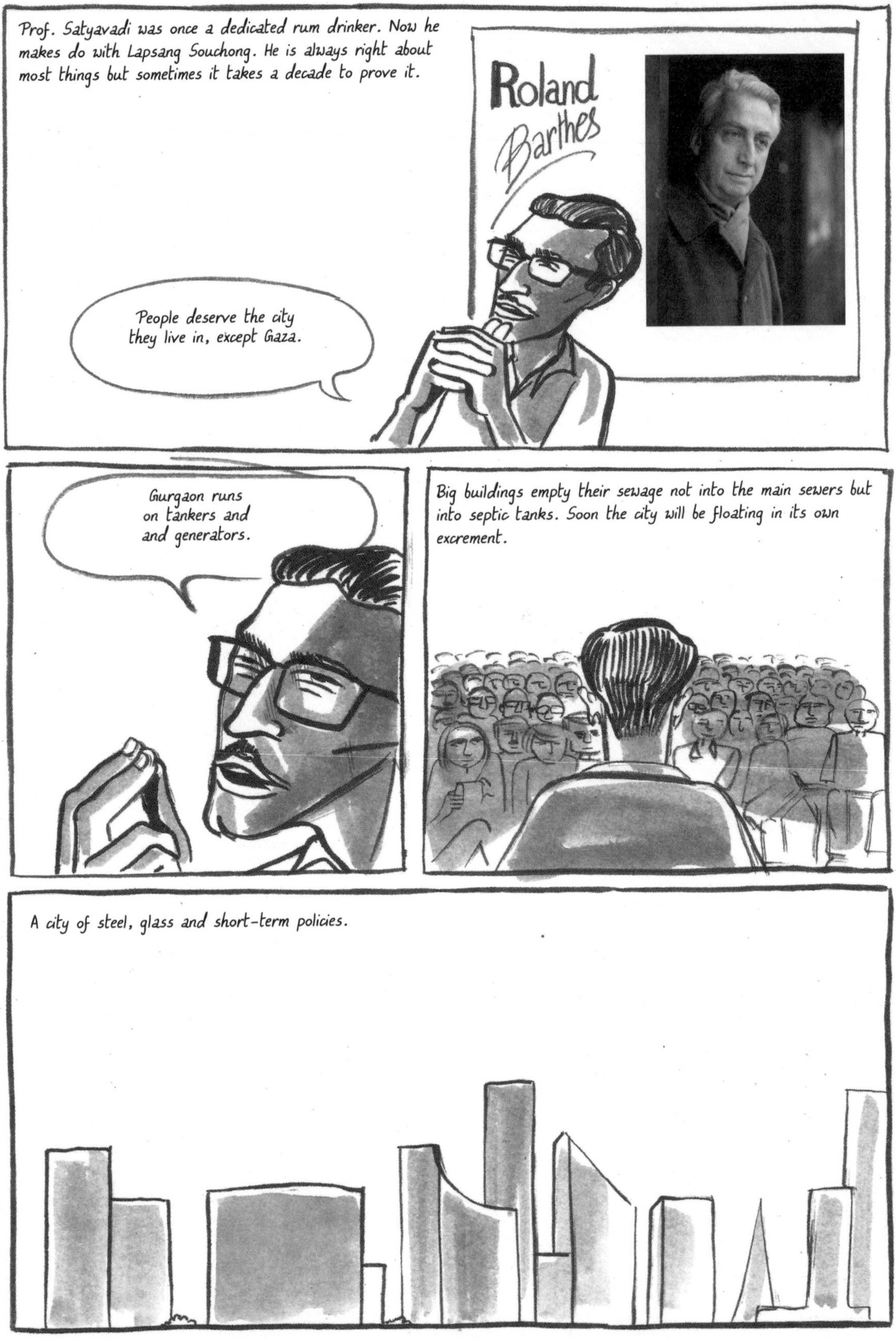
Prof. Satyavadi was once a dedicated rum drinker. Now he makes do with Lapsang Souchong. He is always right about most things but sometimes it takes a decade to prove it.
Roland Barthes
People deserve the city they live in, except Gaza.
Gurgaon runs on tankers and and generators.
Big buildings empty their sewage not into the main sewers but into septic tanks. Soon the city will be floating in its own excrement.
A city of steel, glass and short-term policies.

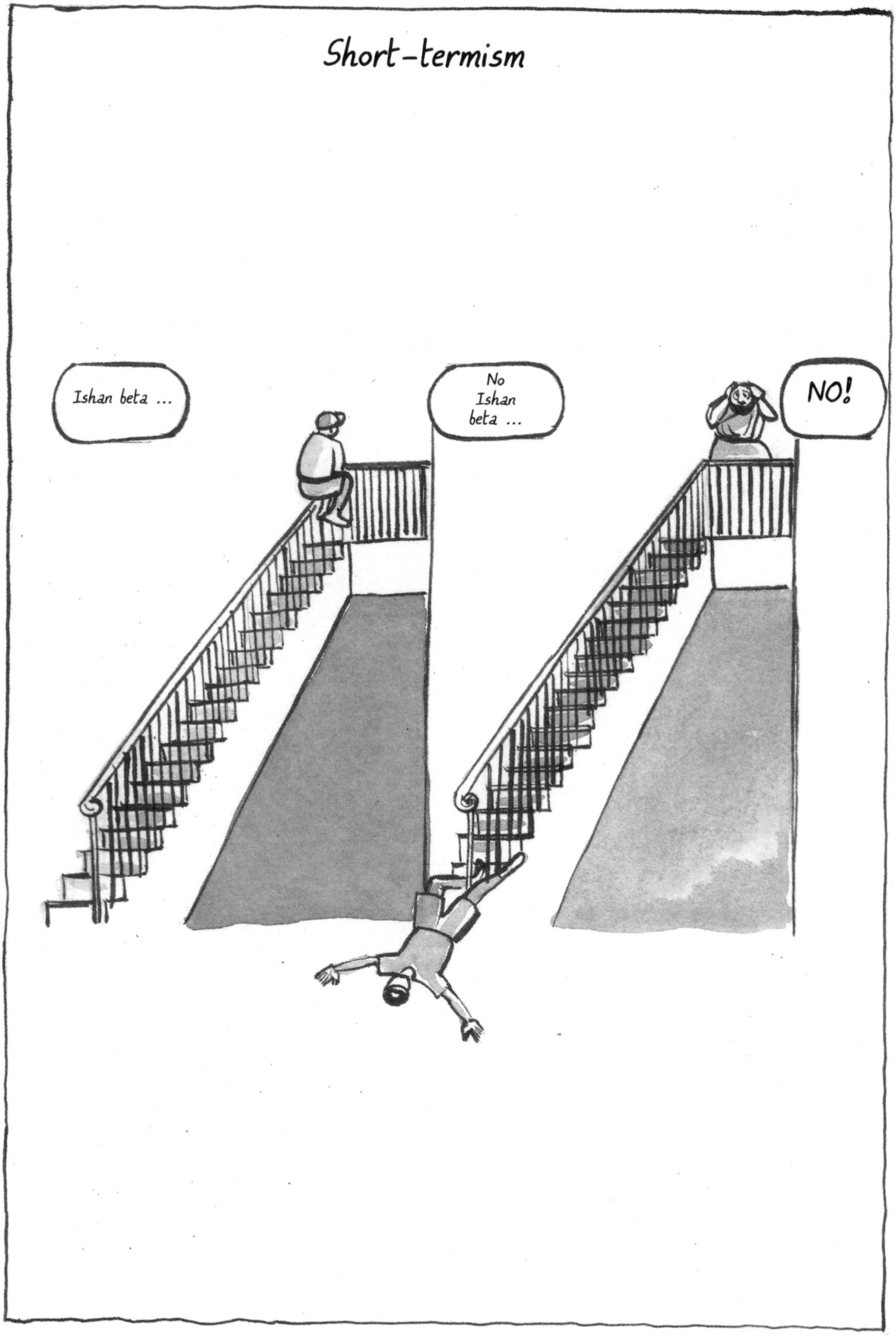
Short-termism
Ishan beta ...
No
Ishan
beta ...
NO!

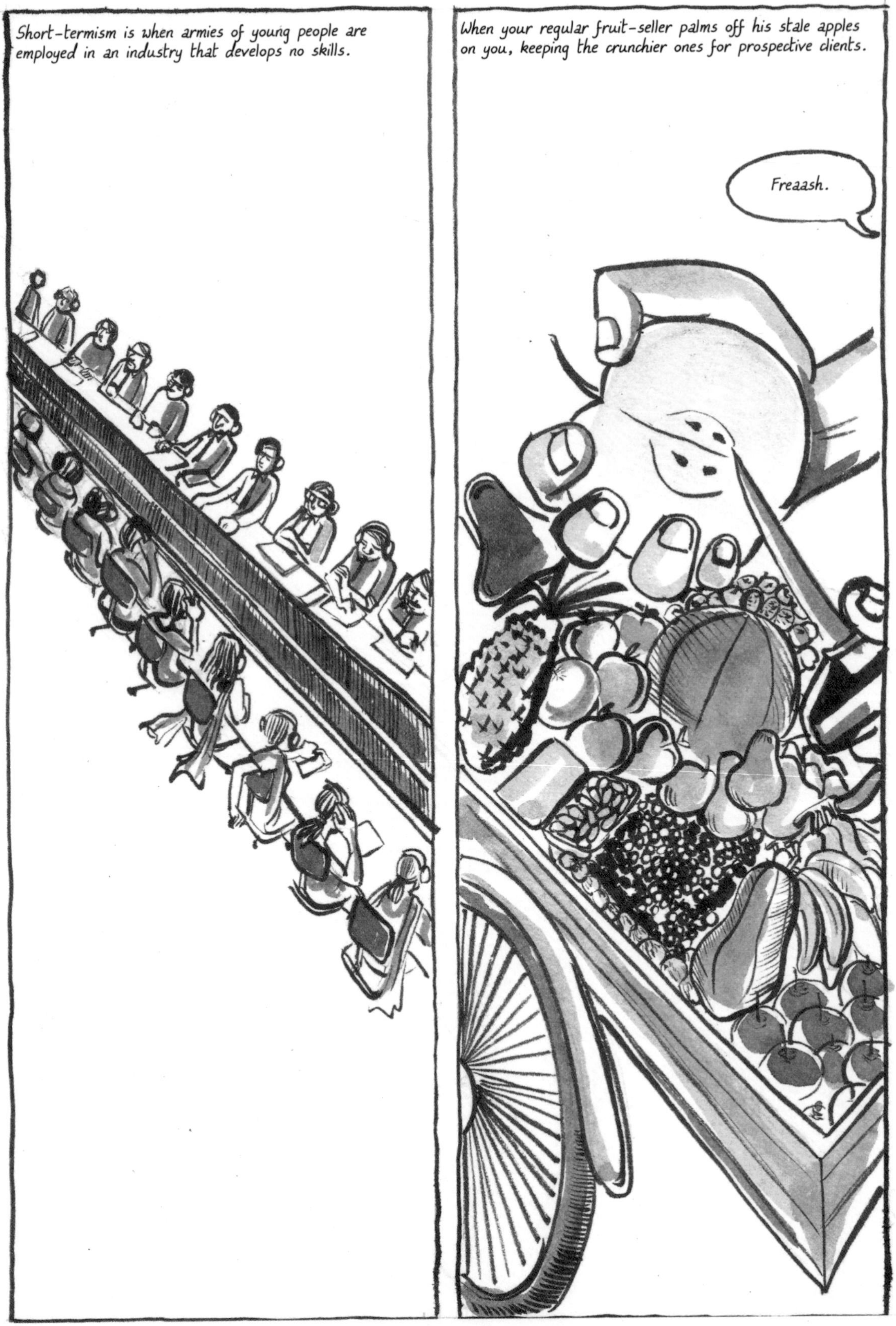
Short-termism is when armies of young people are employed in an industry that develops no skills.
When your regular fruit-seller palms off his stale apples on you, keeping the crunchier ones for prospective clients.
Freaash.

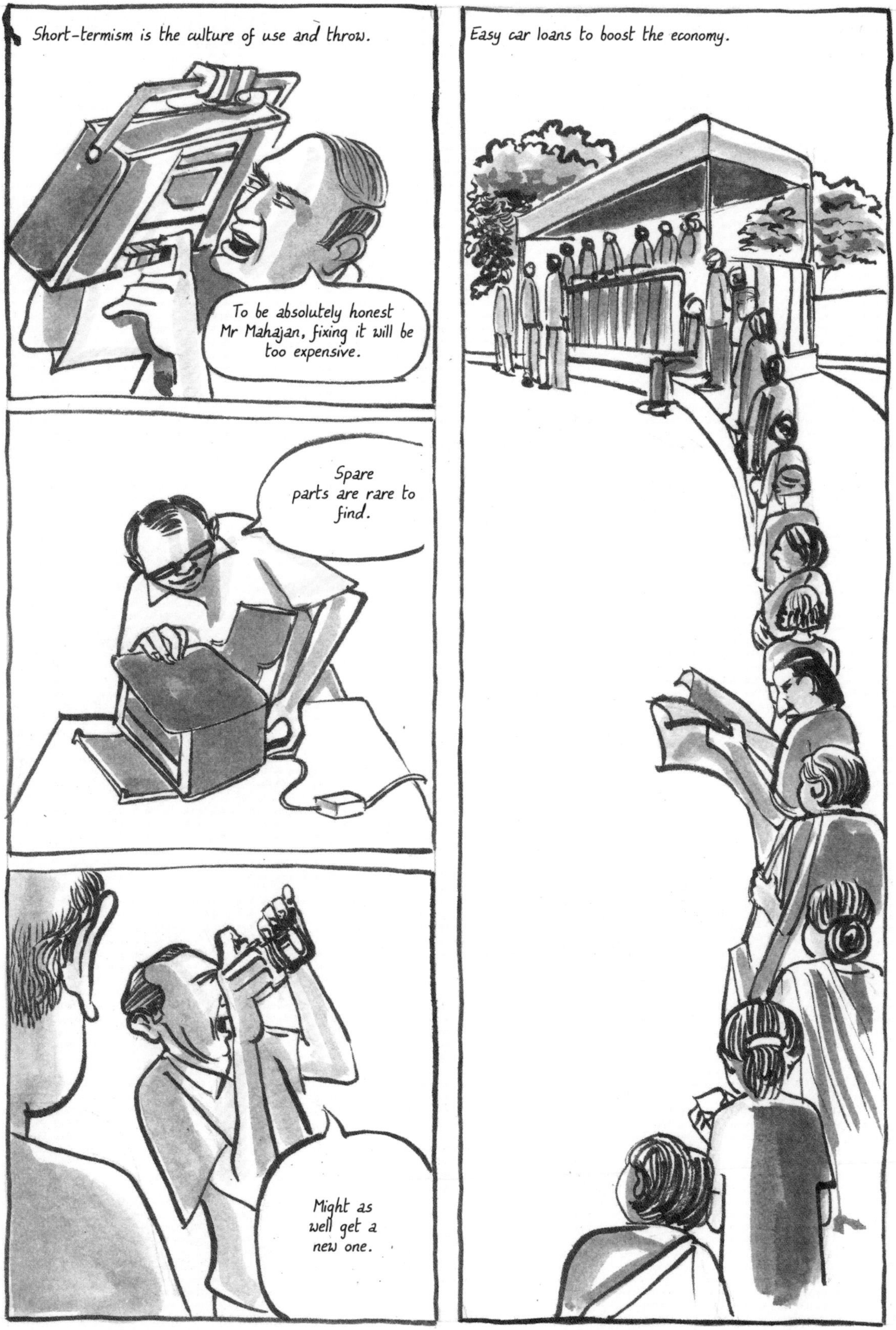
Short-termism is the culture of use and throw.
To be absolutely honest Mr Mahajan, fixing it will be too expensive.
Spare parts are rare to find.
Might as well get a new one.
Easy car loans to boost the economy.

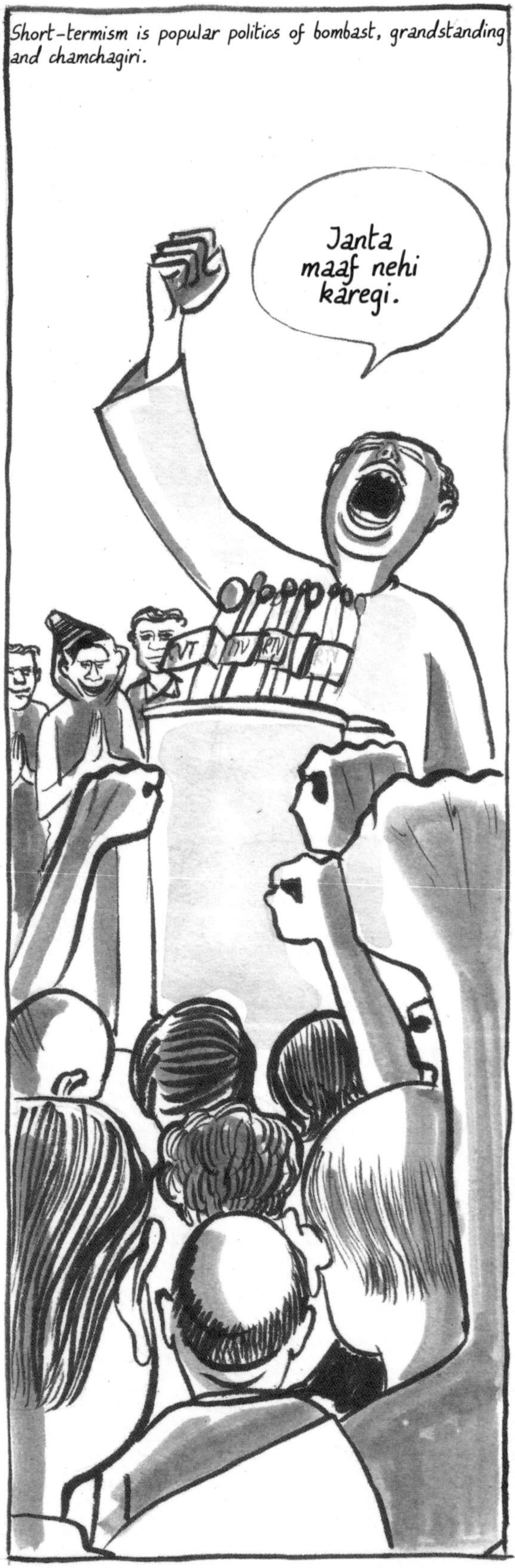
Short-termism is popular politics of bombast, grandstanding and chamchagiri.
Janta maaf nehi karegi.

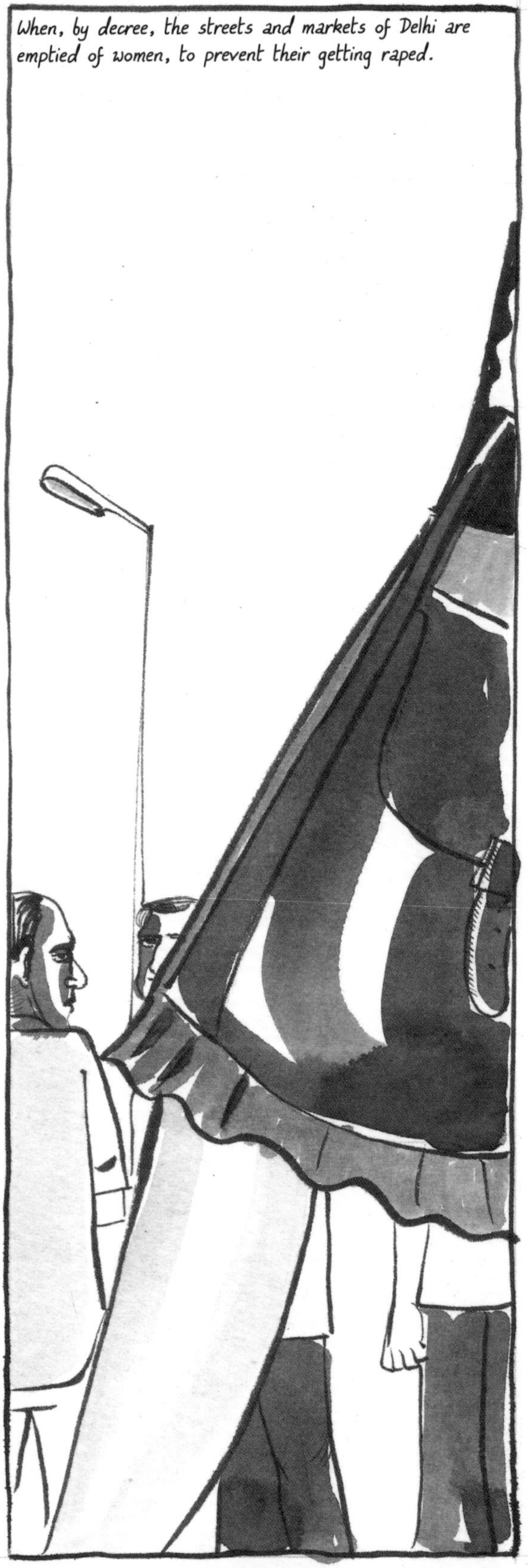
When, by decree, the streets and markets of Delhi are emptied of women, to prevent their getting raped.

Short-terming is when floors upon floors are held together by optimism.

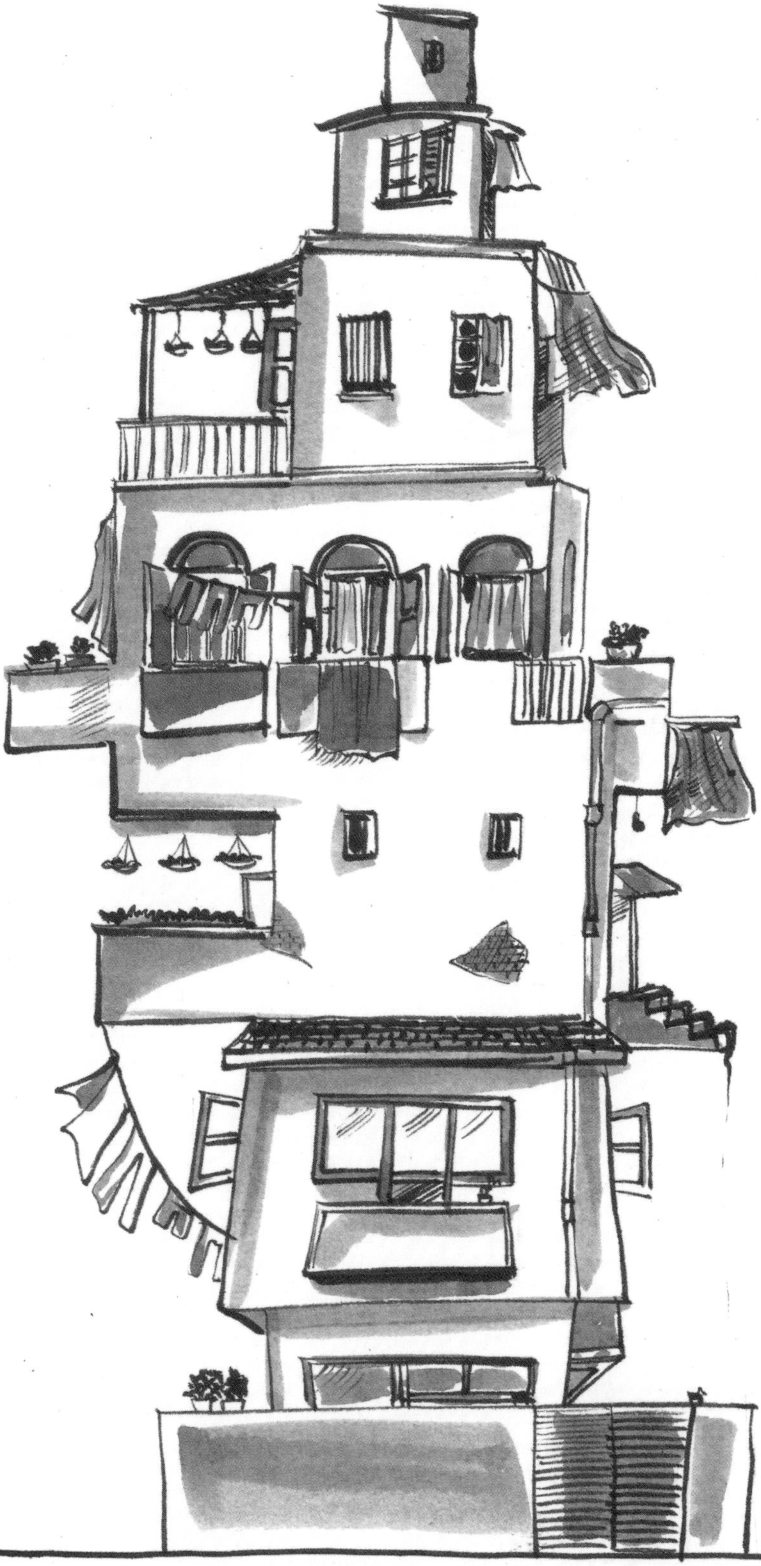

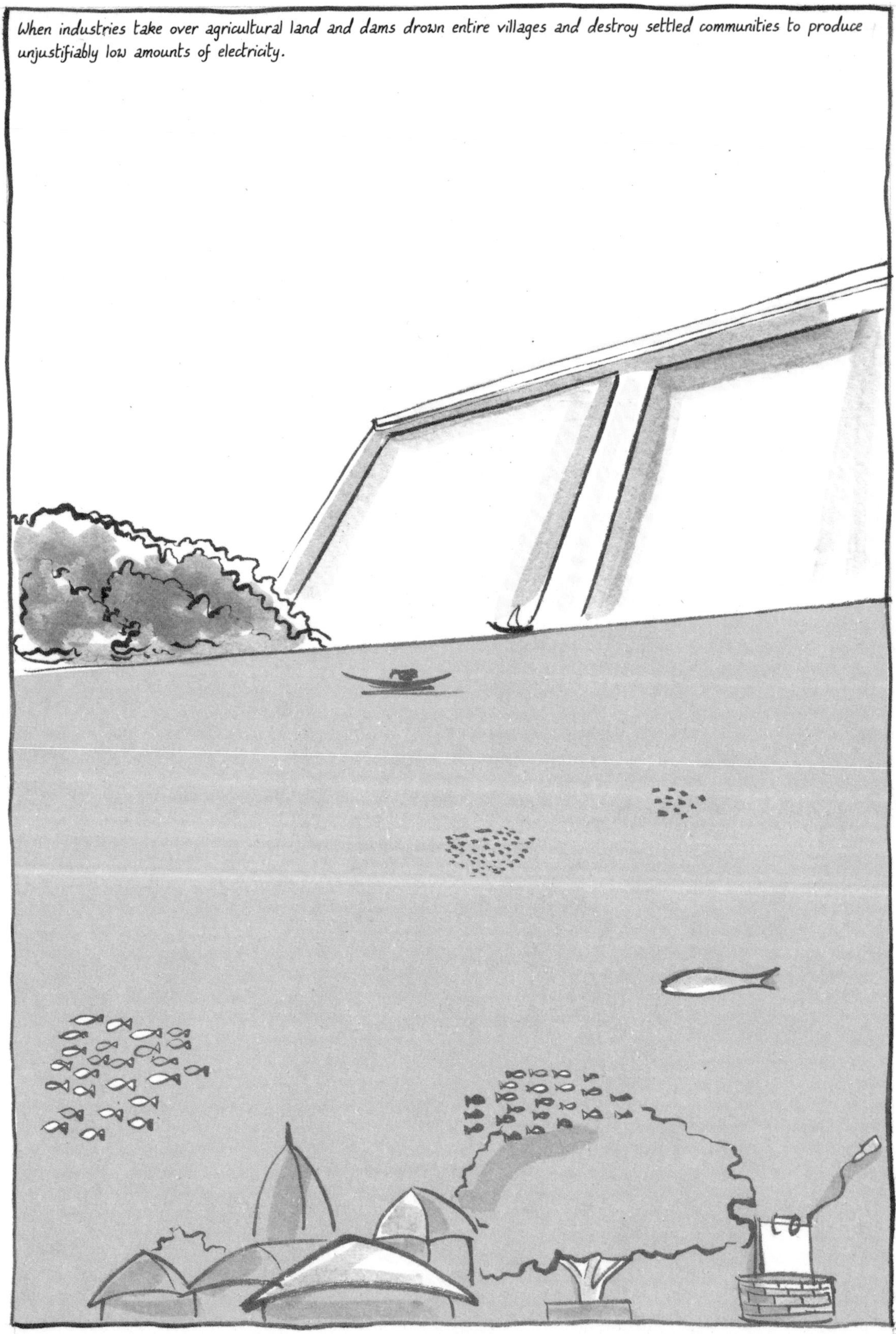
When industries take over agricultural land and dams drown entire villages and destroy settled communities to produce unjustifiably low amounts of electricity.

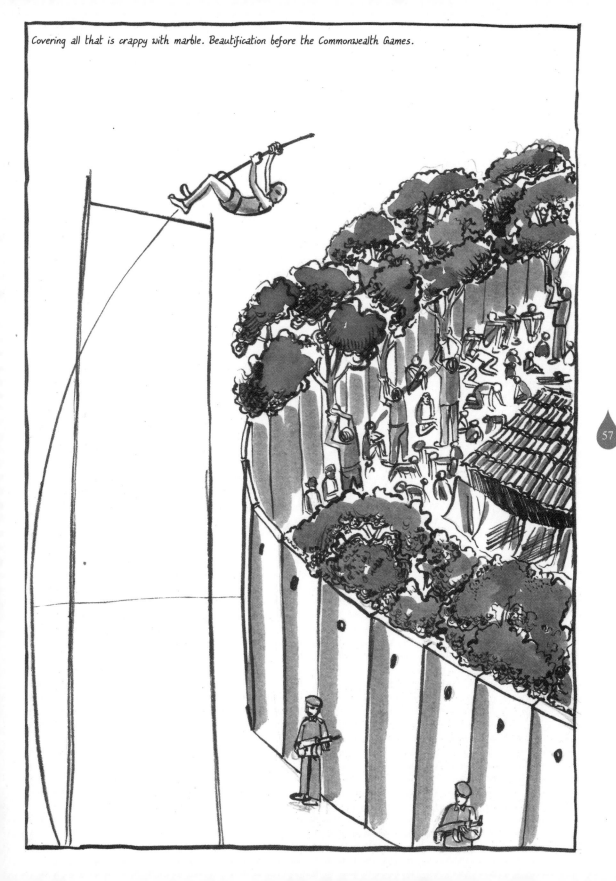

Covering all that is crappy with marble. Beautification before the Commonwealth Games.

57

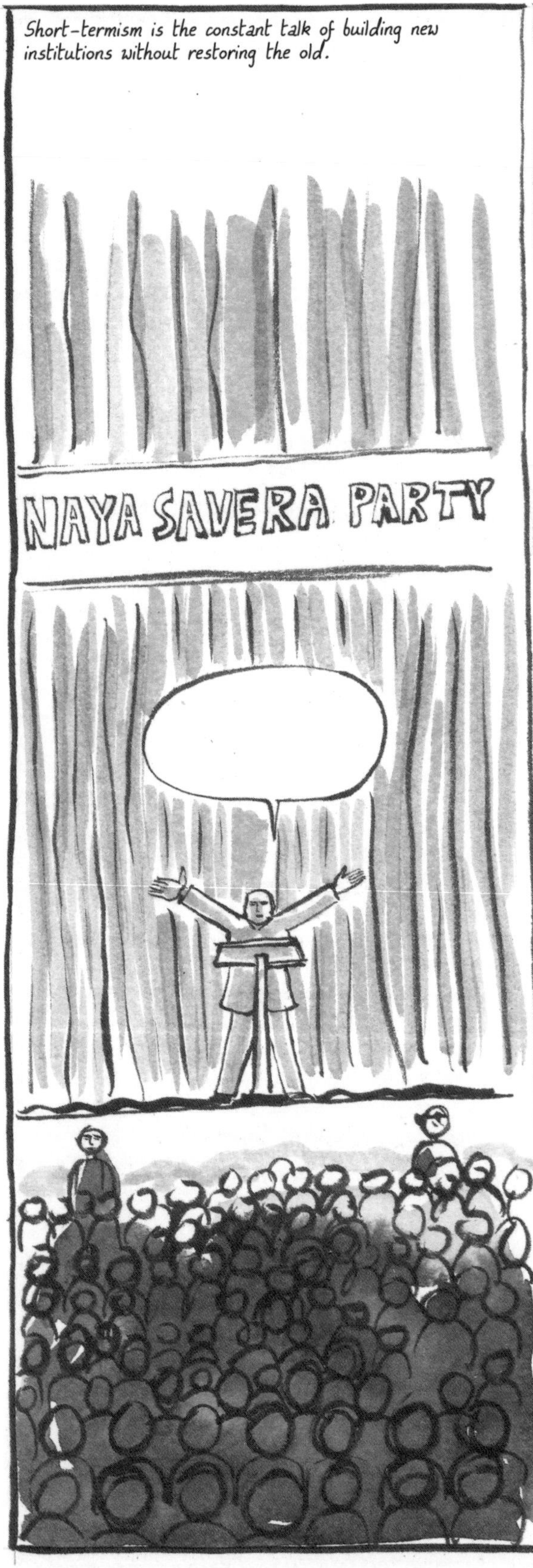
Short-termism is the constant talk of building new institutions without restoring the old.
NAYA SAVERA PARTY

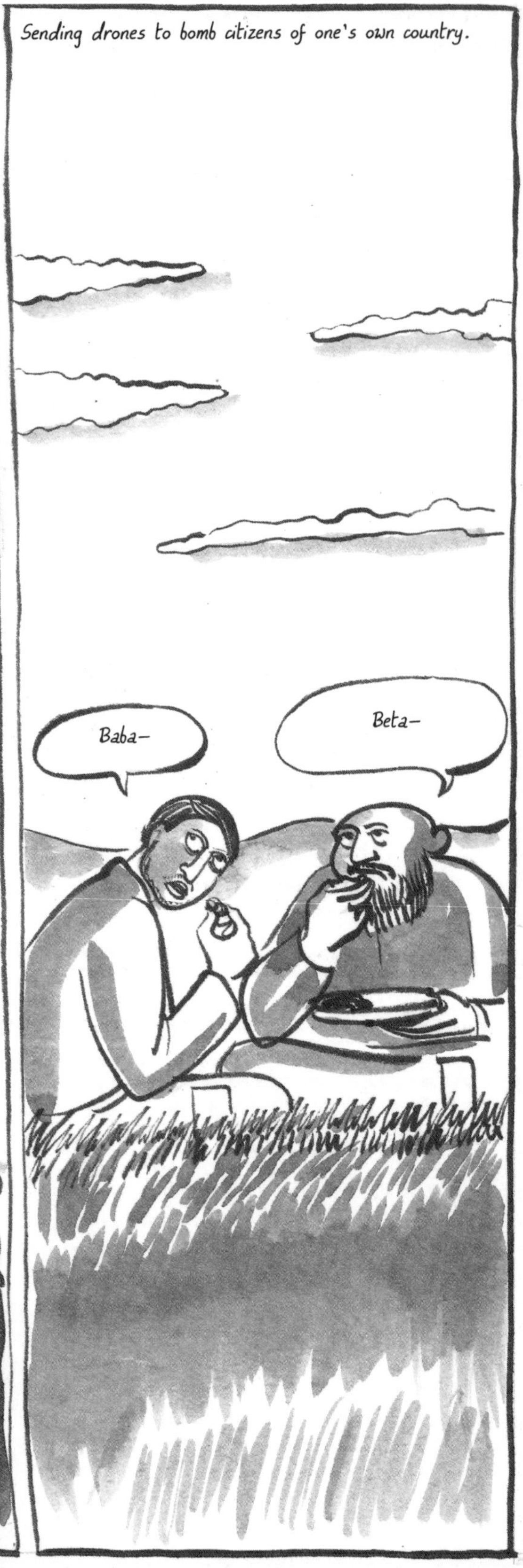
Sending drones to bomb citizens of one's own country.
Baba–
Beta–

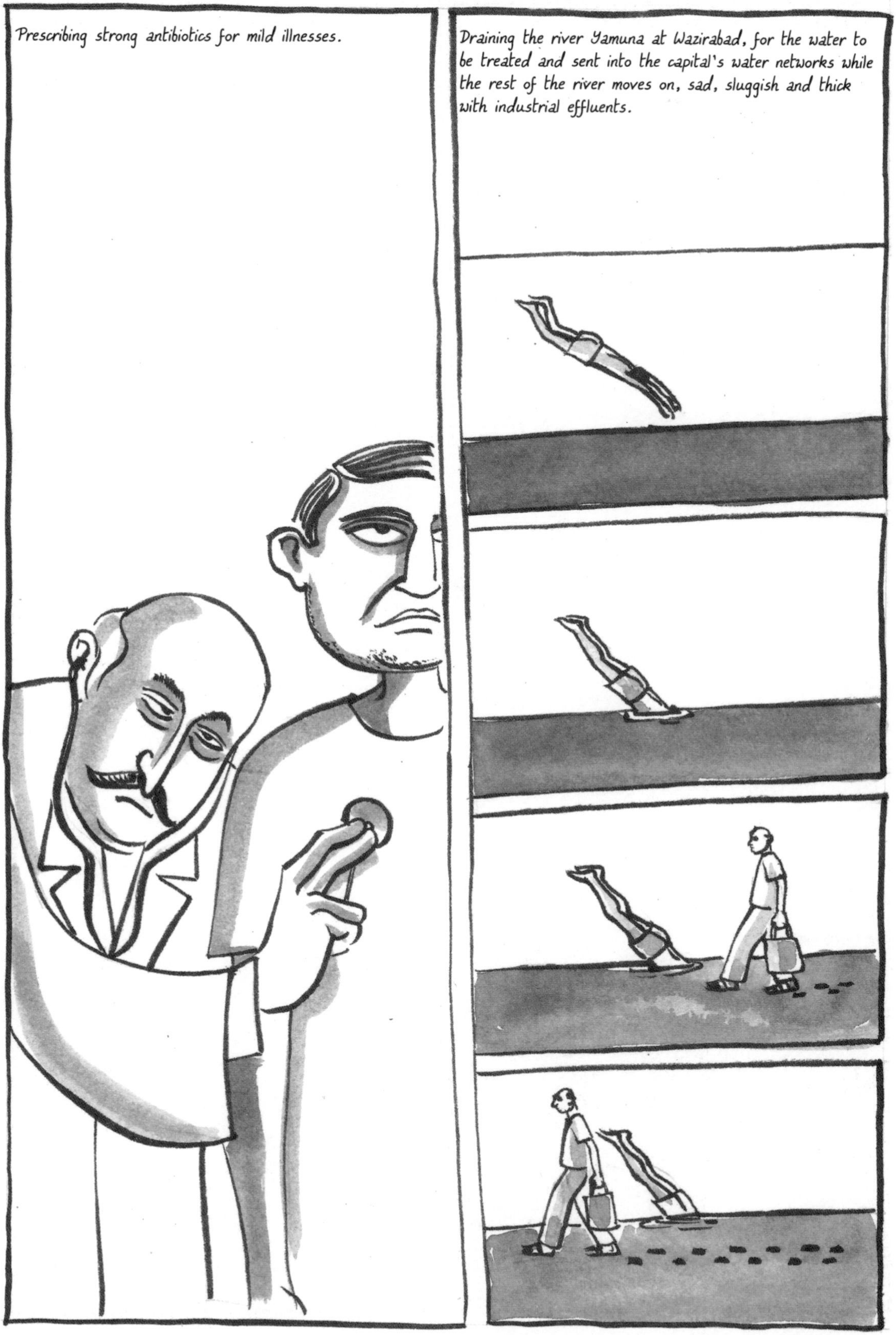
Prescribing strong antibiotics for mild illnesses.
Draining the river Yamuna at Wazirabad, for the water to be treated and sent into the capital's water networks while the rest of the river moves on, sad, sluggish and thick with industrial effluents.

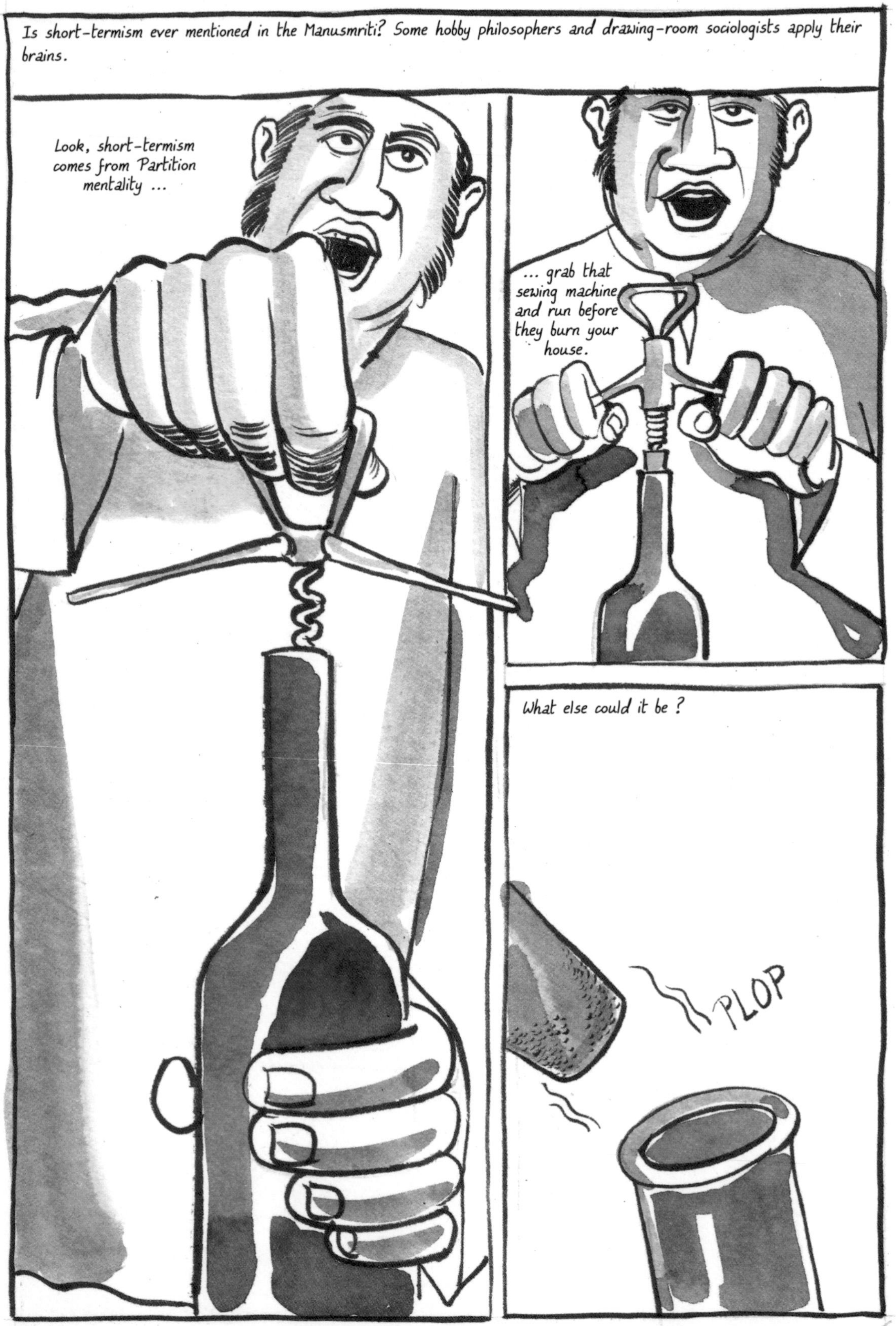
Is short-termism ever mentioned in the Manusmriti? Some hobby philosophers and drawing-room sociologists apply their brains.
Look, short-termism comes from Partition mentality ...
... grab that sewing machine and run before they burn your house.
What else could it be ?
PLOP

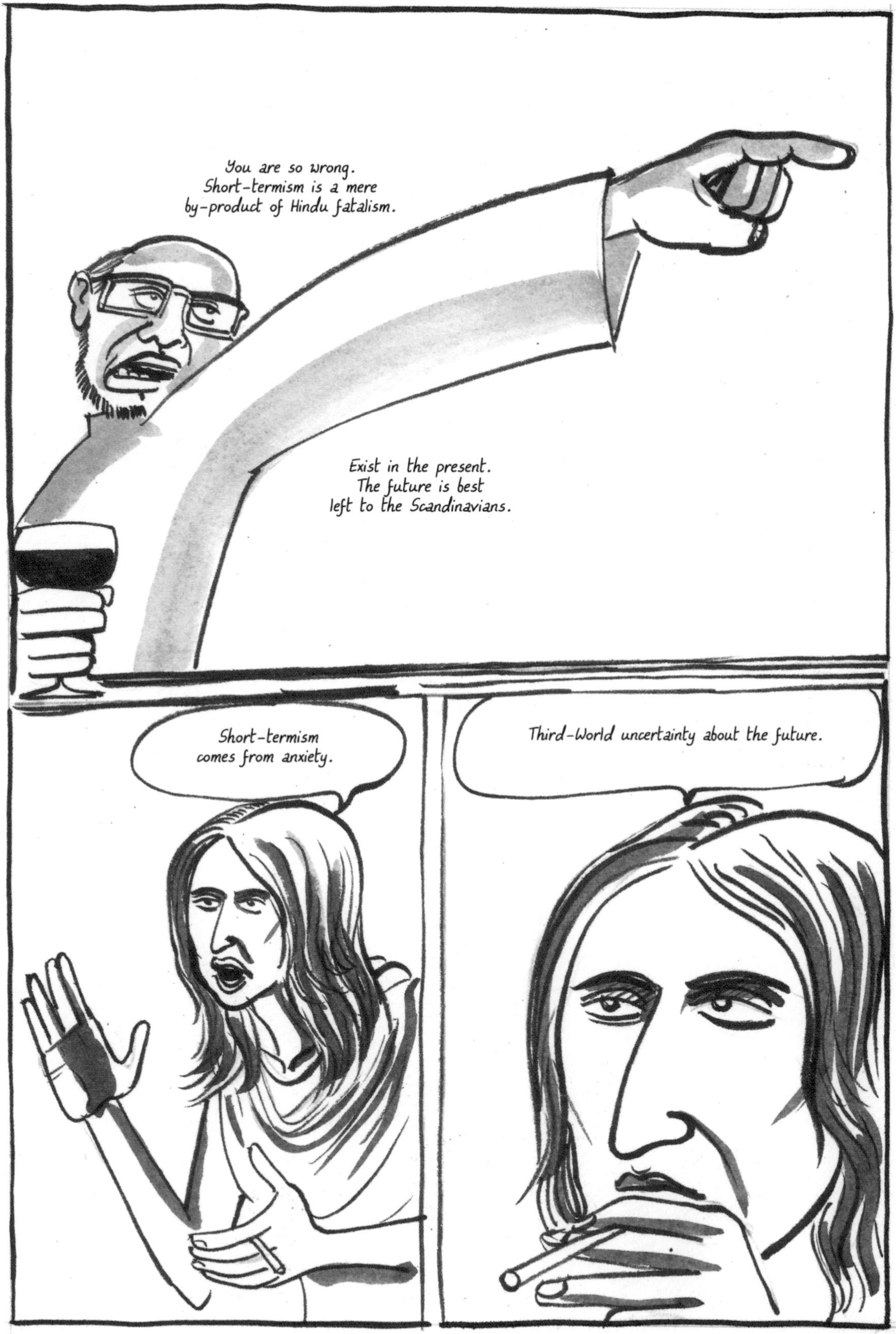
You are so wrong.
Short-termism is a mere
by-product of Hindu fatalism.
Exist in the present.
The future is best
left to the Scandinavians.
Short-termism
comes from anxiety.
Third-World uncertainty about the future.

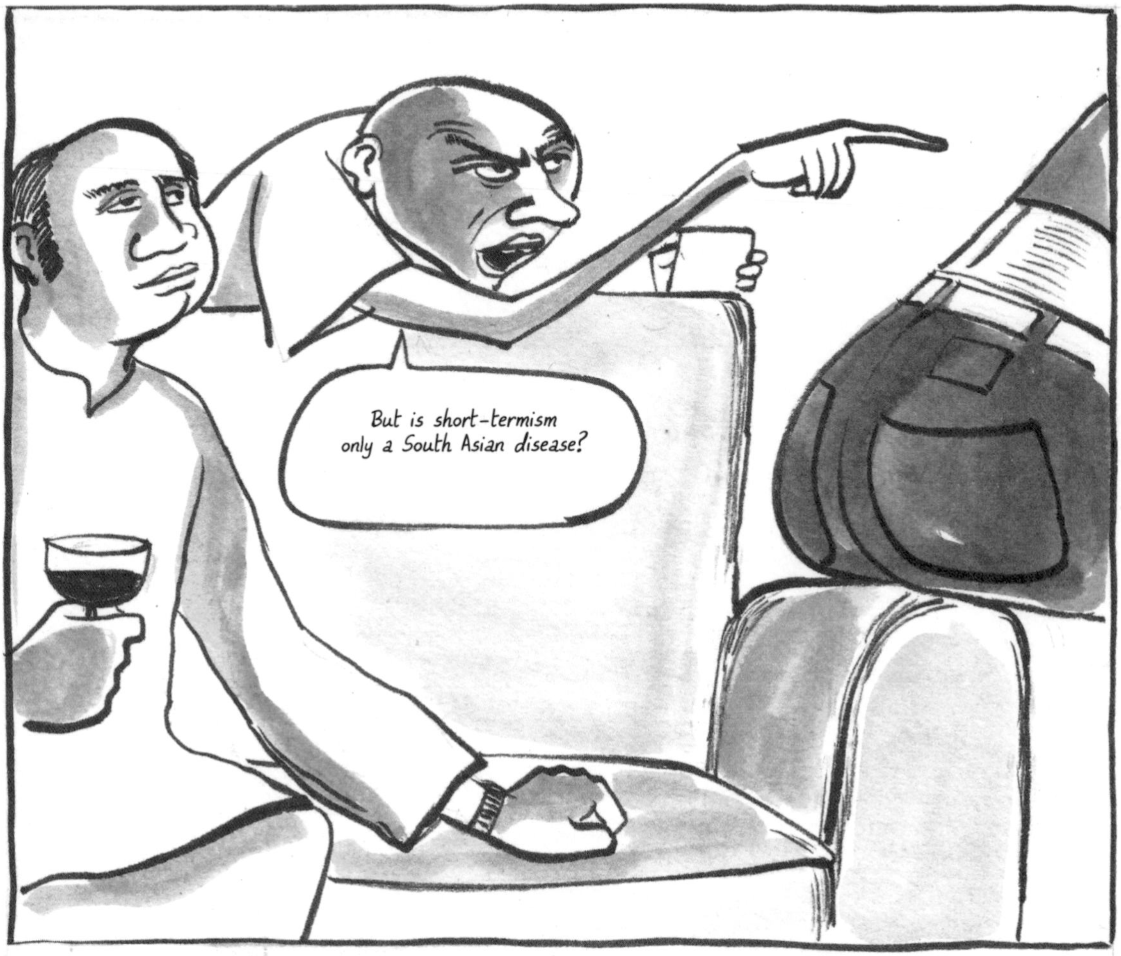
But is short-termism only a South Asian disease?

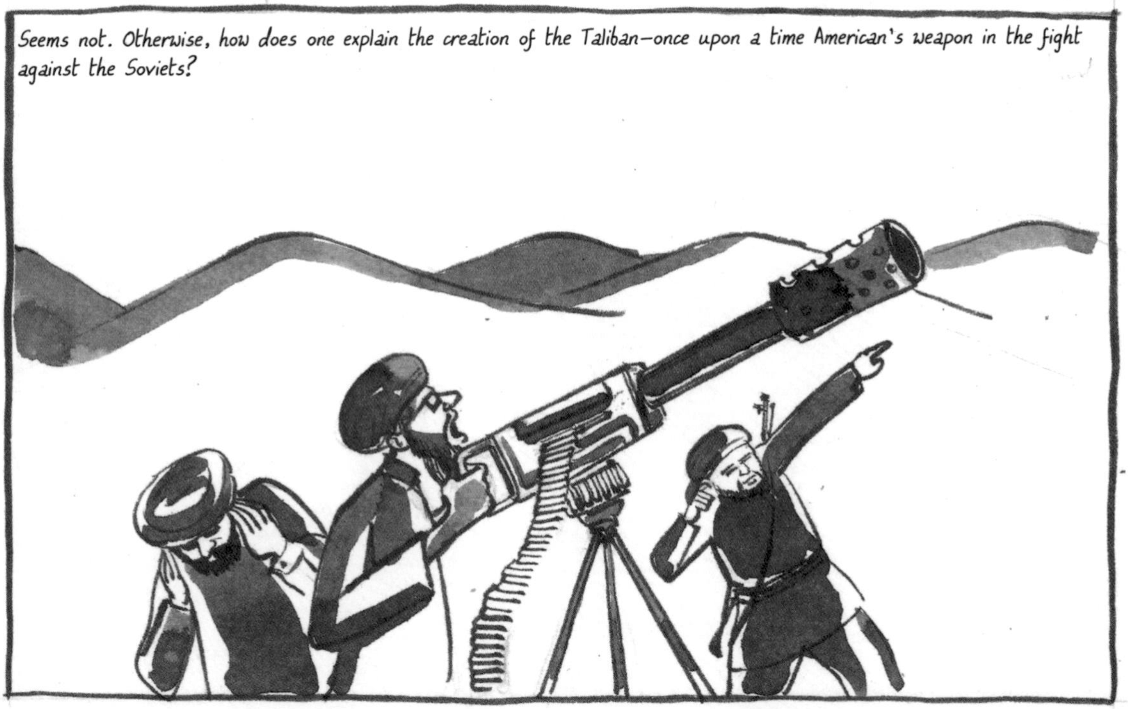
Seems not. Otherwise, how does one explain the creation of the Taliban—once upon a time American's weapon in the fight against the Soviets?

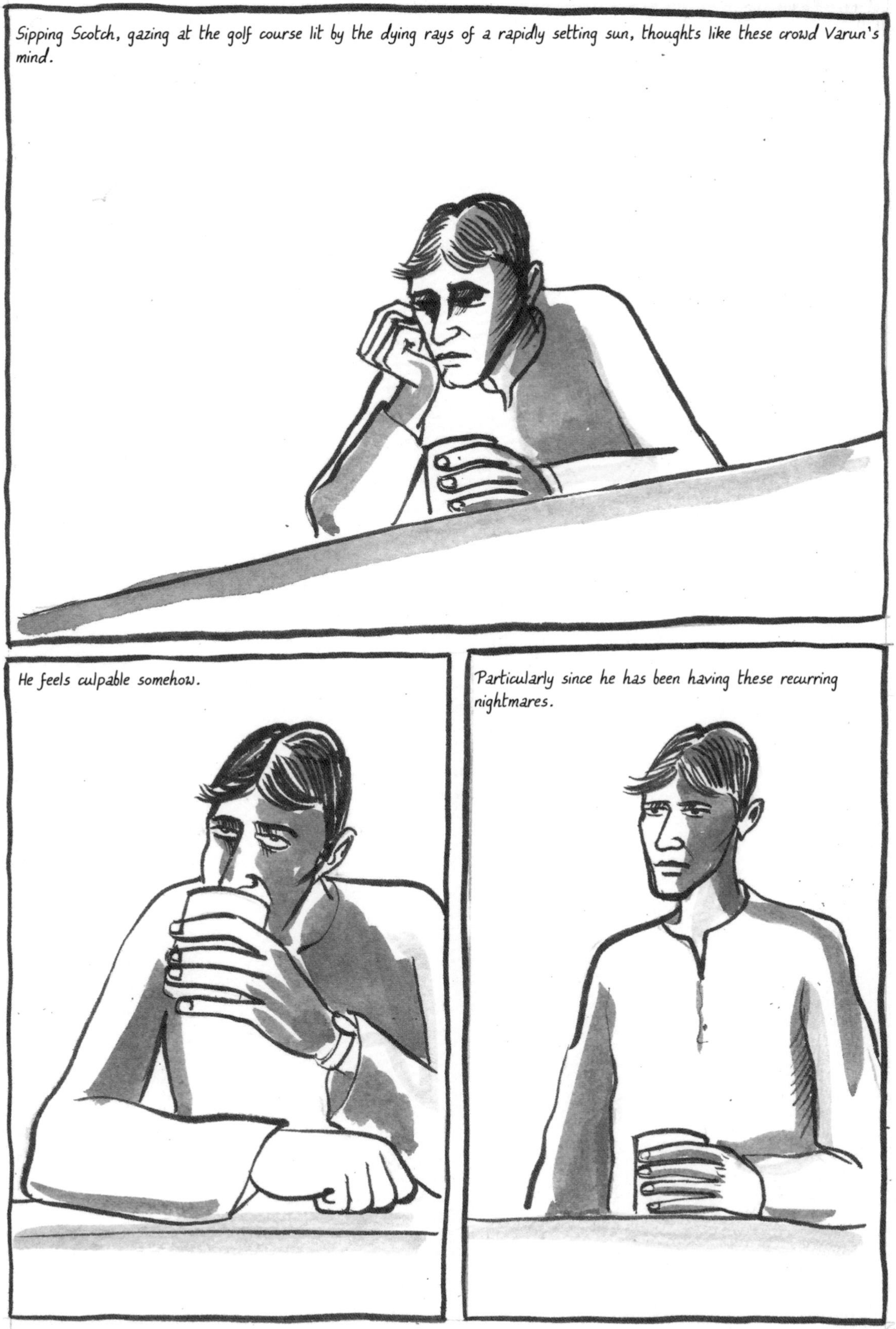
Sipping Scotch, gazing at the golf course lit by the dying rays of a rapidly setting sun, thoughts like these crowd Varun's mind.
He feels culpable somehow.
Particularly since he has been having these recurring nightmares.

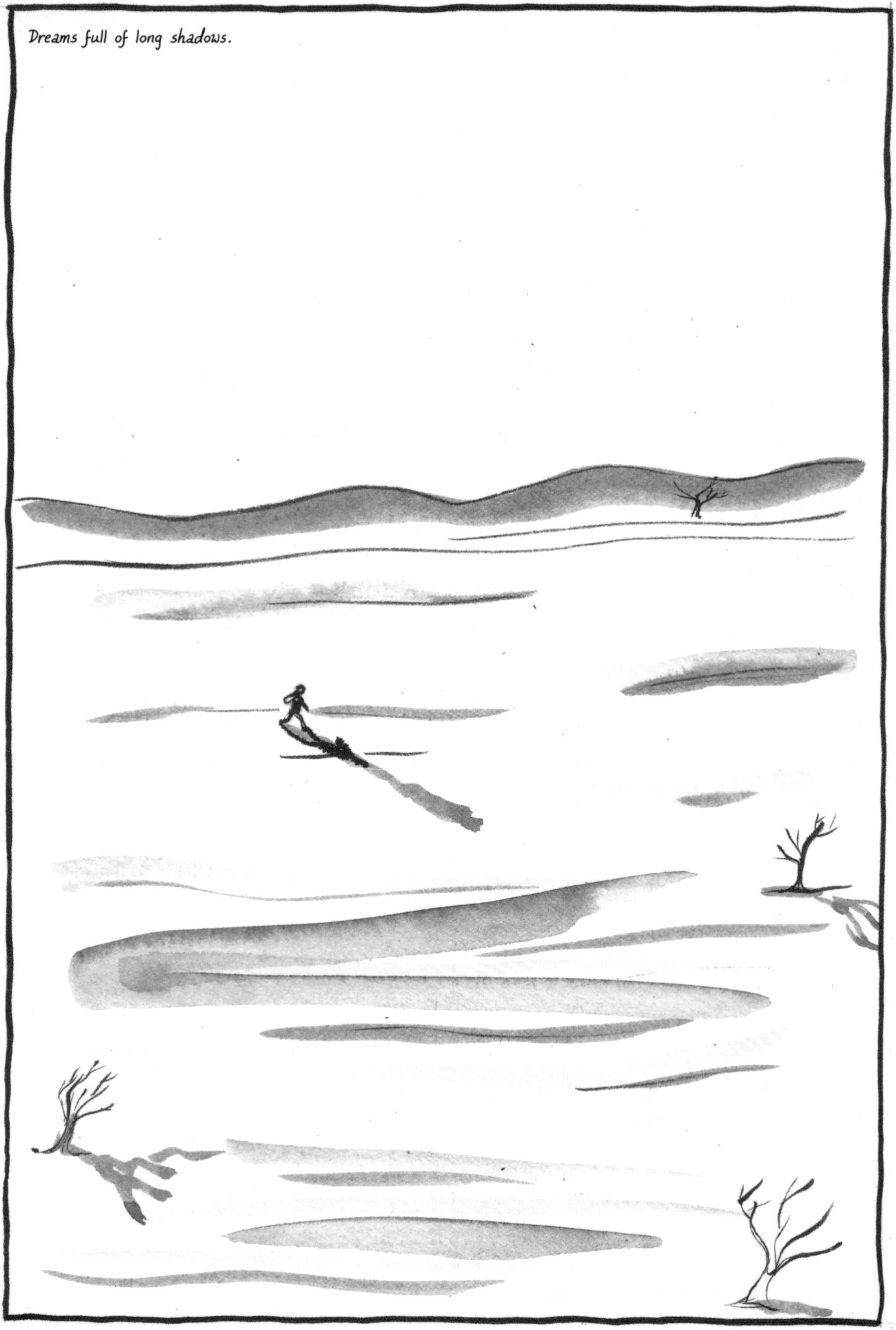
Dreams full of long shadows.

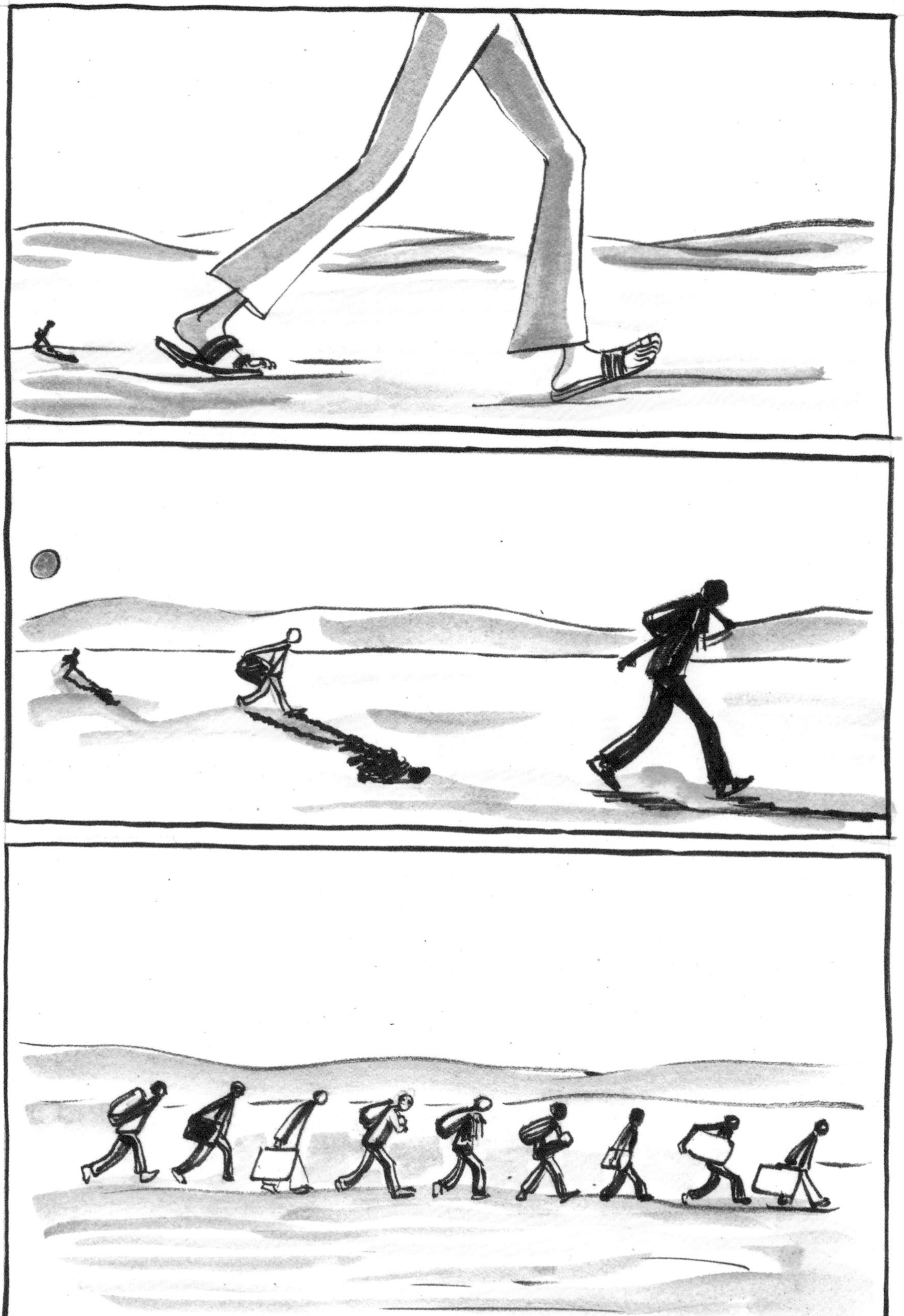

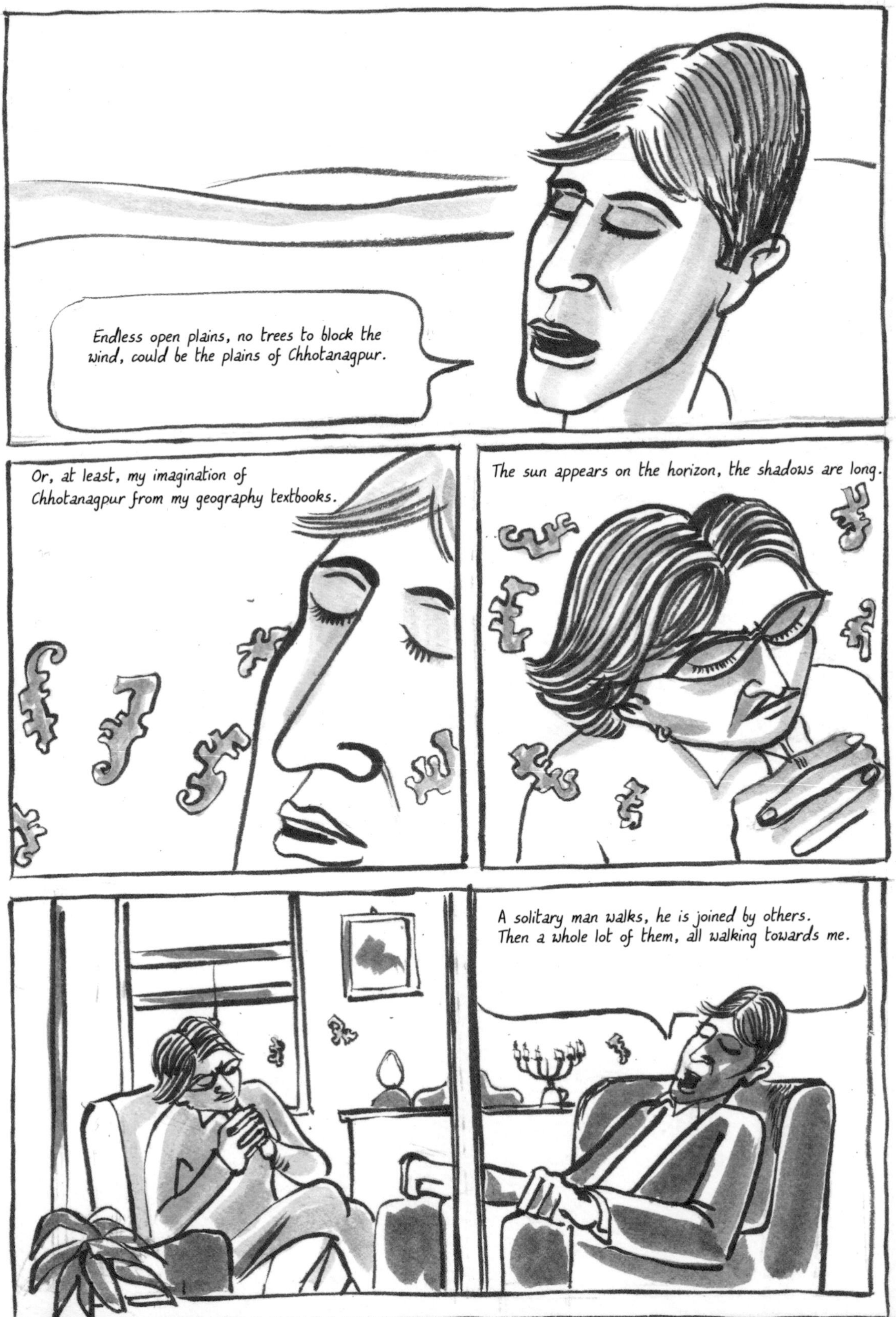
Endless open plains, no trees to block the wind, could be the plains of Chhotanagpur.
Or, at least, my imagination of Chhotanagpur from my geography textbooks.
The sun appears on the horizon, the shadows are long.
A solitary man walks, he is joined by others. Then a whole lot of them, all walking towards me.

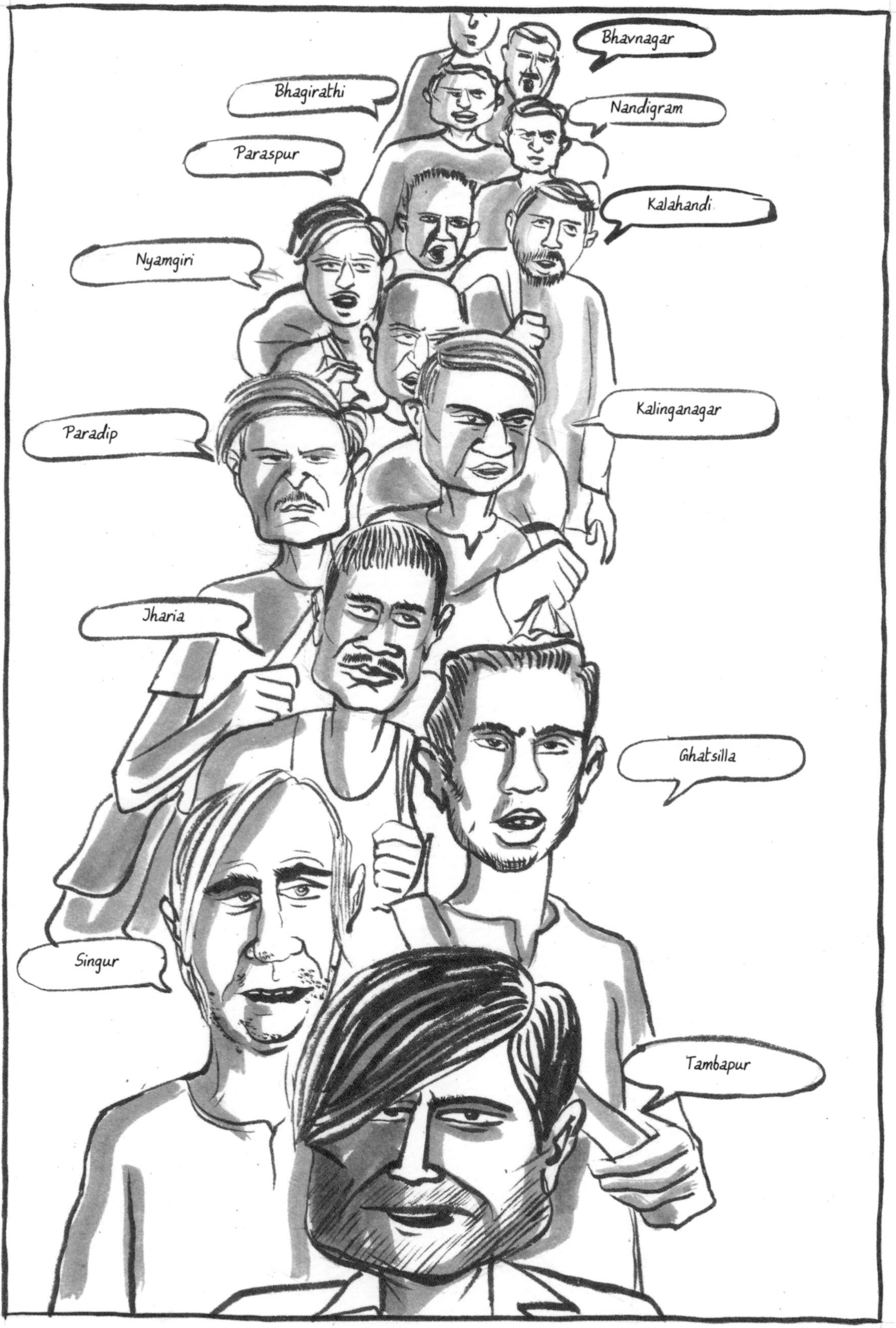
Bhavnagar
Bhagirathi
Nandigram
Paraspur
Kalahandi
Nyamgiri
Kalinganagar
Paradip
Jharia
Ghatsilla
Singur
Tambapur

Market rewards financial returns.

Profit becomes progress.

Government has to become more business friendly.

Tambapur.

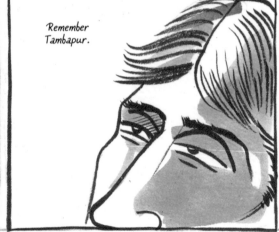

Remember Tambapur.

The sun has set behind the Aravallis, Varun remembers the factory he had helped closing down. Life sucks sometimes.

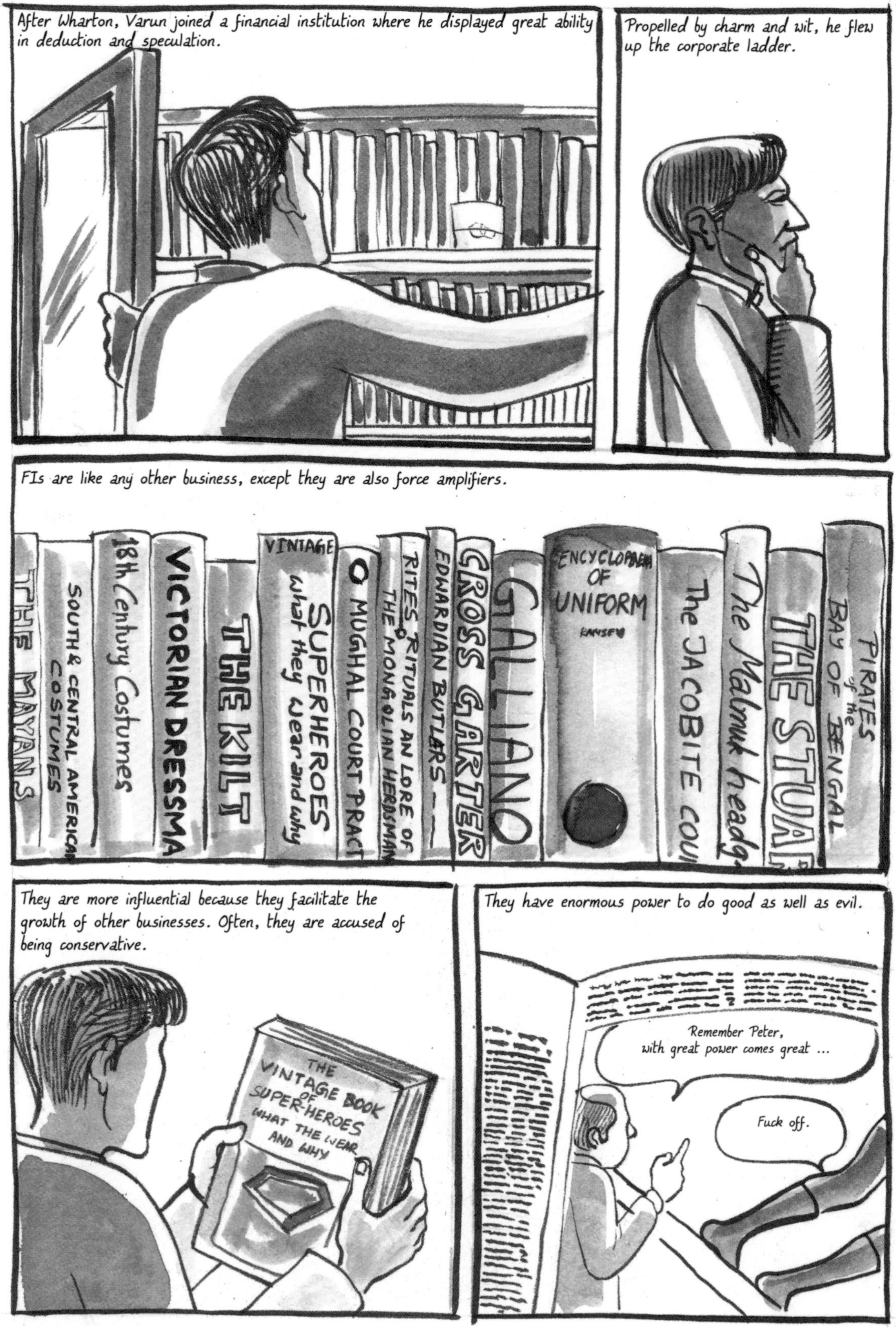

After Wharton, Varun joined a financial institution where he displayed great ability in deduction and speculation.
Propelled by charm and wit, he flew up the corporate ladder.
FIs are like any other business, except they are also force amplifiers.
THE MAYANS
SOUTH & CENTRAL AMERICAN COSTUMES
18th Century Costumes
VICTORIAN DRESSMA
THE KILT
VINTAGE SUPERHEROES what they wear and why
MUGHAL COURT PRACT
RITES RITUALS AN LORE OF THE MONGOLIAN HERDSMAN
EDWARDIAN BUTLERS
CROSS GARTER
GALLIANO
ENCYCLOPAEDIA OF UNIFORM
The JACOBITE COU
The Malmuk headg
THE STUAR
PIRATES of the BAY OF BENGAL
They are more influential because they facilitate the growth of other businesses. Often, they are accused of being conservative.
THE VINTAGE BOOK OF SUPER-HEROES WHAT THE WEAR AND WHY
They have enormous power to do good as well as evil.
Remember Peter, with great power comes great ...
Fuck off.

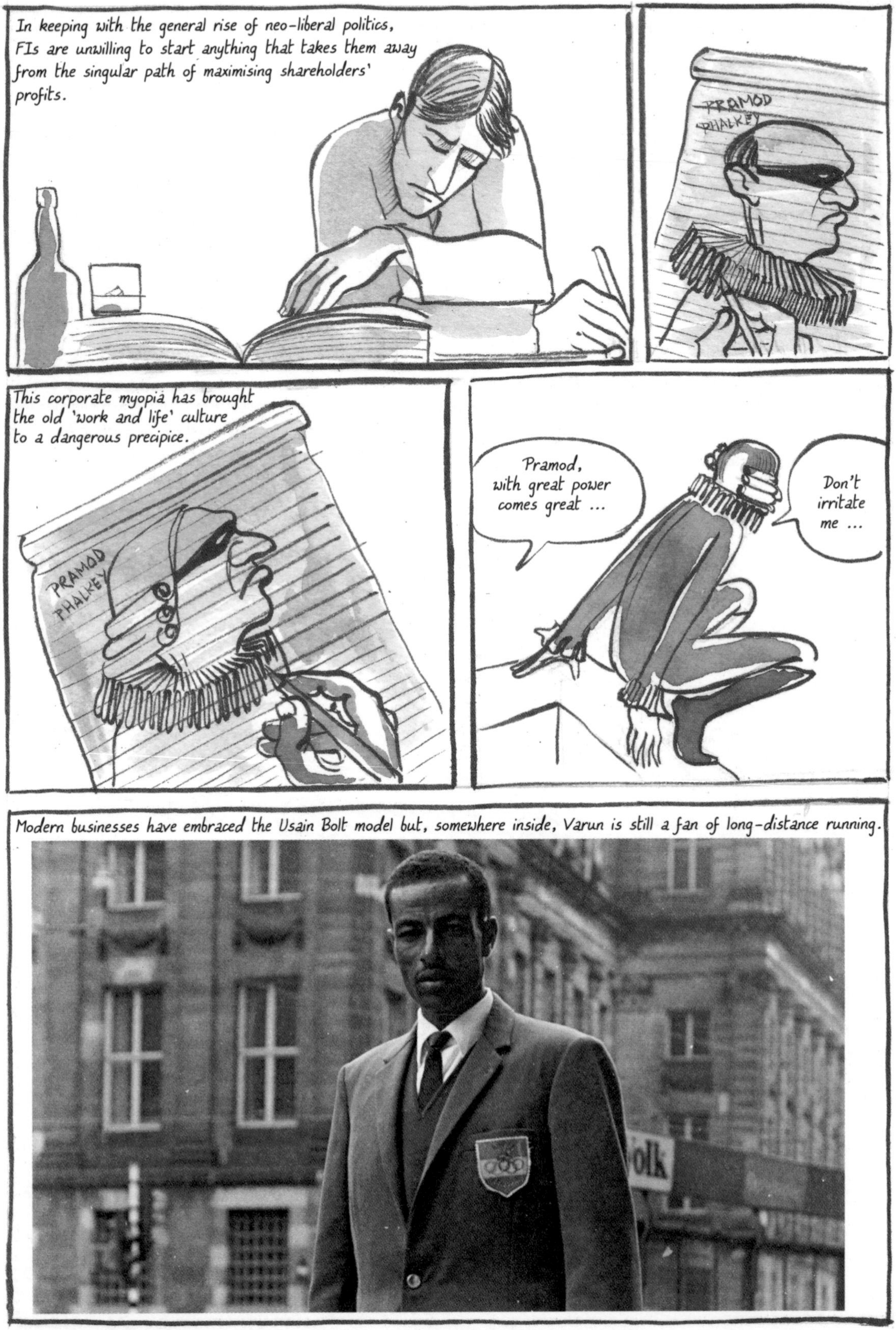
In keeping with the general rise of neo-liberal politics, FIs are unwilling to start anything that takes them away from the singular path of maximising shareholders' profits.
PRAMOD PHALKEY
This corporate myopia has brought the old 'work and life' culture to a dangerous precipice.
PRAMOD PHALKEY
Pramod, with great power comes great ...
Don't irritate me ...
Modern businesses have embraced the Usain Bolt model but, somewhere inside, Varun is still a fan of long-distance running.

He knows that, thanks to some FIs, companies like Platypus Group have amassed massive wealth. But where's the honour in that?

What a powerful speech!

I feel horny.

Many FIs are notorious for creating the briefest time horizons which privilege companies that are looking for short-term profit than those that take the long view.

Academic institutions too, in general, are producing not visionaries but templates.

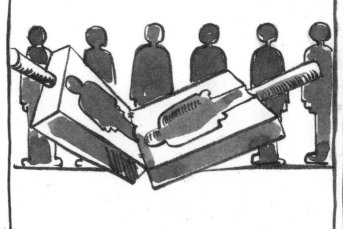

Visionaries can be very annoying.

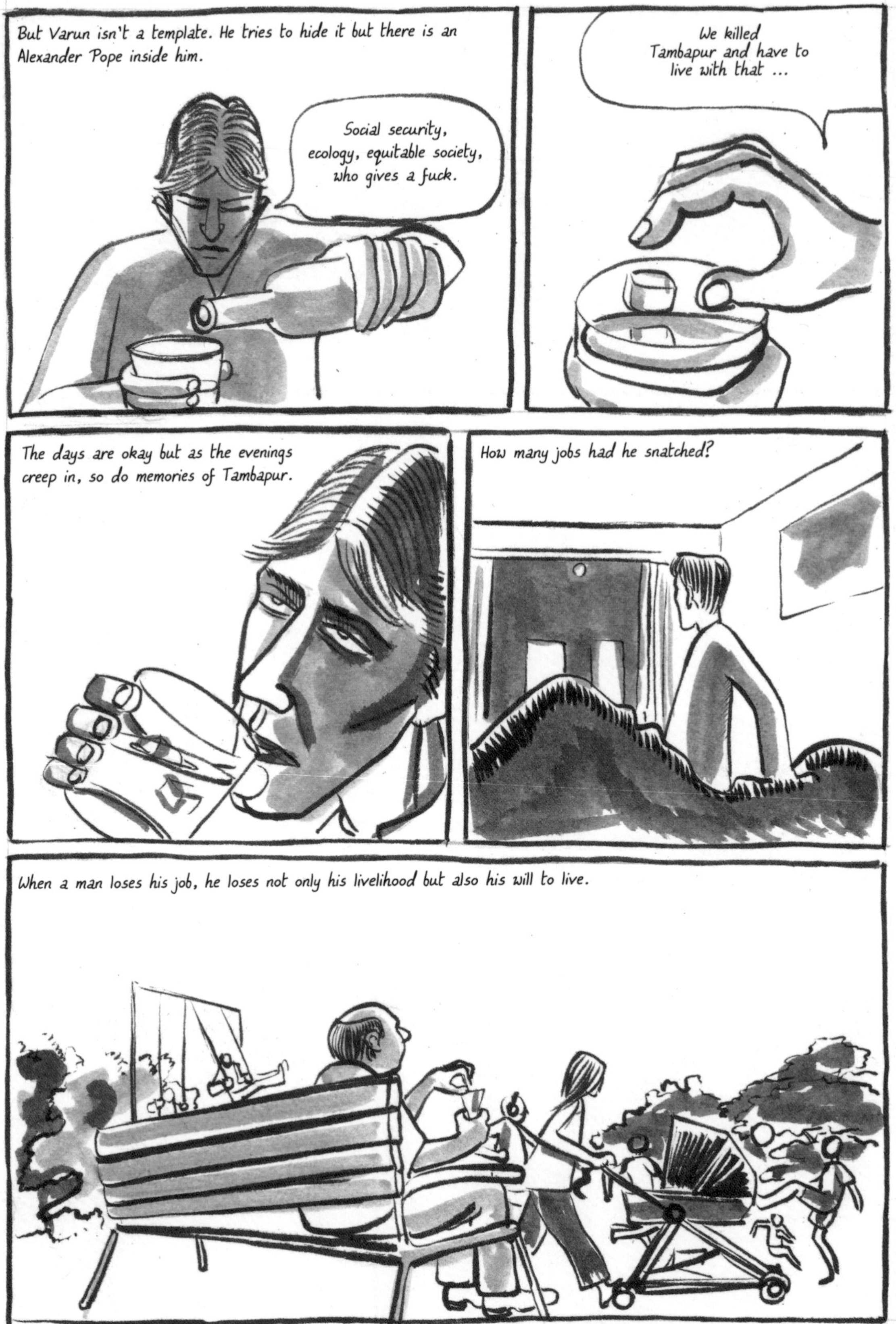
But Varun isn't a template. He tries to hide it but there is an Alexander Pope inside him.
Social security, ecology, equitable society, who gives a fuck.
We killed Tambapur and have to live with that ...
The days are okay but as the evenings creep in, so do memories of Tambapur.
How many jobs had he snatched?
When a man loses his job, he loses not only his livelihood but also his will to live.

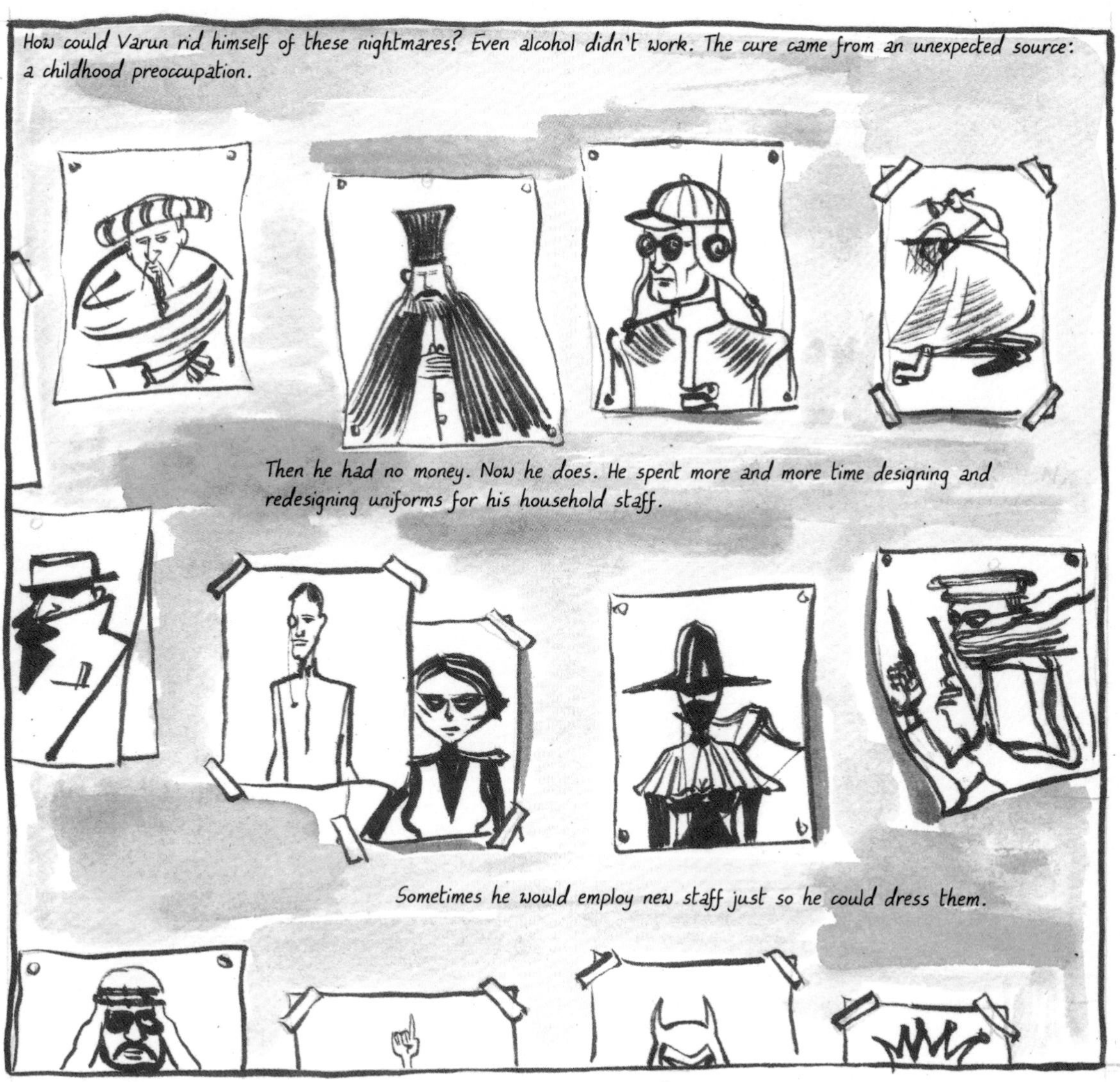
How could Varun rid himself of these nightmares? Even alcohol didn't work. The cure came from an unexpected source: a childhood preoccupation.
Then he had no money. Now he does. He spent more and more time designing and redesigning uniforms for his household staff.
Sometimes he would employ new staff just so he could dress them.

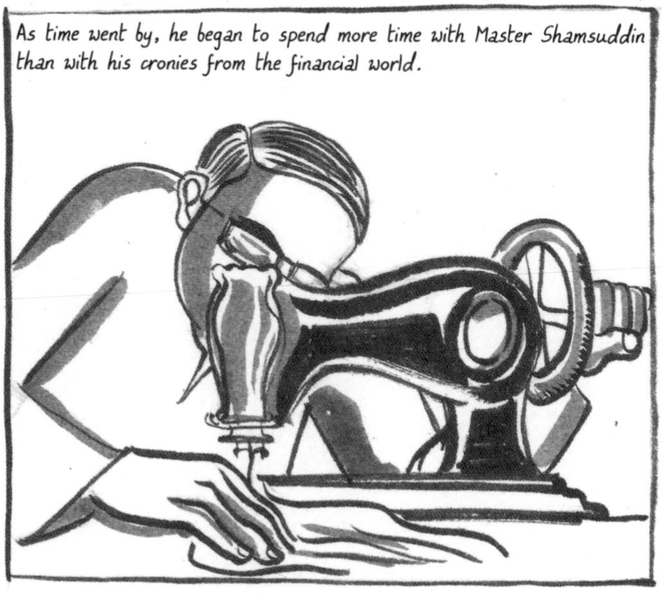
As time went by, he began to spend more time with Master Shamsuddin than with his cronies from the financial world.

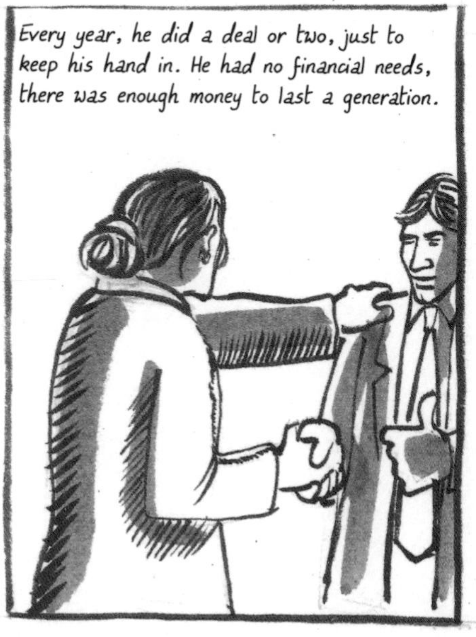
Every year, he did a deal or two, just to keep his hand in. He had no financial needs, there was enough money to last a generation.

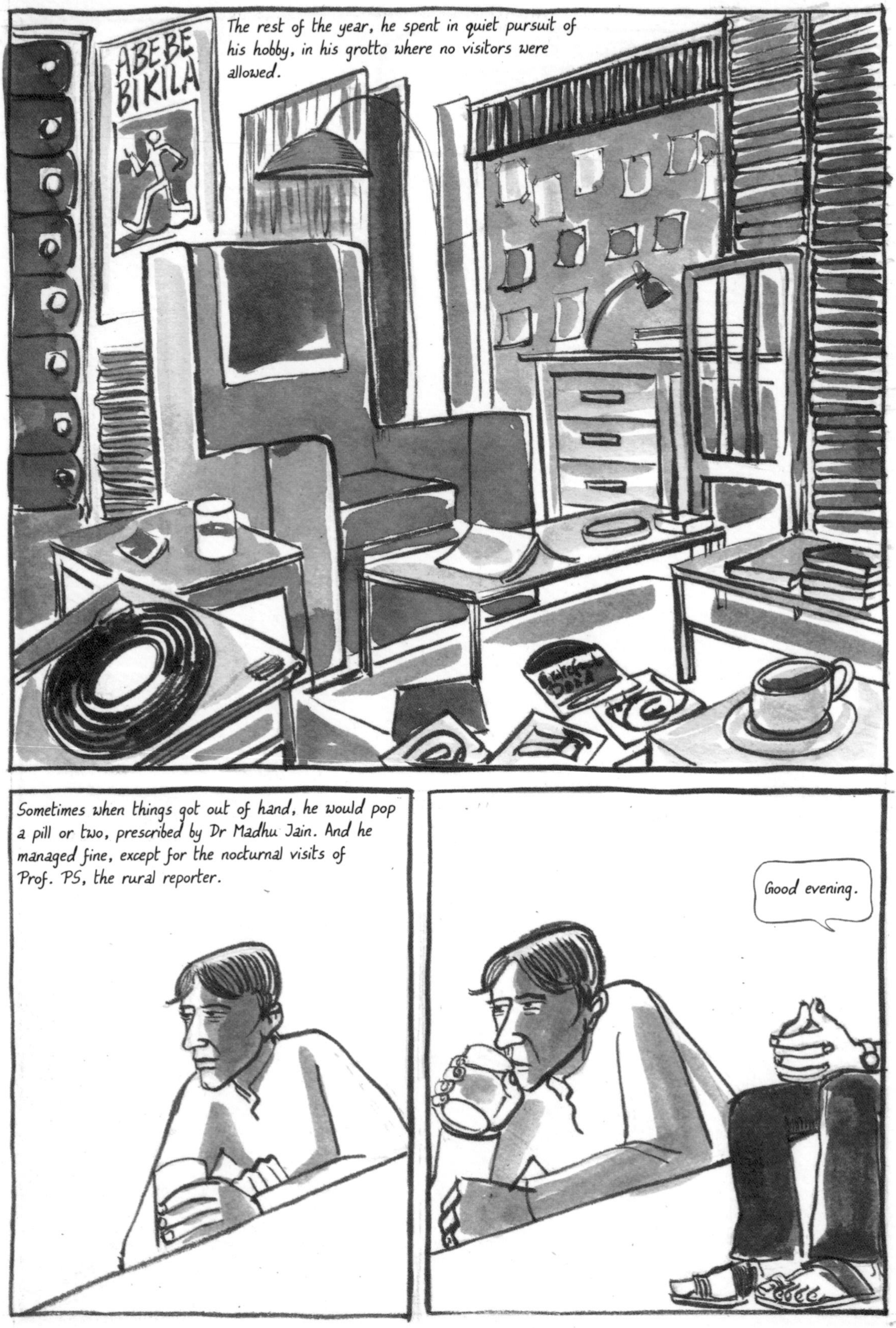
The rest of the year, he spent in quiet pursuit of his hobby, in his grotto where no visitors were allowed.
ABEBE BIKILA
Sometimes when things got out of hand, he would pop a pill or two, prescribed by Dr Madhu Jain. And he managed fine, except for the nocturnal visits of Prof. PS, the rural reporter.
Good evening.

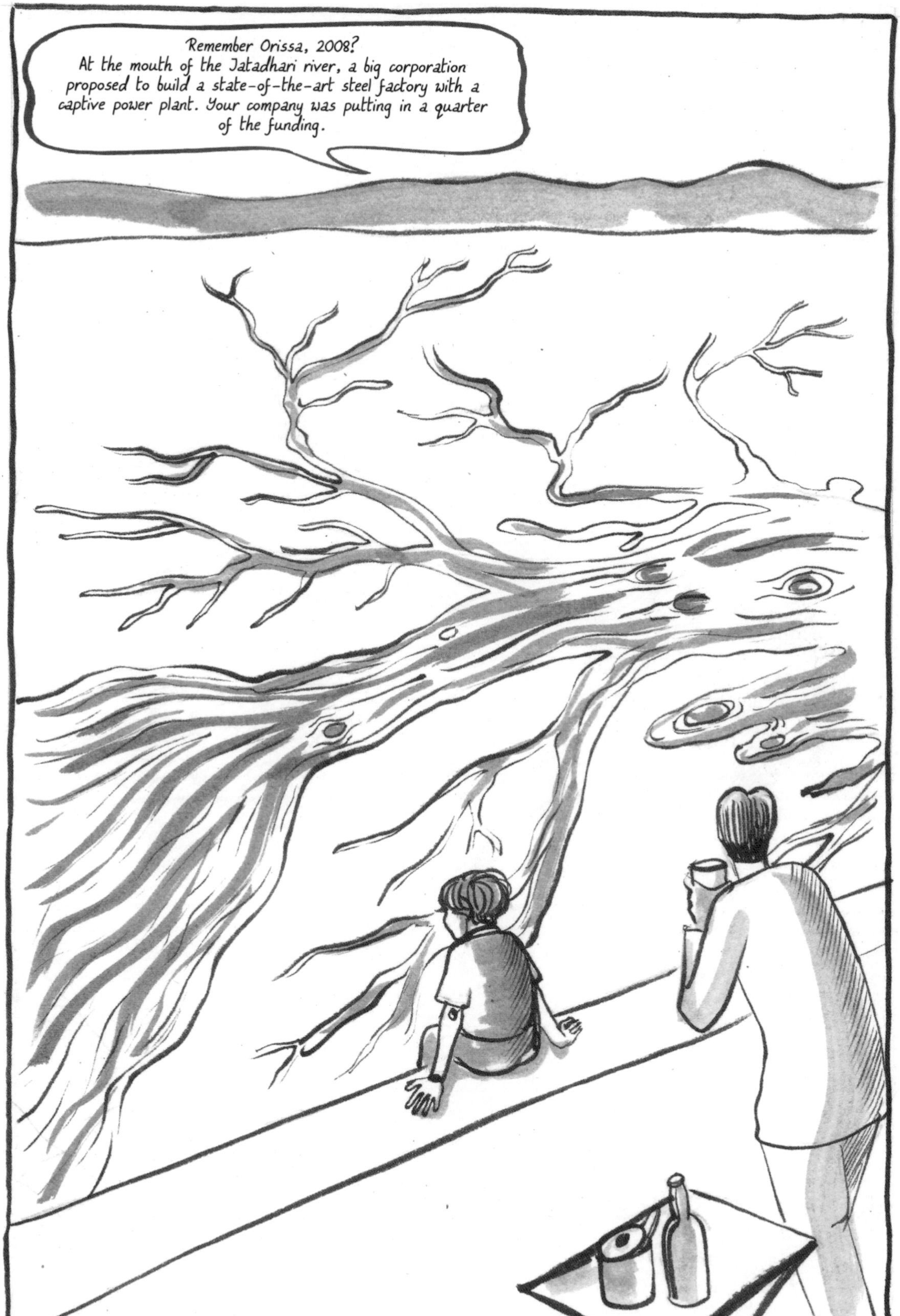
Remember Orissa, 2008? At the mouth of the Jatadhari river, a big corporation proposed to build a state-of-the-art steel factory with a captive power plant. Your company was putting in a quarter of the funding.

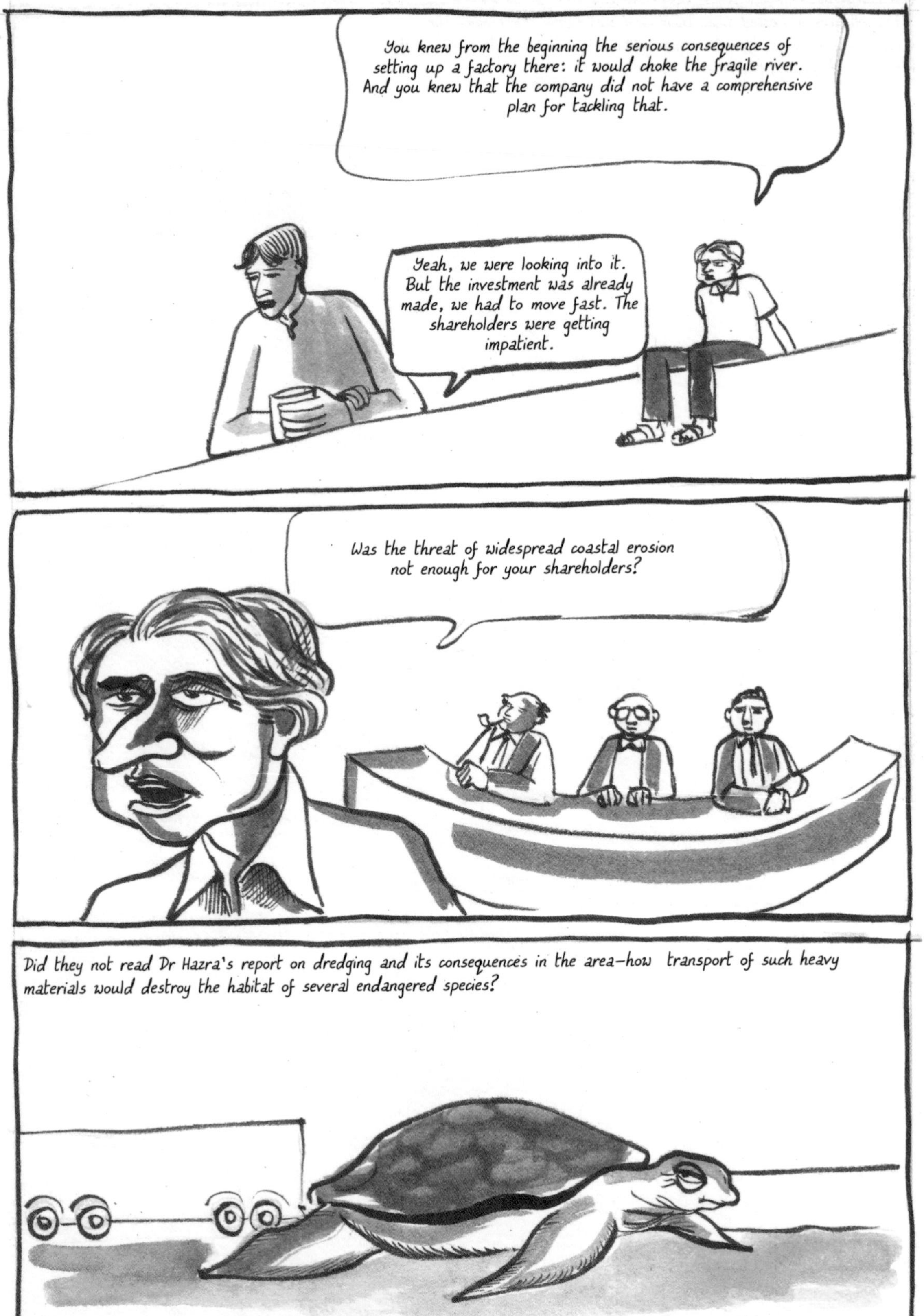

You knew from the beginning the serious consequences of setting up a factory there: it would choke the fragile river. And you knew that the company did not have a comprehensive plan for tackling that.
Yeah, we were looking into it. But the investment was already made, we had to move fast. The shareholders were getting impatient.
Was the threat of widespread coastal erosion not enough for your shareholders?
Did they not read Dr Hazra's report on dredging and its consequences in the area—how transport of such heavy materials would destroy the habitat of several endangered species?

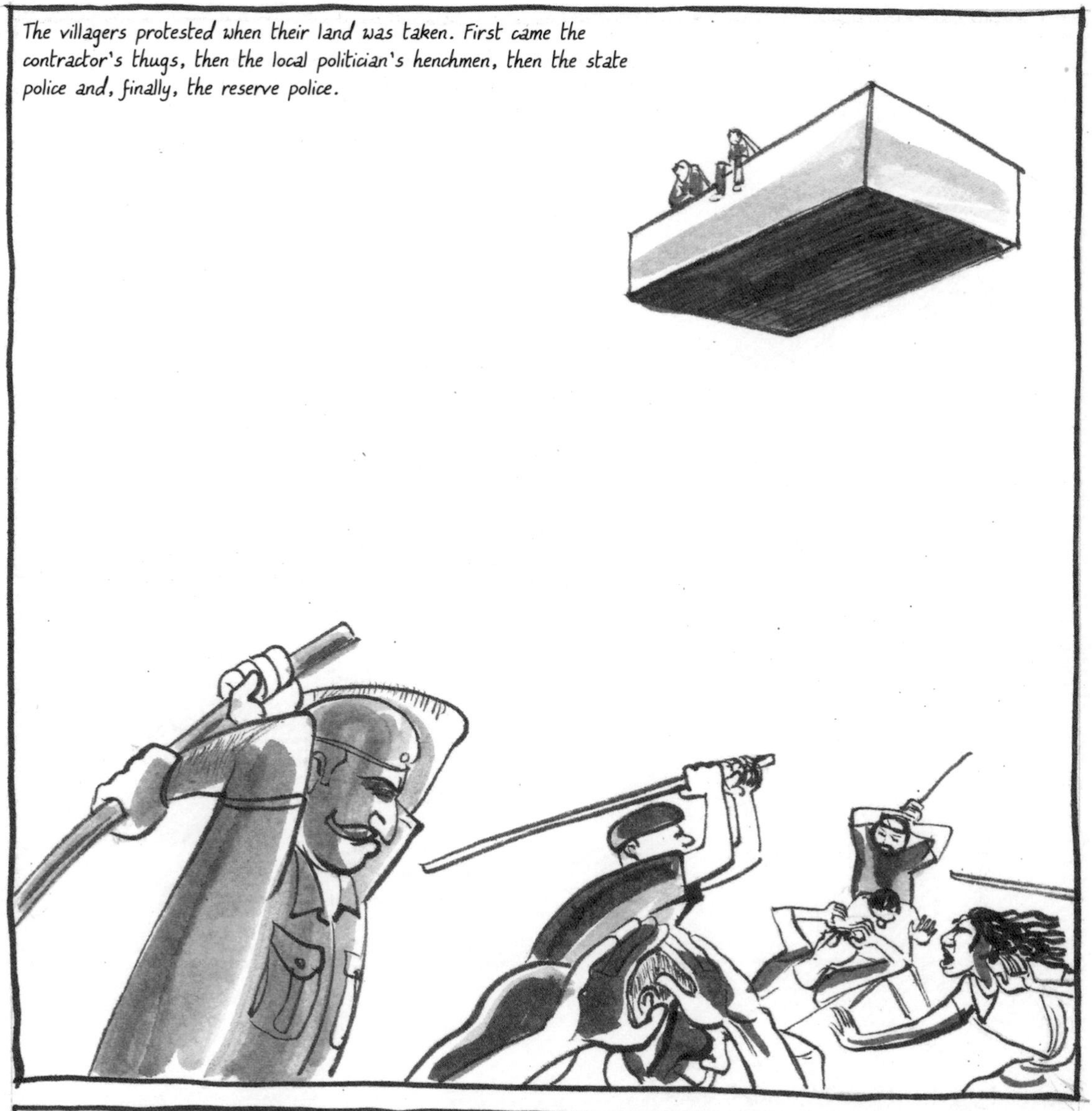
The villagers protested when their land was taken. First came the contractor's thugs, then the local politician's henchmen, then the state police and, finally, the reserve police.

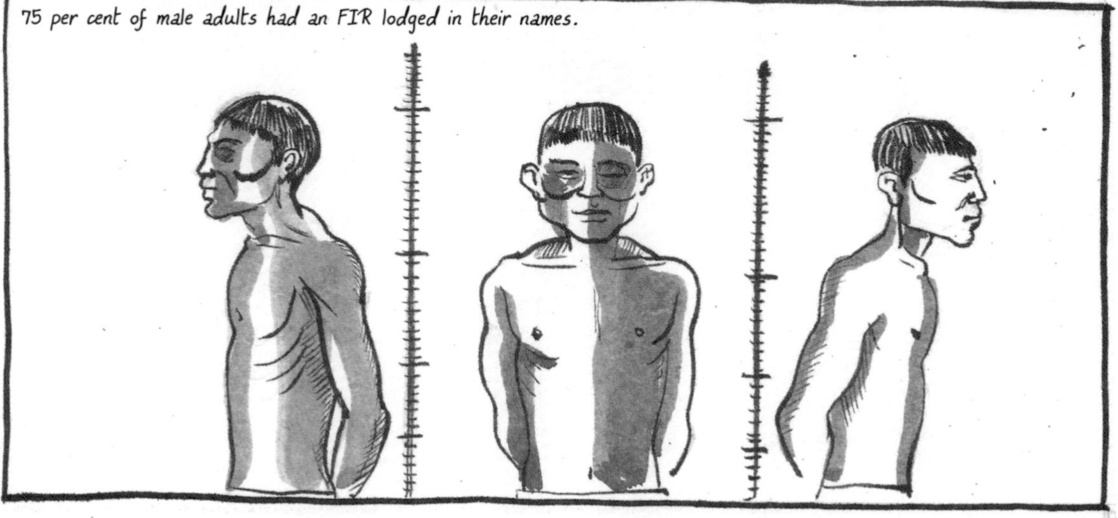
75 per cent of male adults had an FIR lodged in their names.

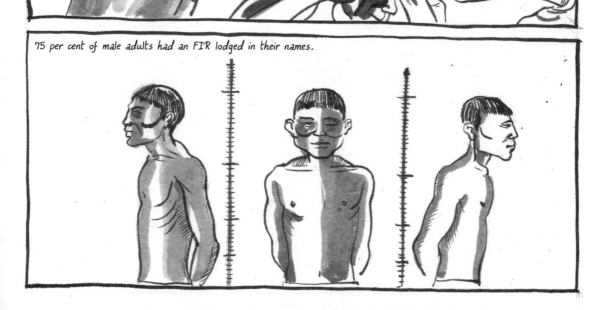

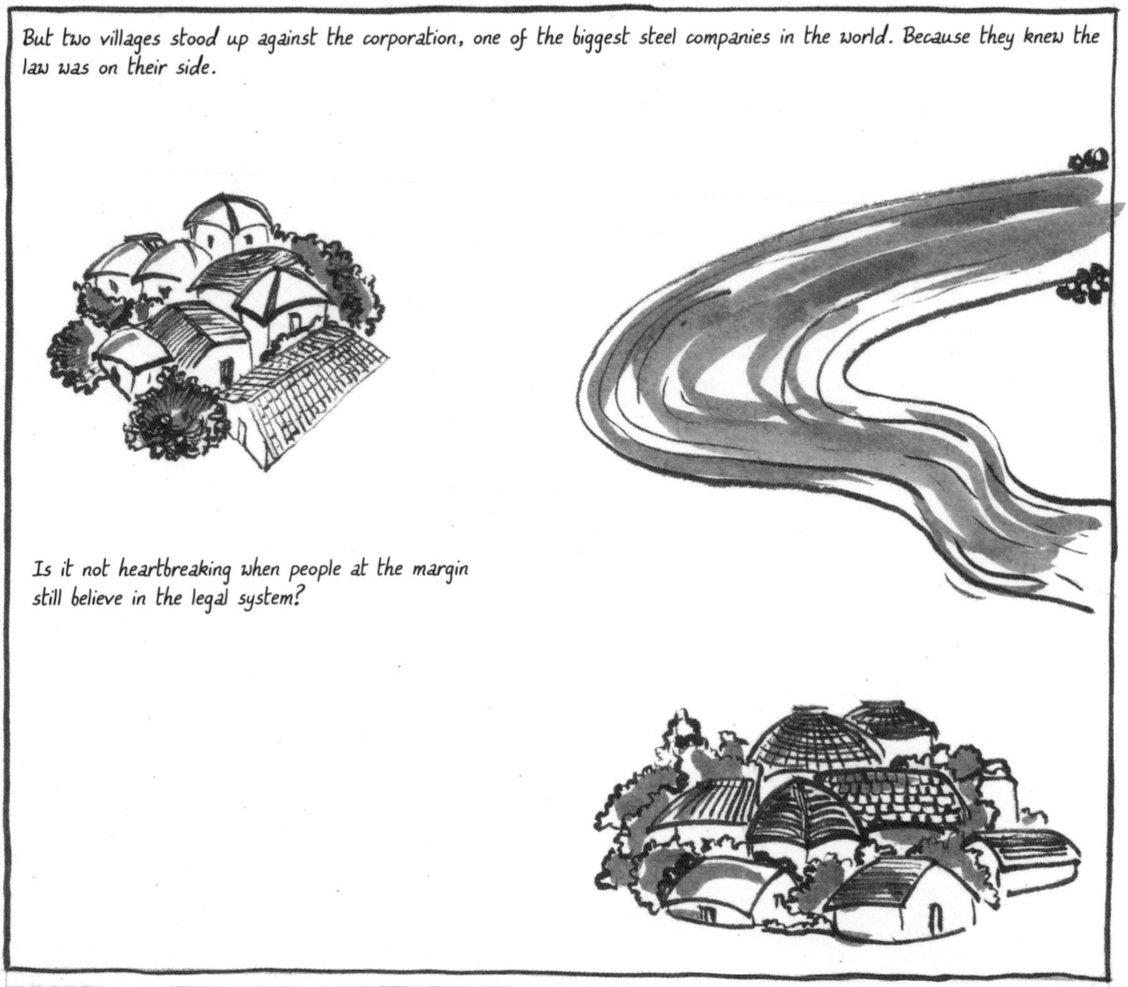
But two villages stood up against the corporation, one of the biggest steel companies in the world. Because they knew the law was on their side.
Is it not heartbreaking when people at the margin still believe in the legal system?

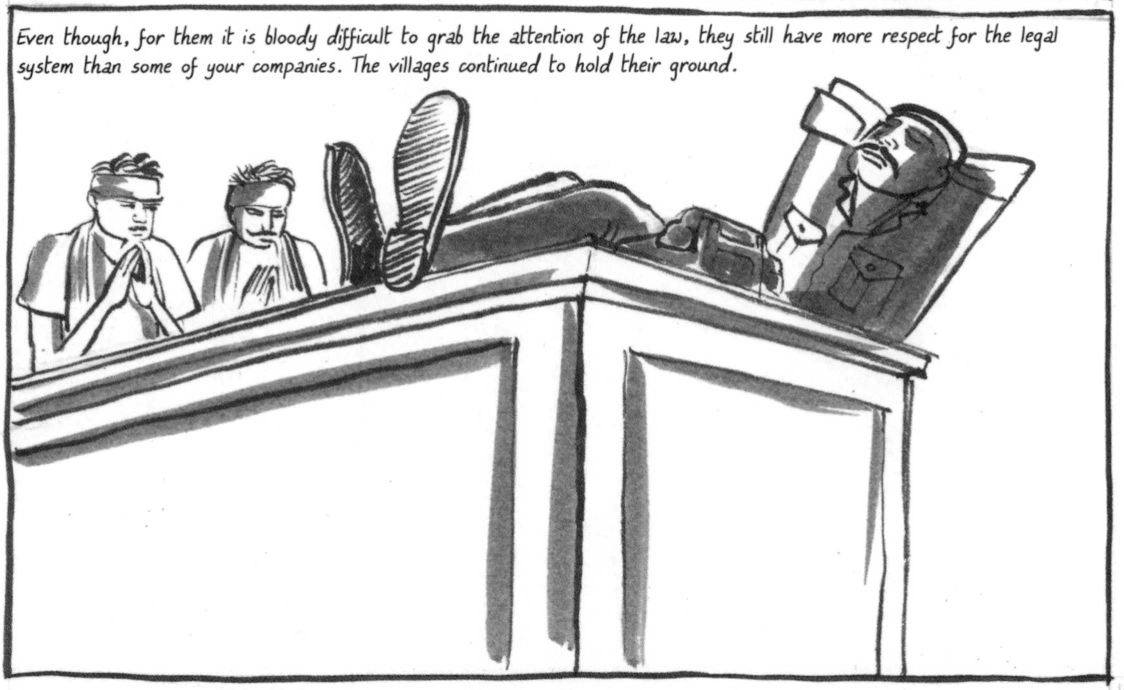
Even though, for them it is bloody difficult to grab the attention of the law, they still have more respect for the legal system than some of your companies. The villages continued to hold their ground.

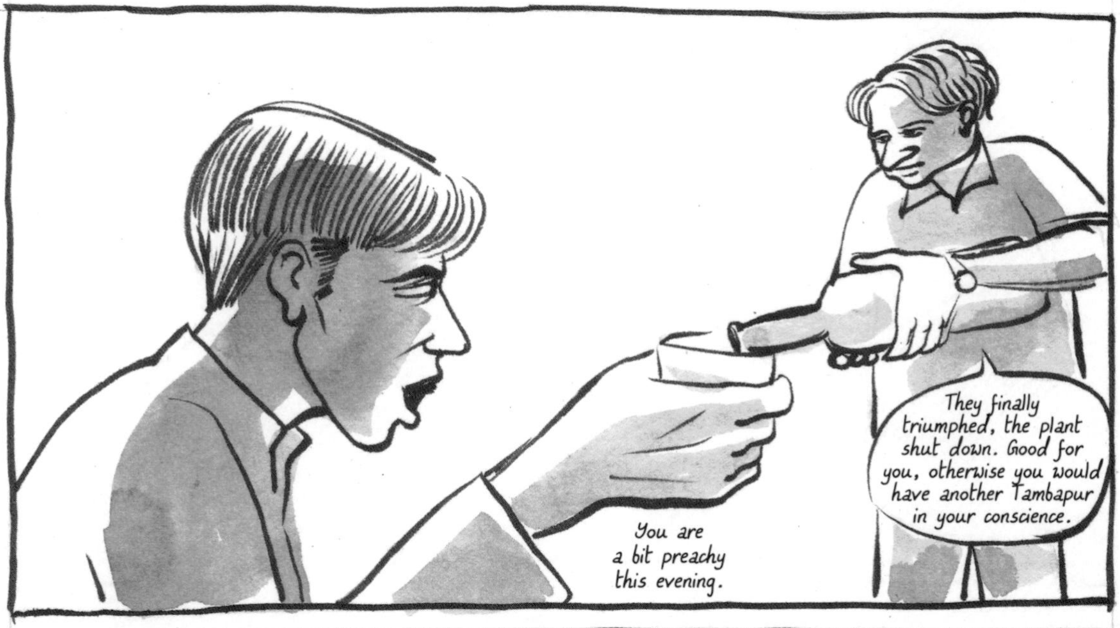
They finally triumphed, the plant shut down. Good for you, otherwise you would have another Tambapur in your conscience.
You are a bit preachy this evening.

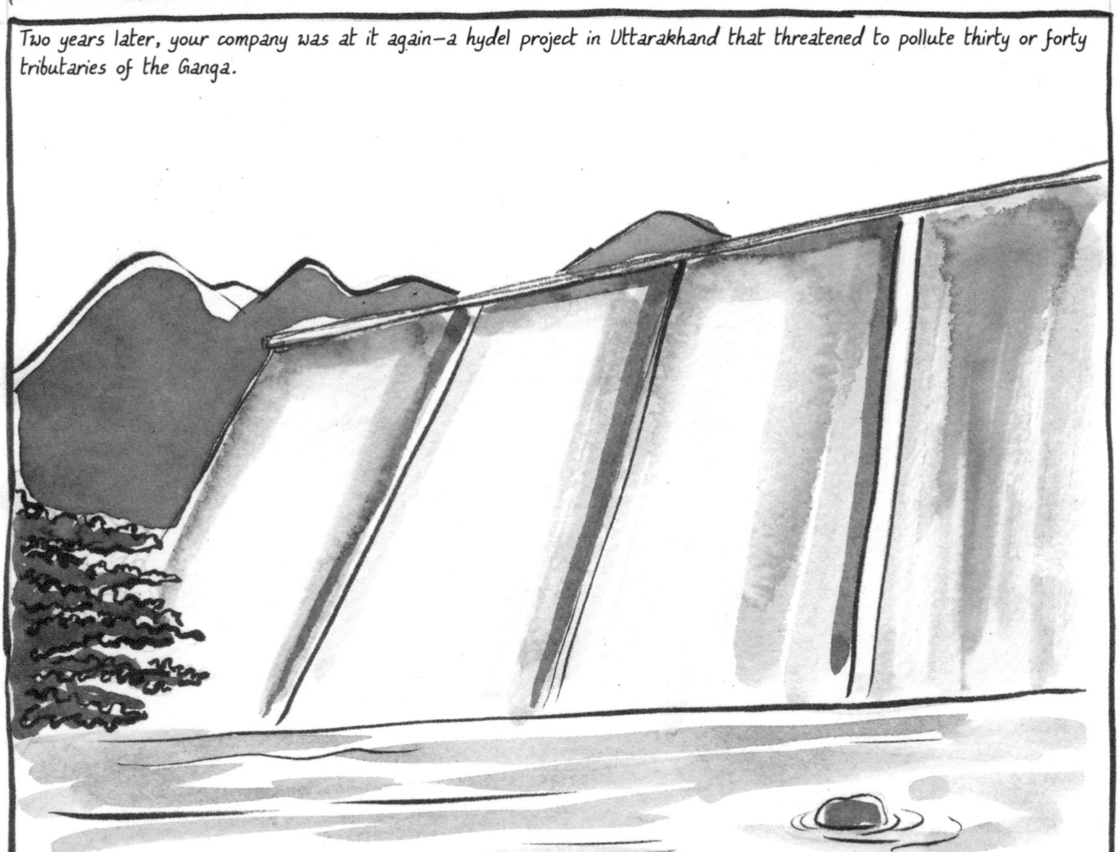
Two years later, your company was at it again—a hydel project in Uttarakhand that threatened to pollute thirty or forty tributaries of the Ganga.

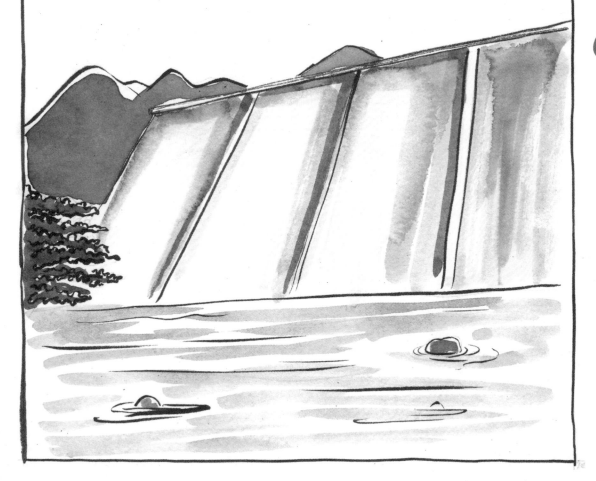

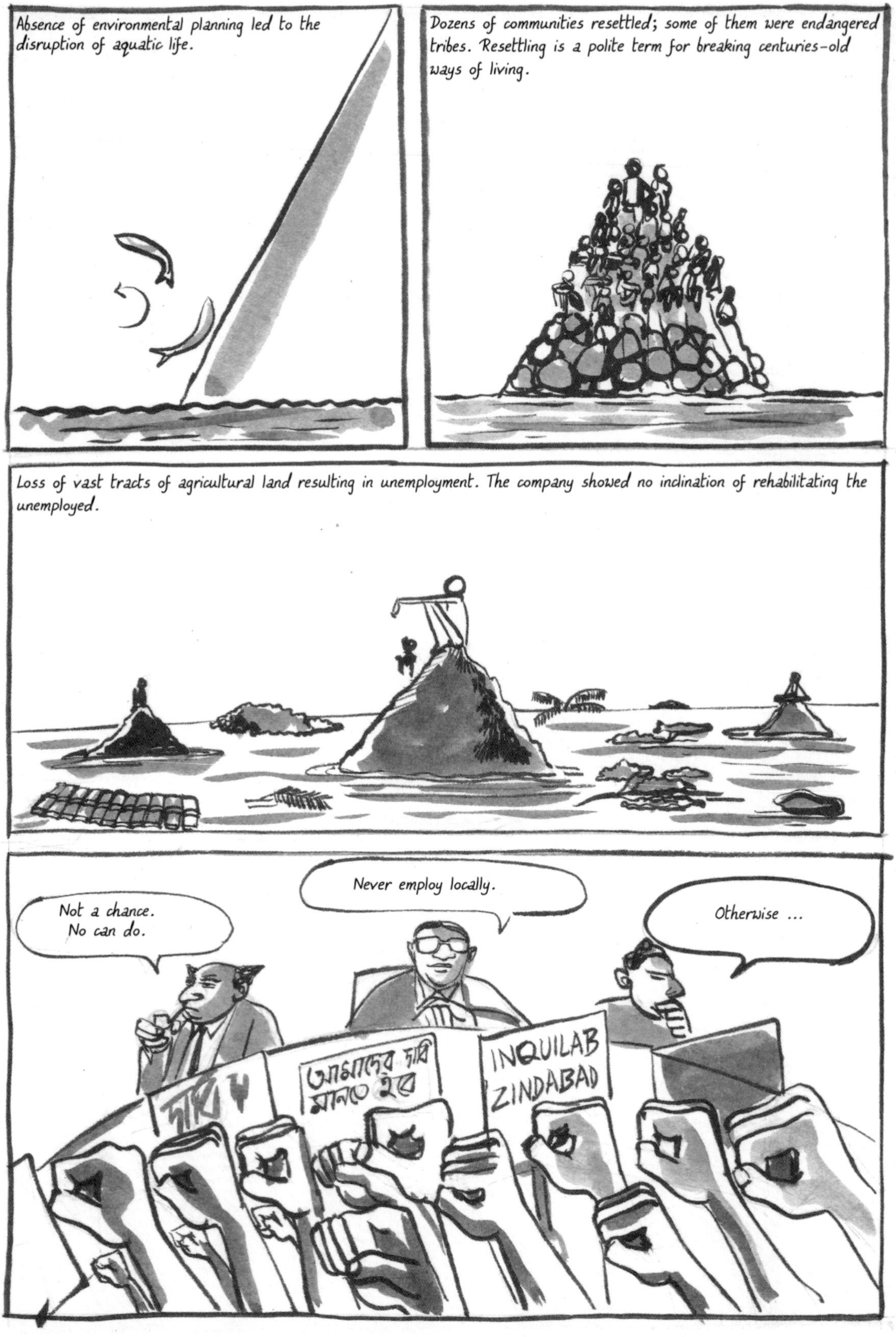
Absence of environmental planning led to the disruption of aquatic life.
Dozens of communities resettled; some of them were endangered tribes. Resettling is a polite term for breaking centuries-old ways of living.
Loss of vast tracts of agricultural land resulting in unemployment. The company showed no inclination of rehabilitating the unemployed.
Not a chance. No can do.
Never employ locally.
Otherwise ...
আমাদের দাবি মানতে হবে
INQUILAB ZINDABAD

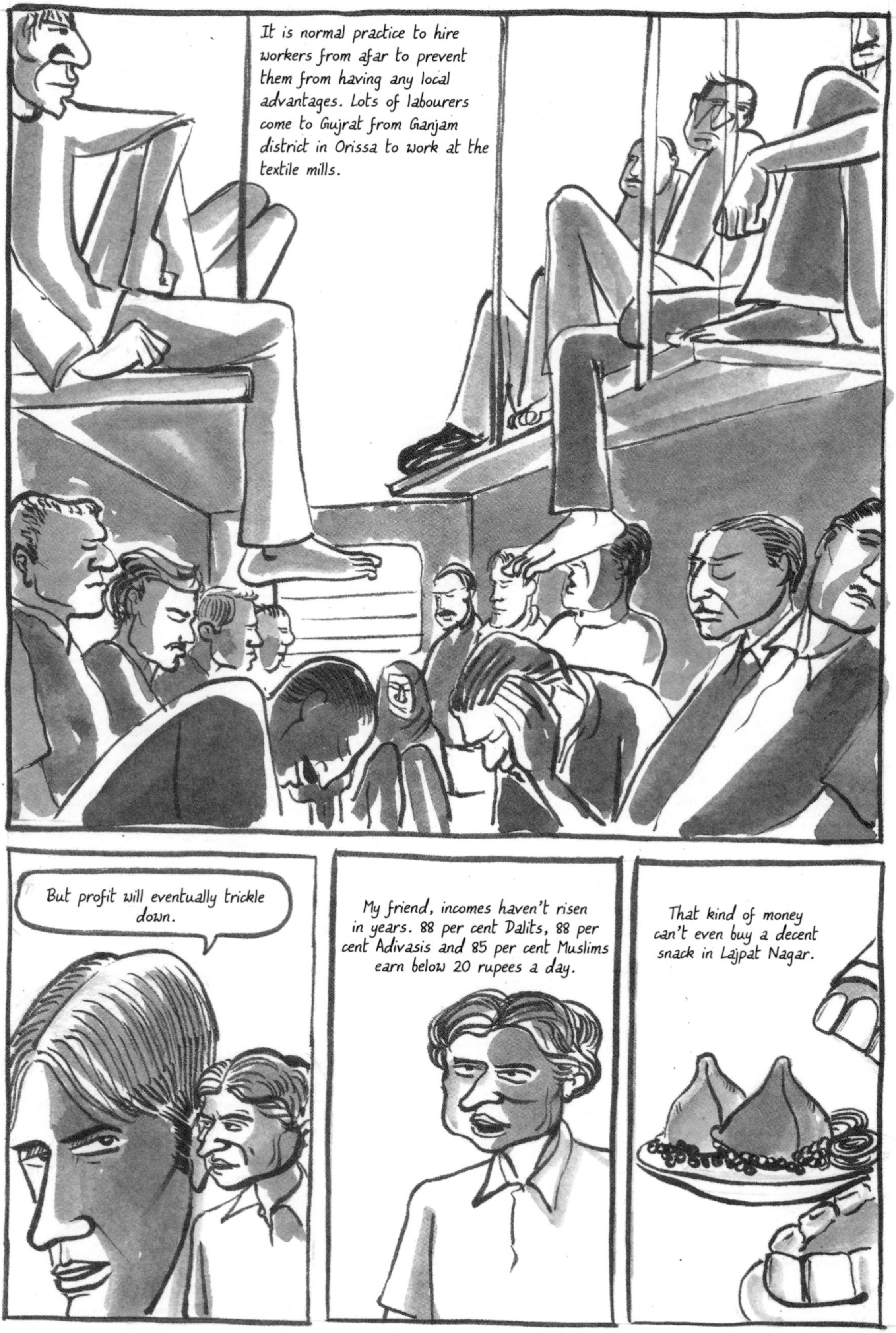

It is normal practice to hire workers from afar to prevent them from having any local advantages. Lots of labourers come to Gujrat from Ganjam district in Orissa to work at the textile mills.
But profit will eventually trickle down.
My friend, incomes haven't risen in years. 88 per cent Dalits, 88 per cent Adivasis and 85 per cent Muslims earn below 20 rupees a day.
That kind of money can't even buy a decent snack in Lajpat Nagar.

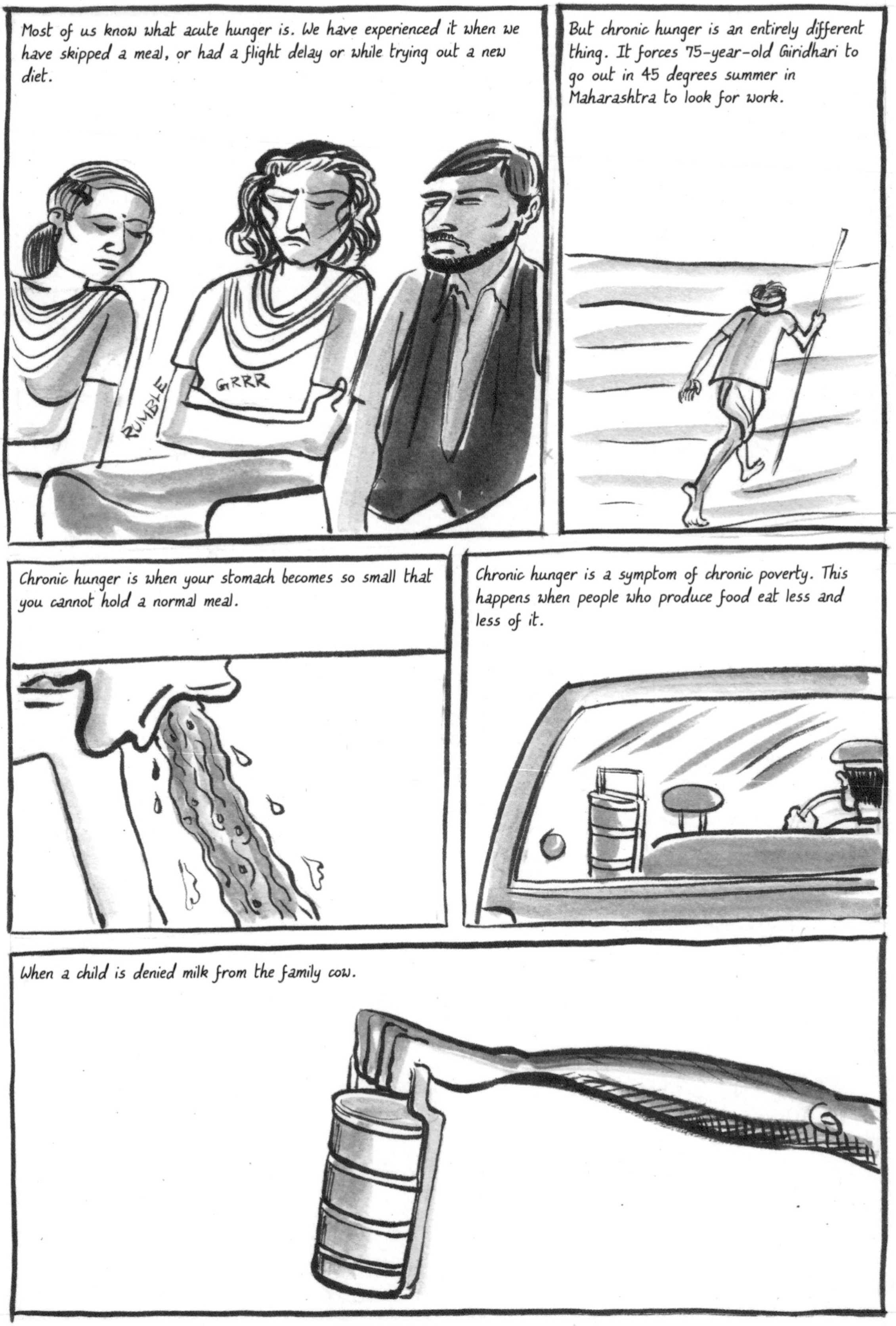
Most of us know what acute hunger is. We have experienced it when we have skipped a meal, or had a flight delay or while trying out a new diet.
RUMBLE
GRRR
But chronic hunger is an entirely different thing. It forces 75-year-old Giridhari to go out in 45 degrees summer in Maharashtra to look for work.
Chronic hunger is when your stomach becomes so small that you cannot hold a normal meal.
Chronic hunger is a symptom of chronic poverty. This happens when people who produce food eat less and less of it.
When a child is denied milk from the family cow.

In a village in Bihar, under the midday meal scheme, teachers demanded double ration for the students on Mondays because they would not have eaten all weekend and could not concentrate on their studies.

In another district, parents were agitated about the temporary closure of a school due to a heat wave. The parents said it was better to die of a heat stroke than from an empty stomach. These were your people too.

You say trickle down effect, but some of the most privatised states have the lowest human index.

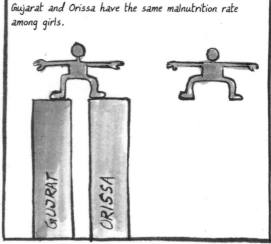

Gujarat and Orissa have the same malnutrition rate among girls.

GUJRAT

ORISSA

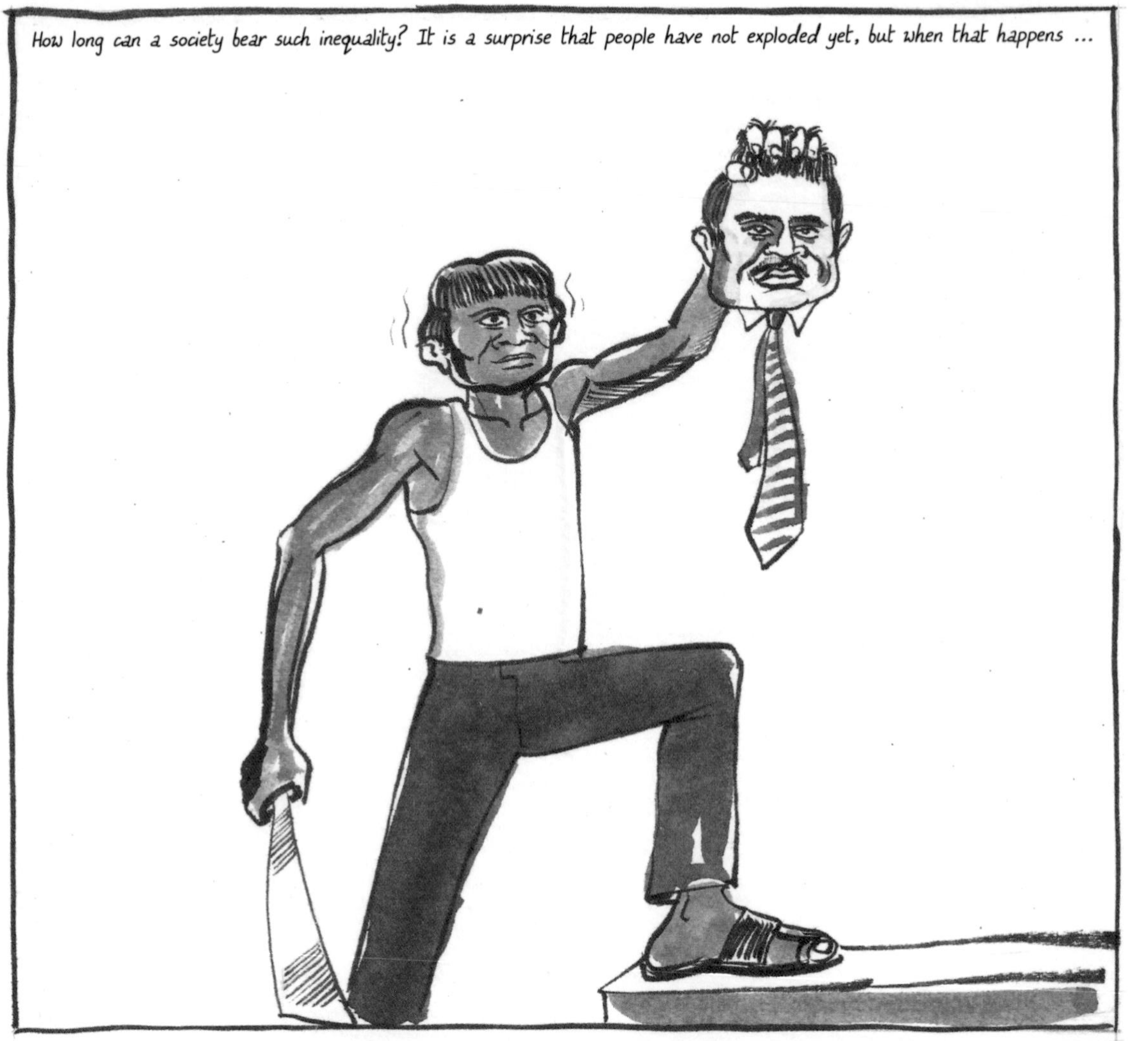
How long can a society bear such inequality? It is a surprise that people have not exploded yet, but when that happens ...

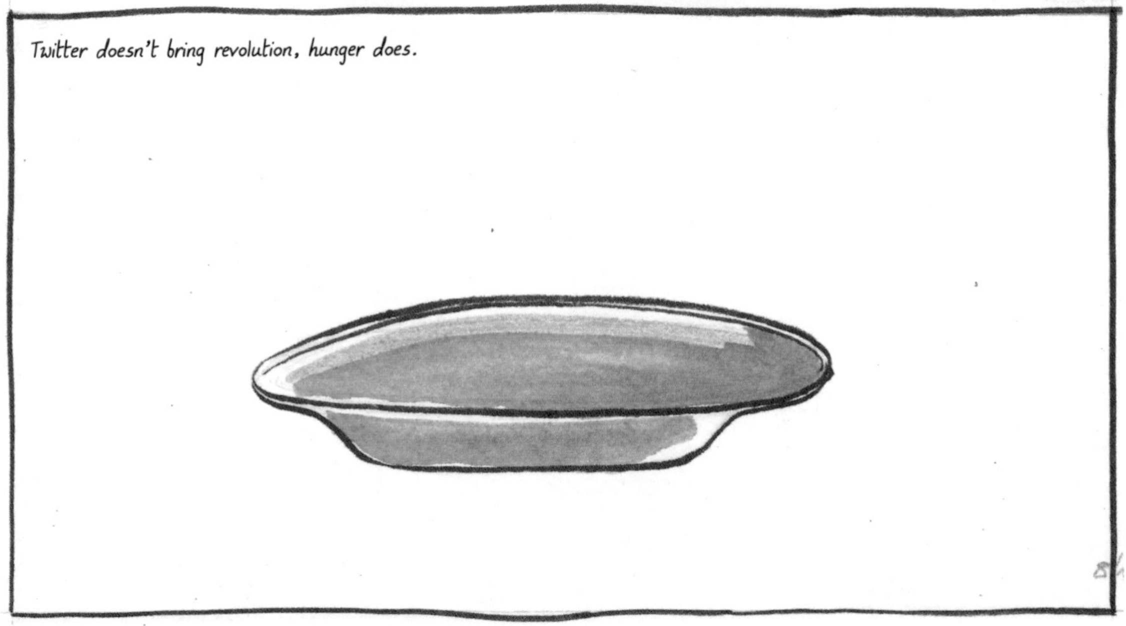
Twitter doesn't bring revolution, hunger does.

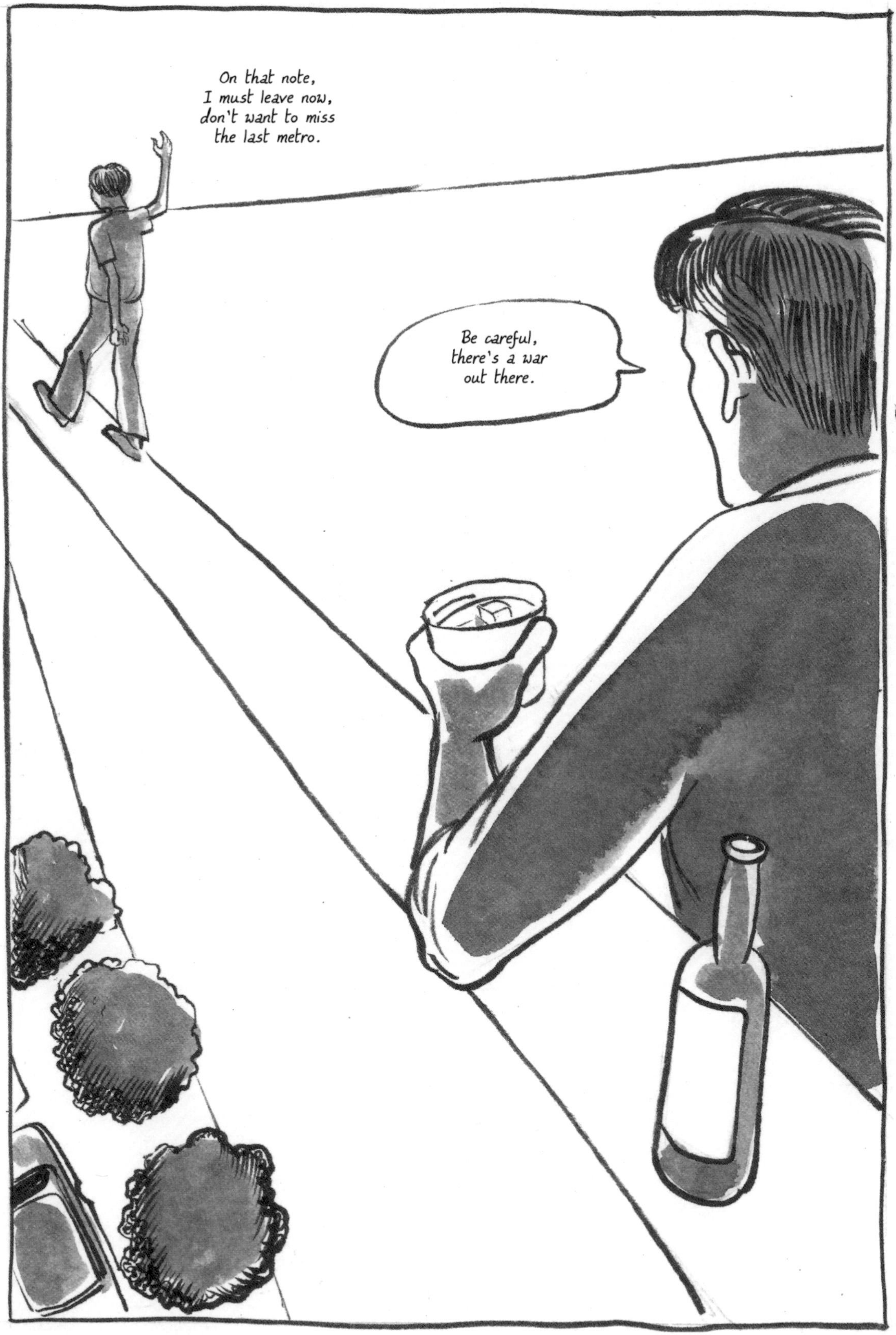
On that note, I must leave now, don't want to miss the last metro.
Be careful, there's a war out there.

All Quiet in Vikaspuri

The war seems to be over, sir.

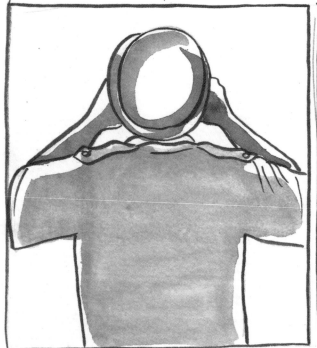

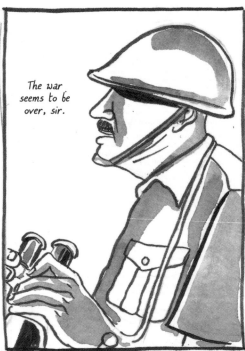

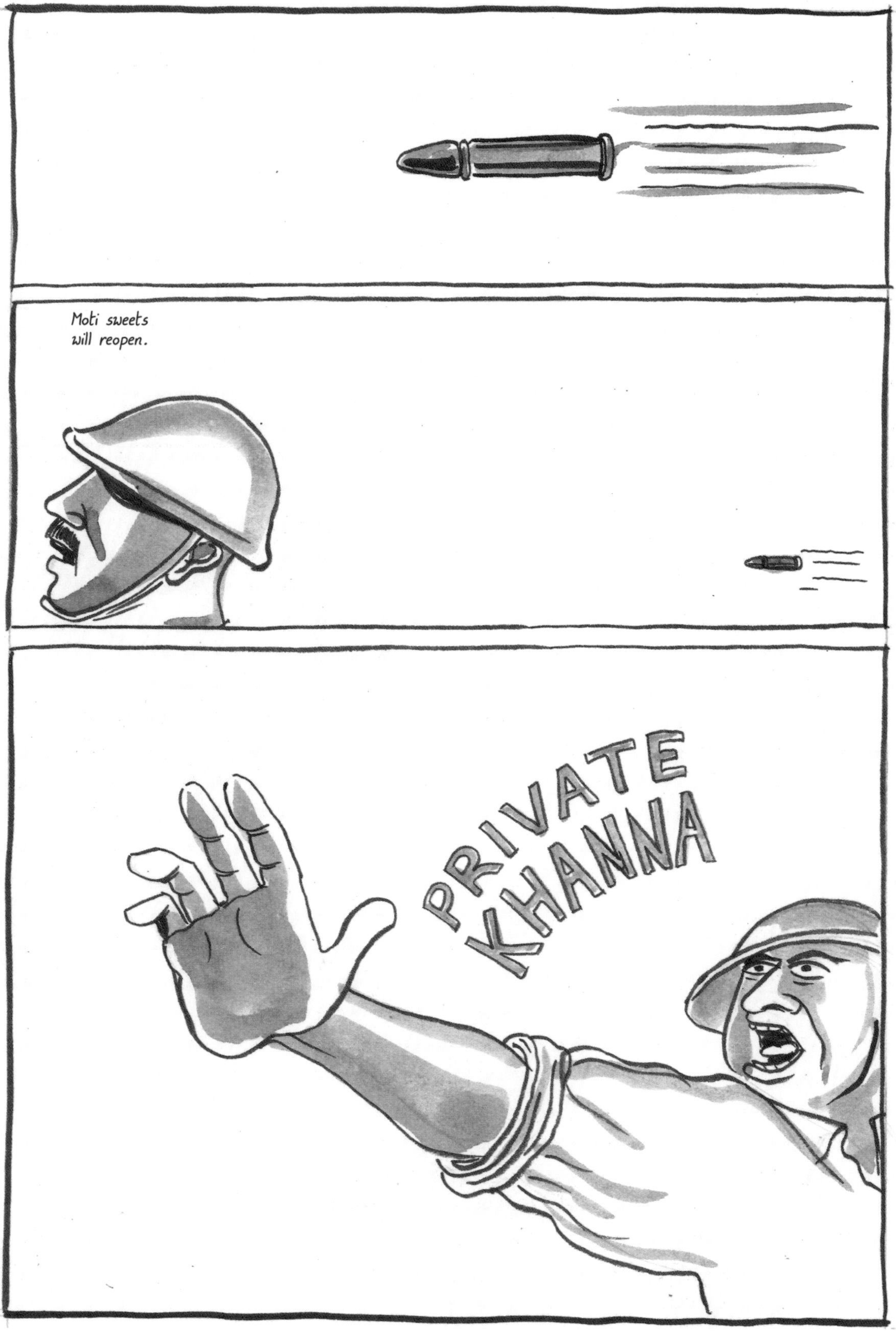
Moti sweets
will reopen.
PRIVATE
KHANNA

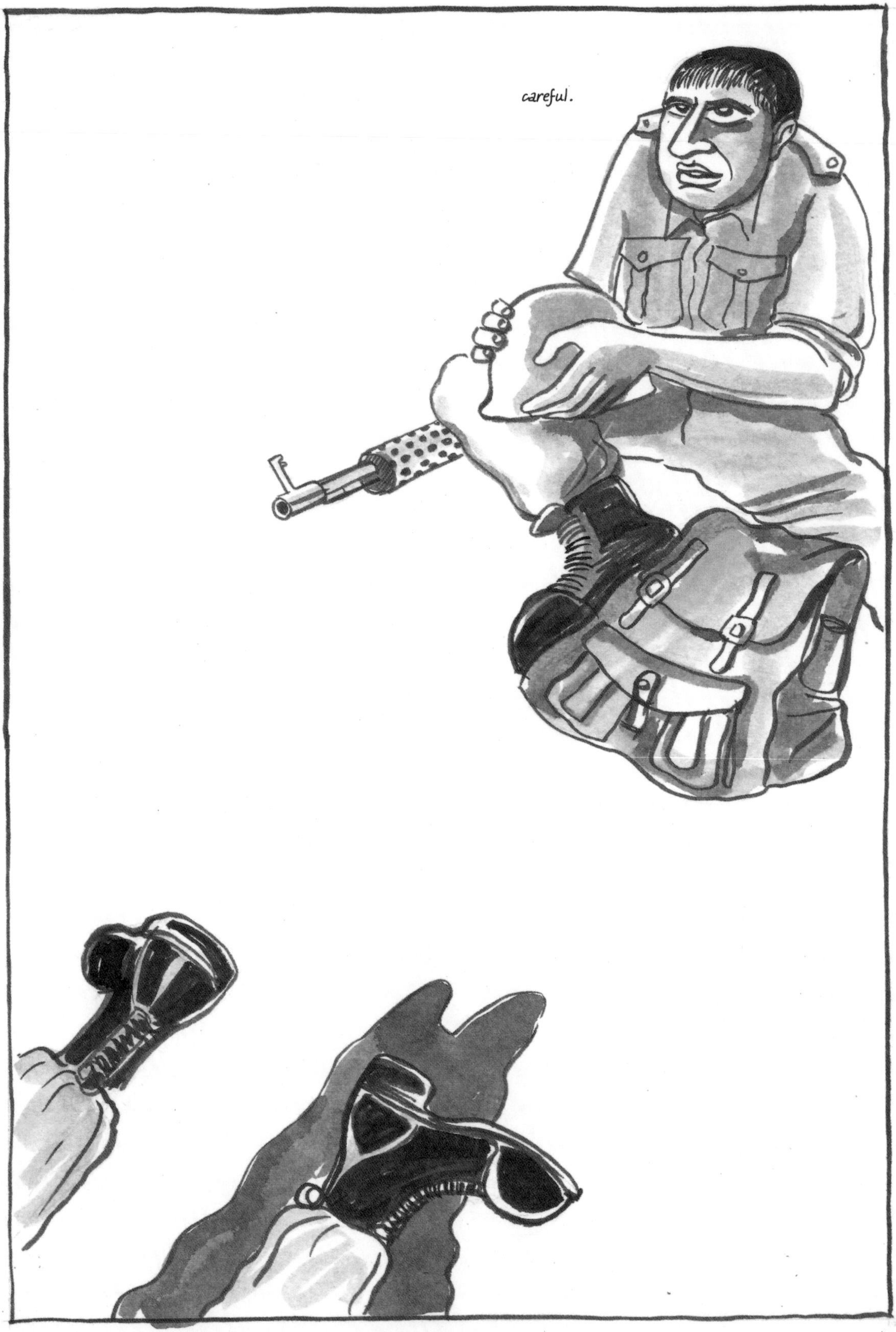
careful.

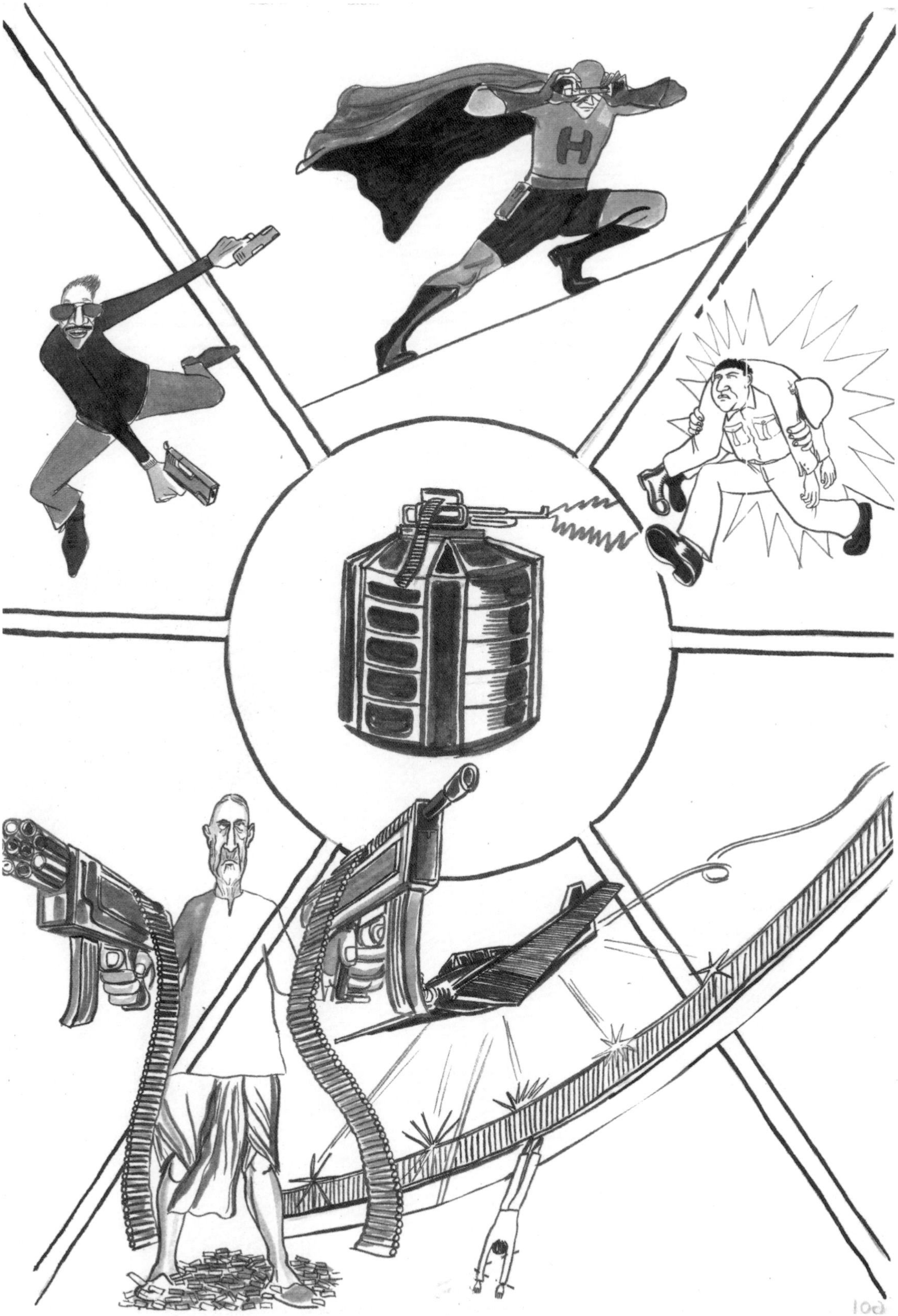

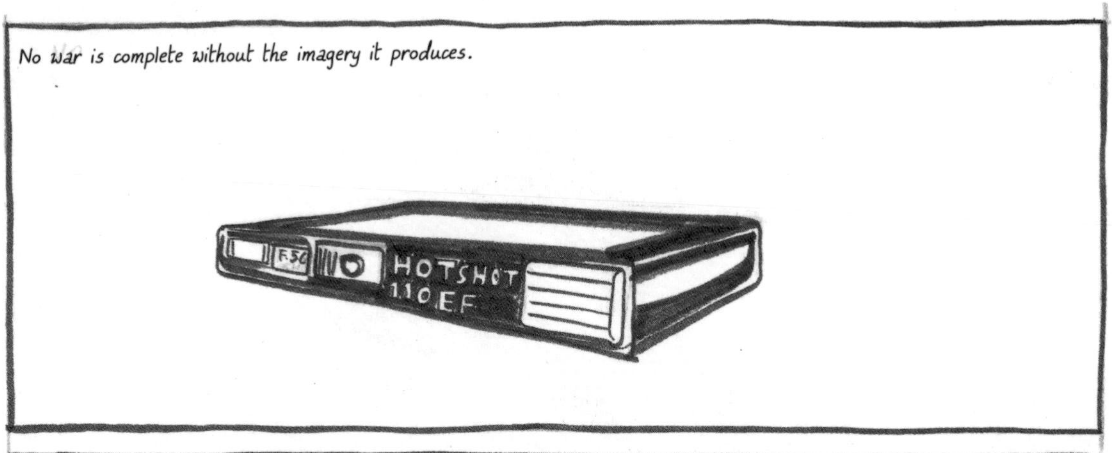
No war is complete without the imagery it produces.
HOTSHOT
110EF

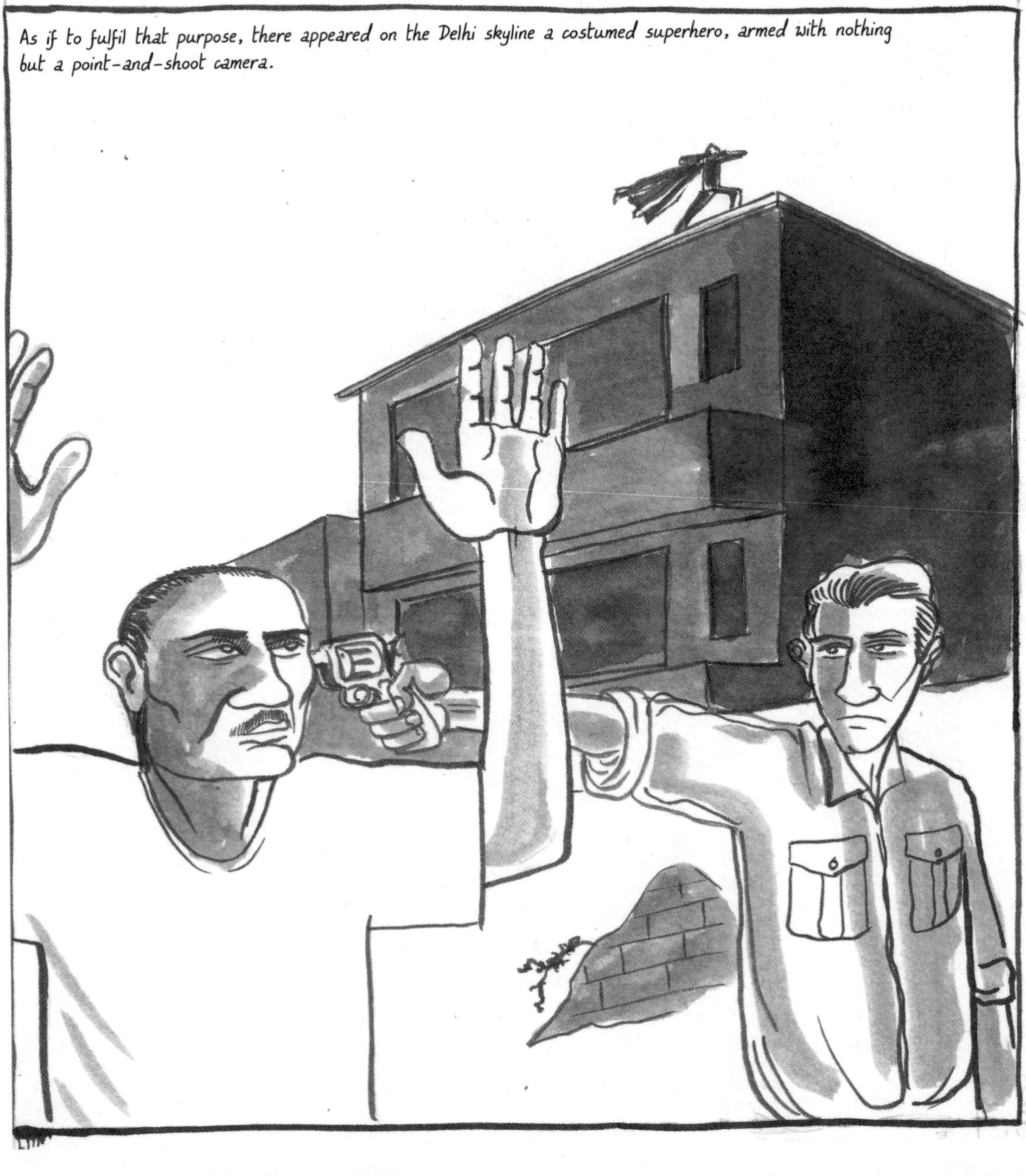
As if to fulfil that purpose, there appeared on the Delhi skyline a costumed superhero, armed with nothing but a point-and-shoot camera.

His dispatches will provide the most important visual documentation of the Second Battle of Kalkaji.

91

The following are some examples, the titles were put together by the astute copy editor Percy M.L.

Saving Private Arora: A story of valour and eternal friendship.

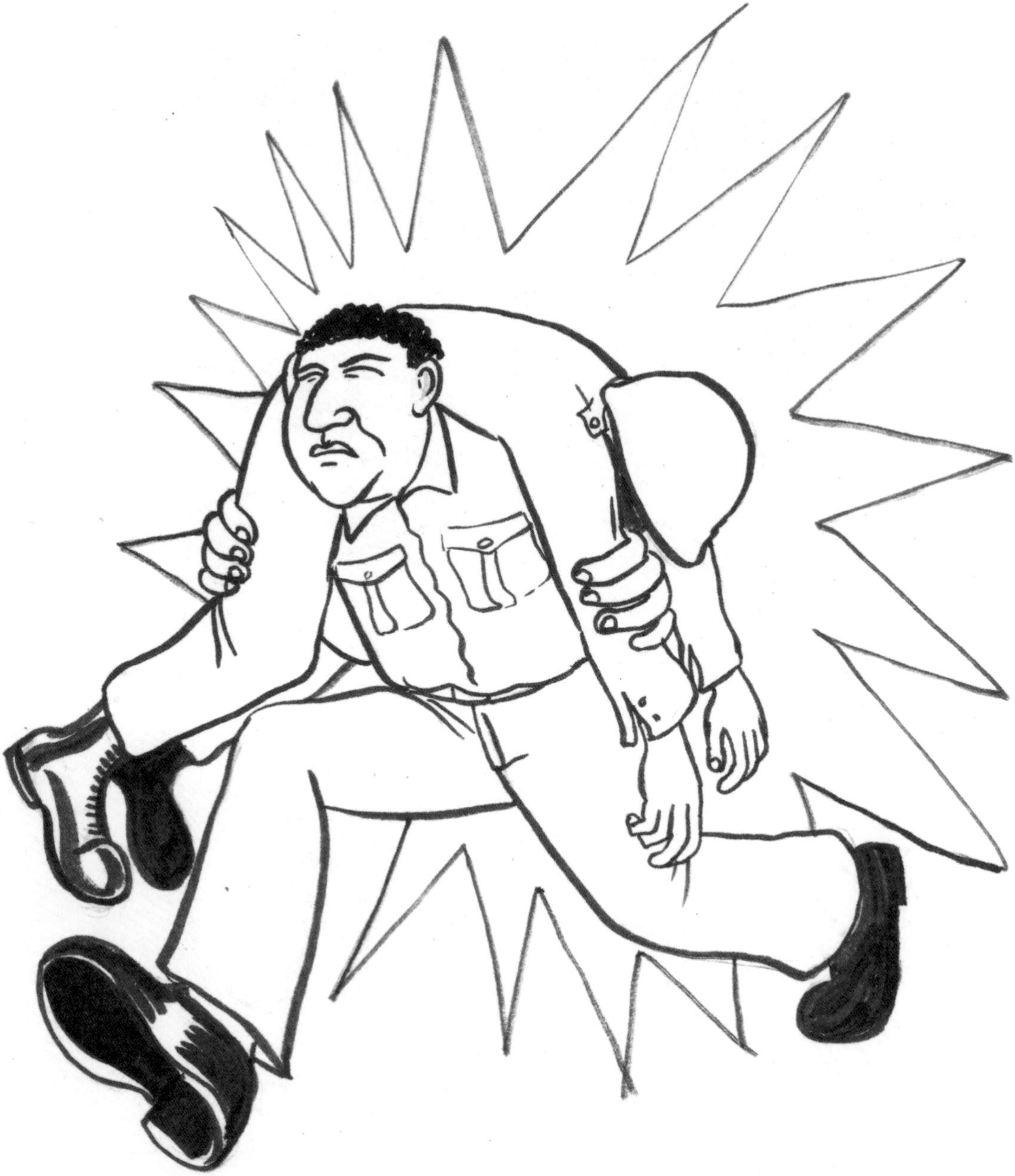

Bridge on the River Yamuna: Where man and machine battle it out to the very end.

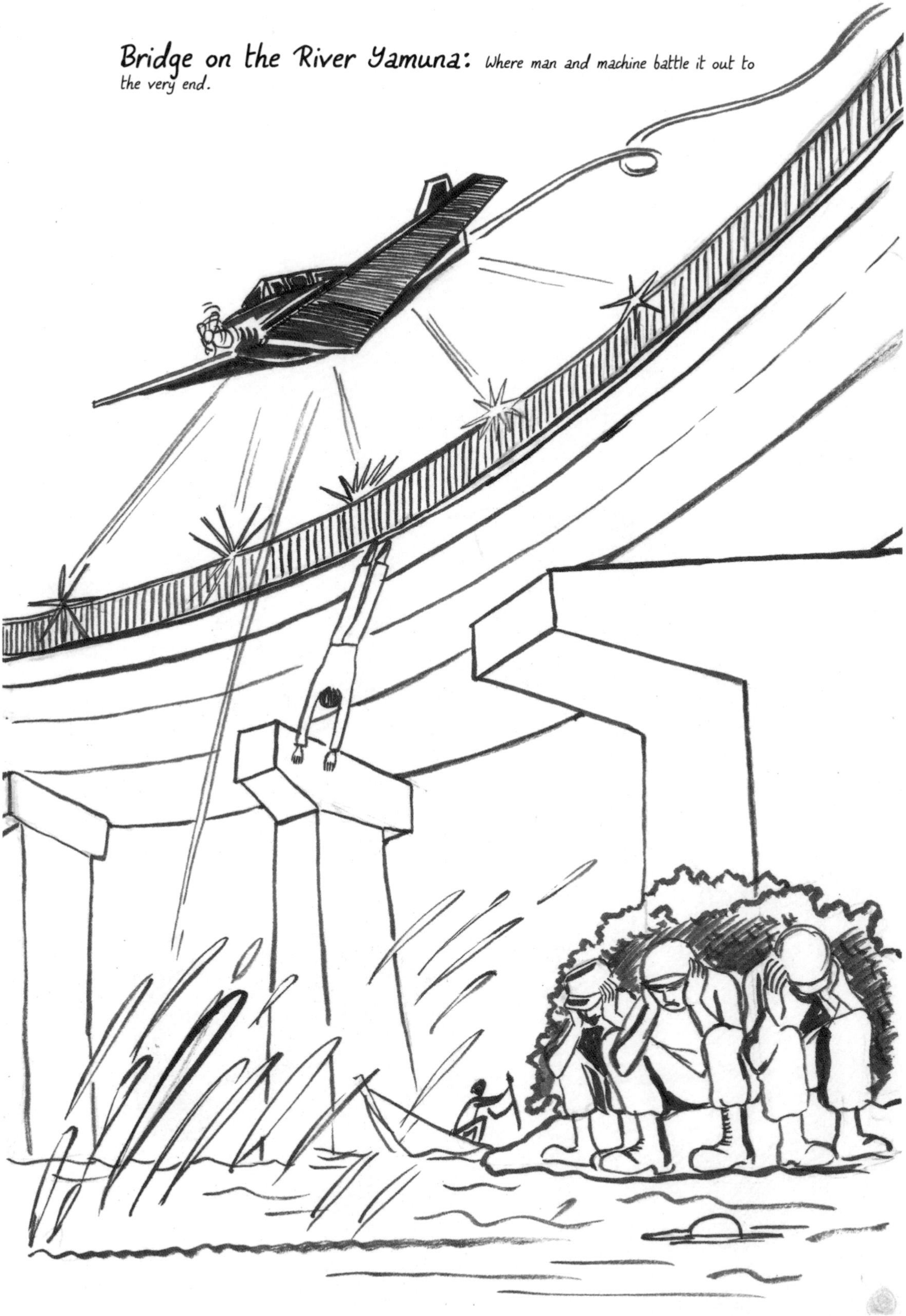

Khurana's List: *One man's crusade to save a community of Punjabi Khatris of New Rajendra Nagar against the onslaught of Paschim Vihar.*

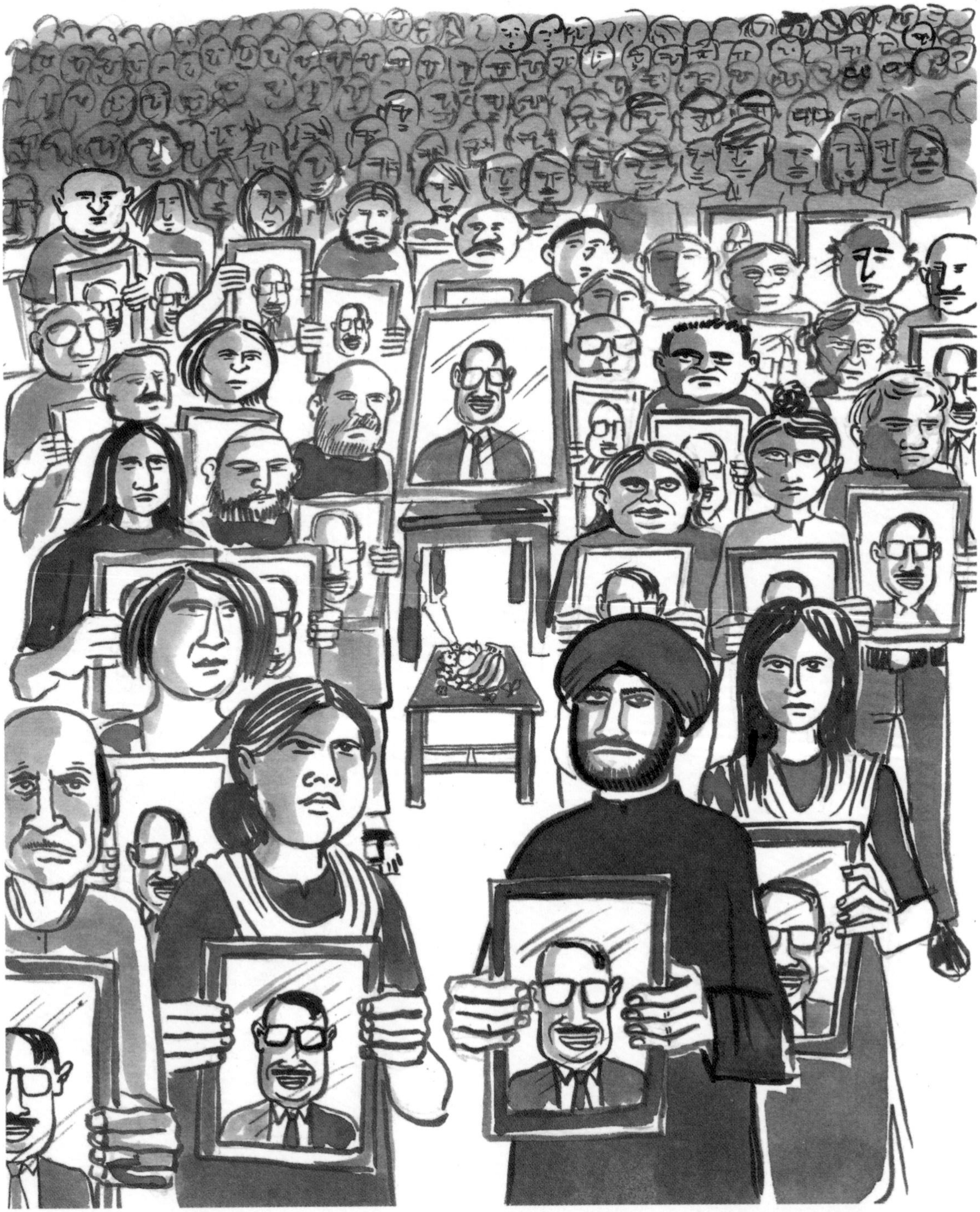

Bhatora! Bhatora! Bhatora!: The siege of INA market.

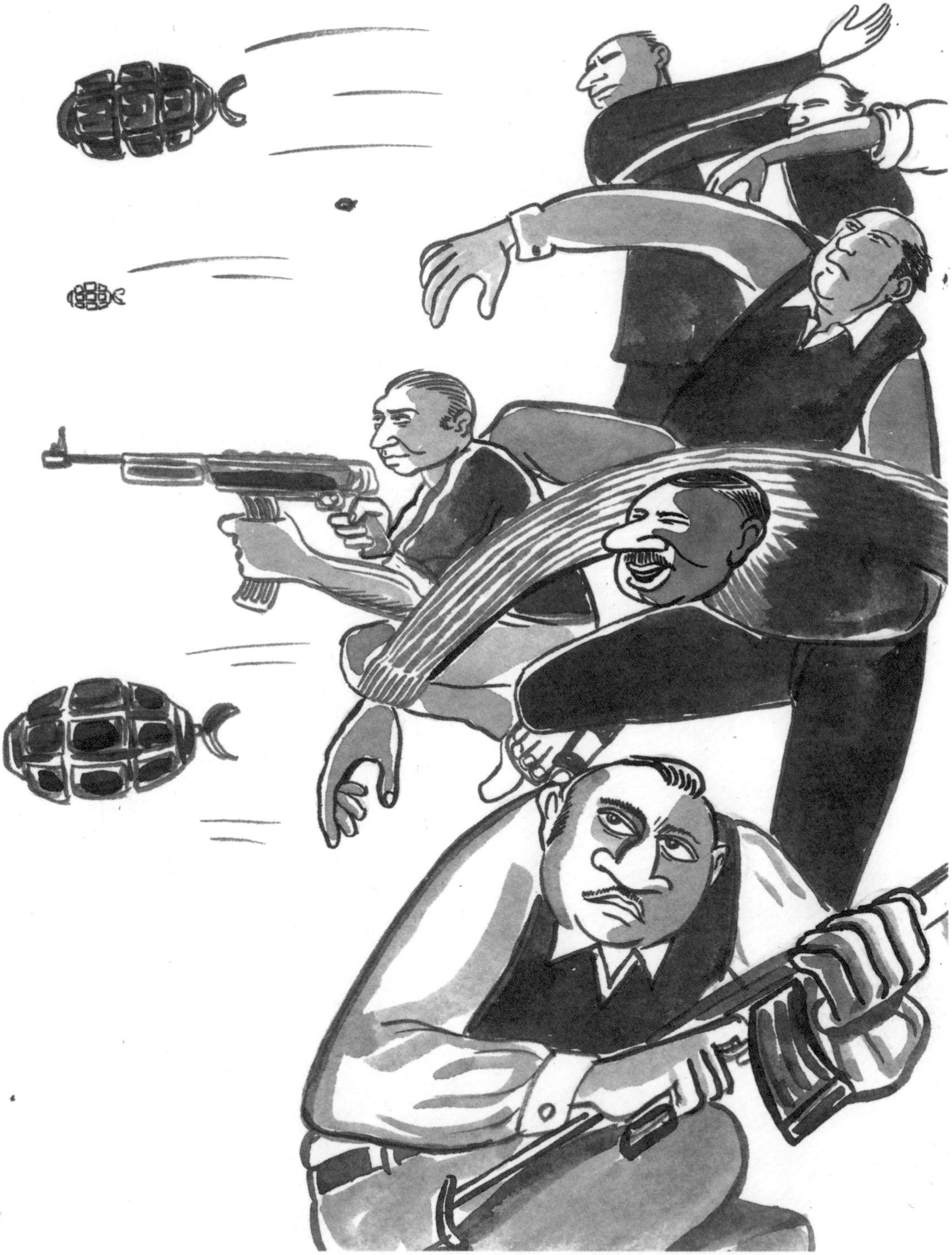

The Guns of Ghantaghar: *How three sisters took control of something that was thought to be invincible.*

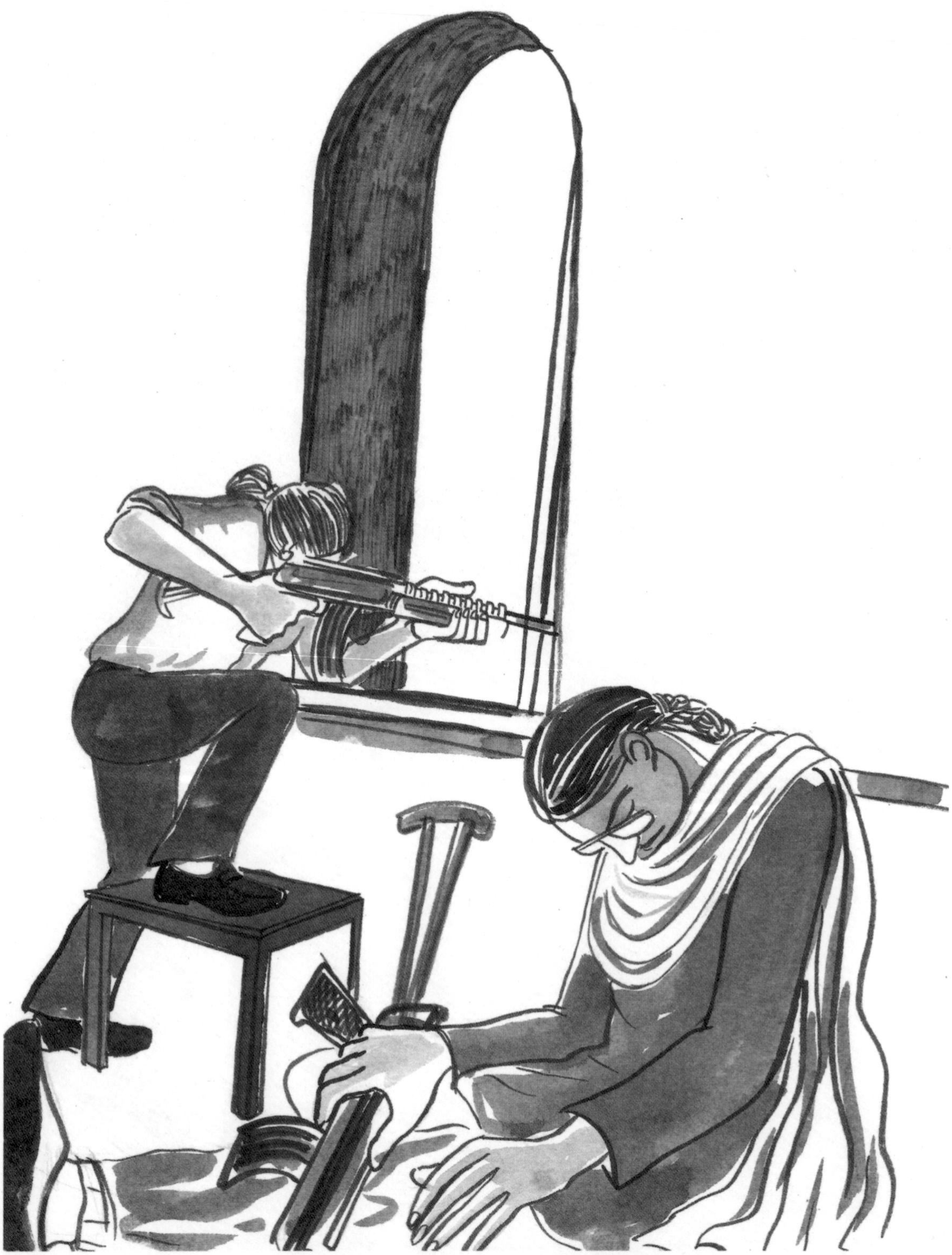

Bhullar's War: One man's war on Soami Nagar.

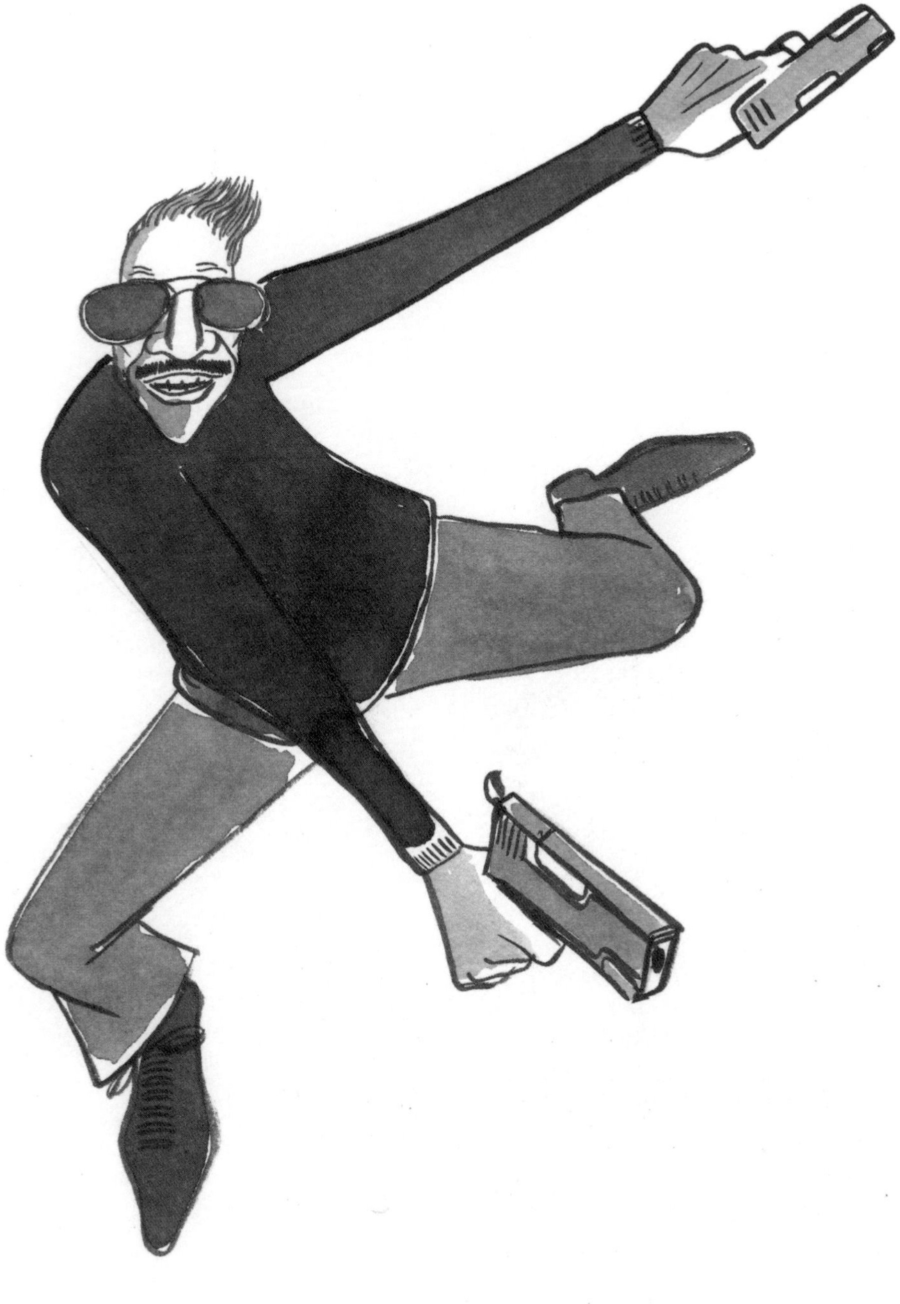

Chronicles of Narayana: Non-Resident Narayanans return home from Canada, US and the Gulf to fight Pitampura alongside their brothers.

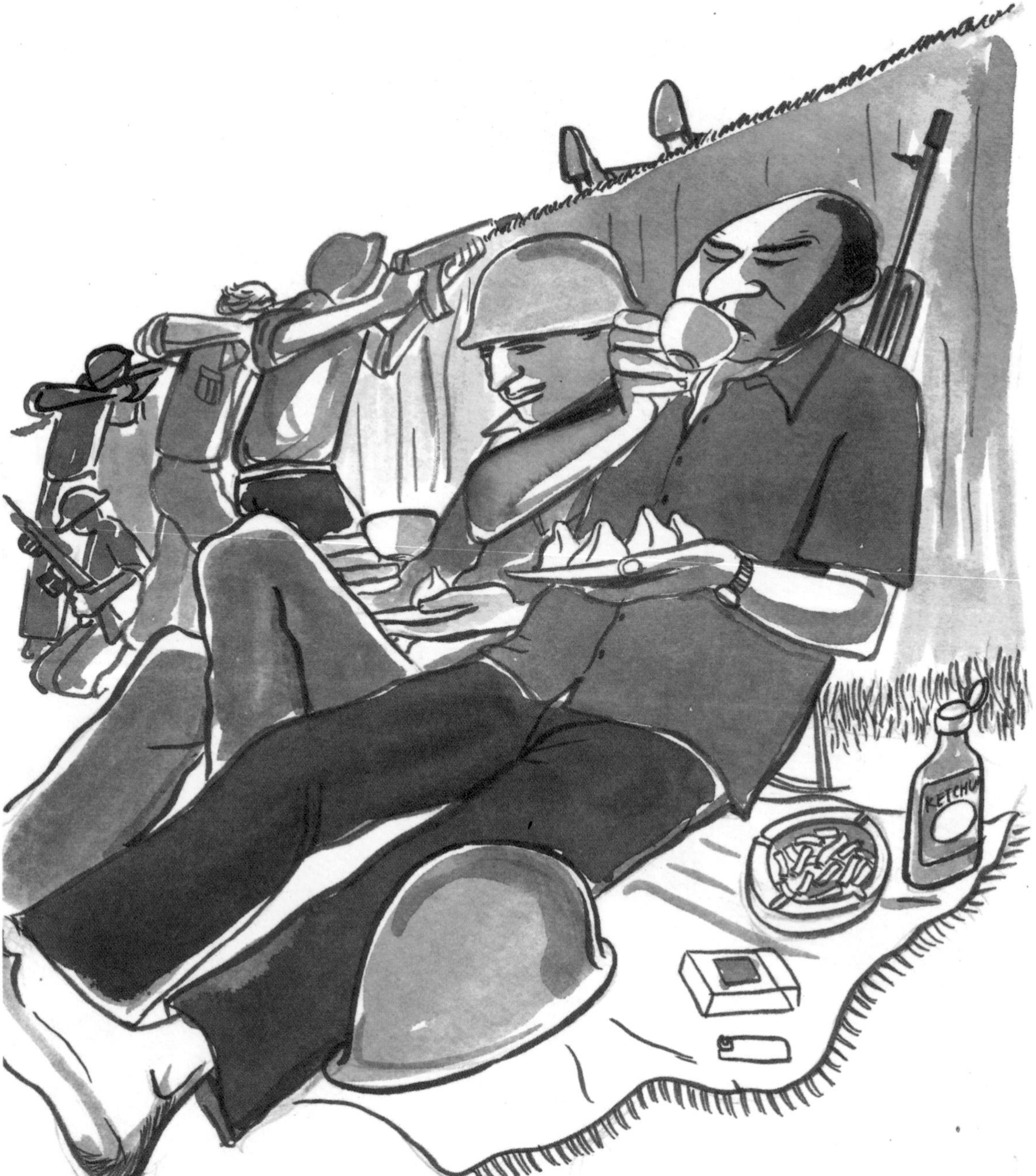
KETCHU

Where Mallus Dare: How a small army of Malayali guerrillas from Gautam Nagar challenged the might of Gulmohar park.

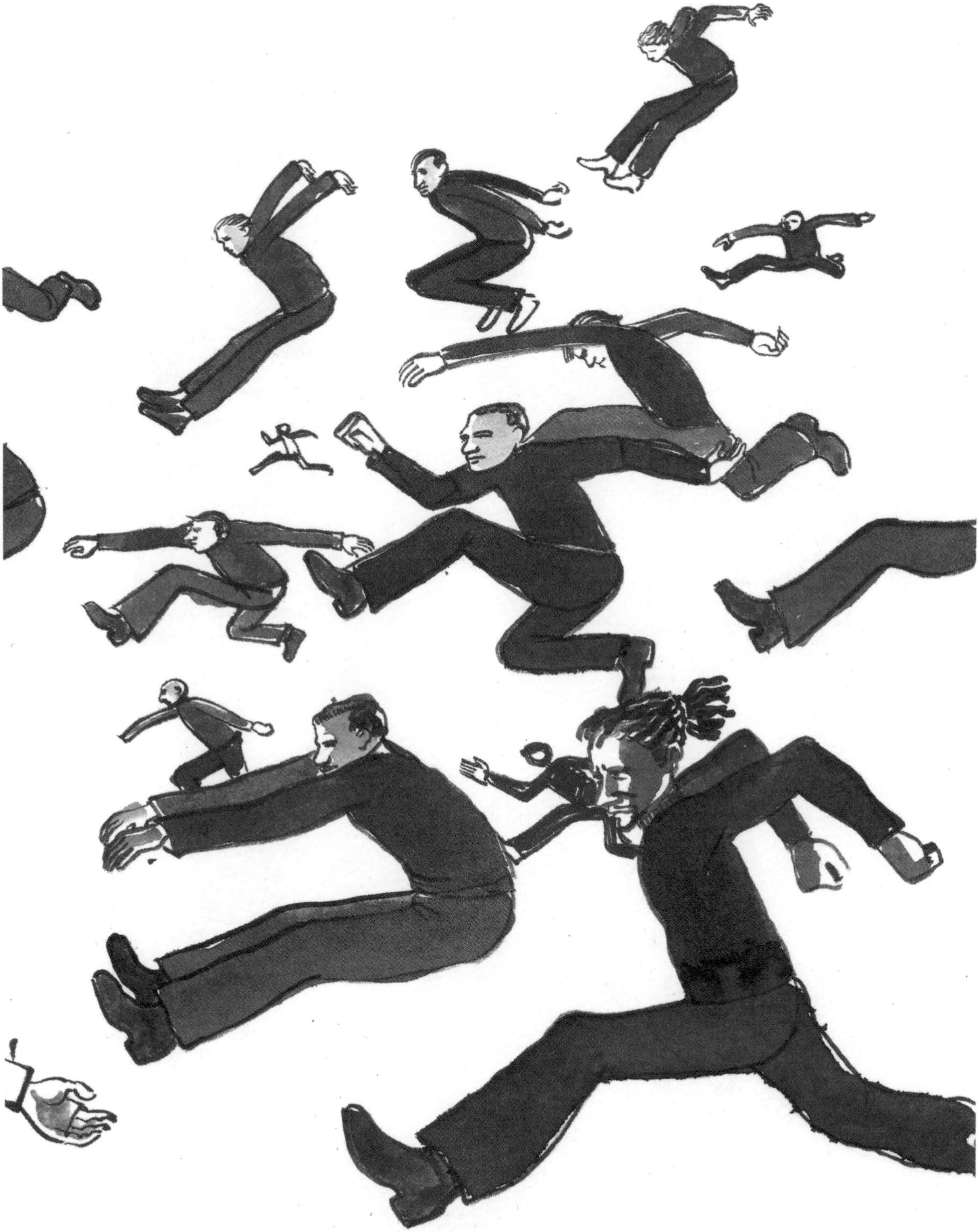

Justice Bipin Bose: The butcher of Safdarjung.

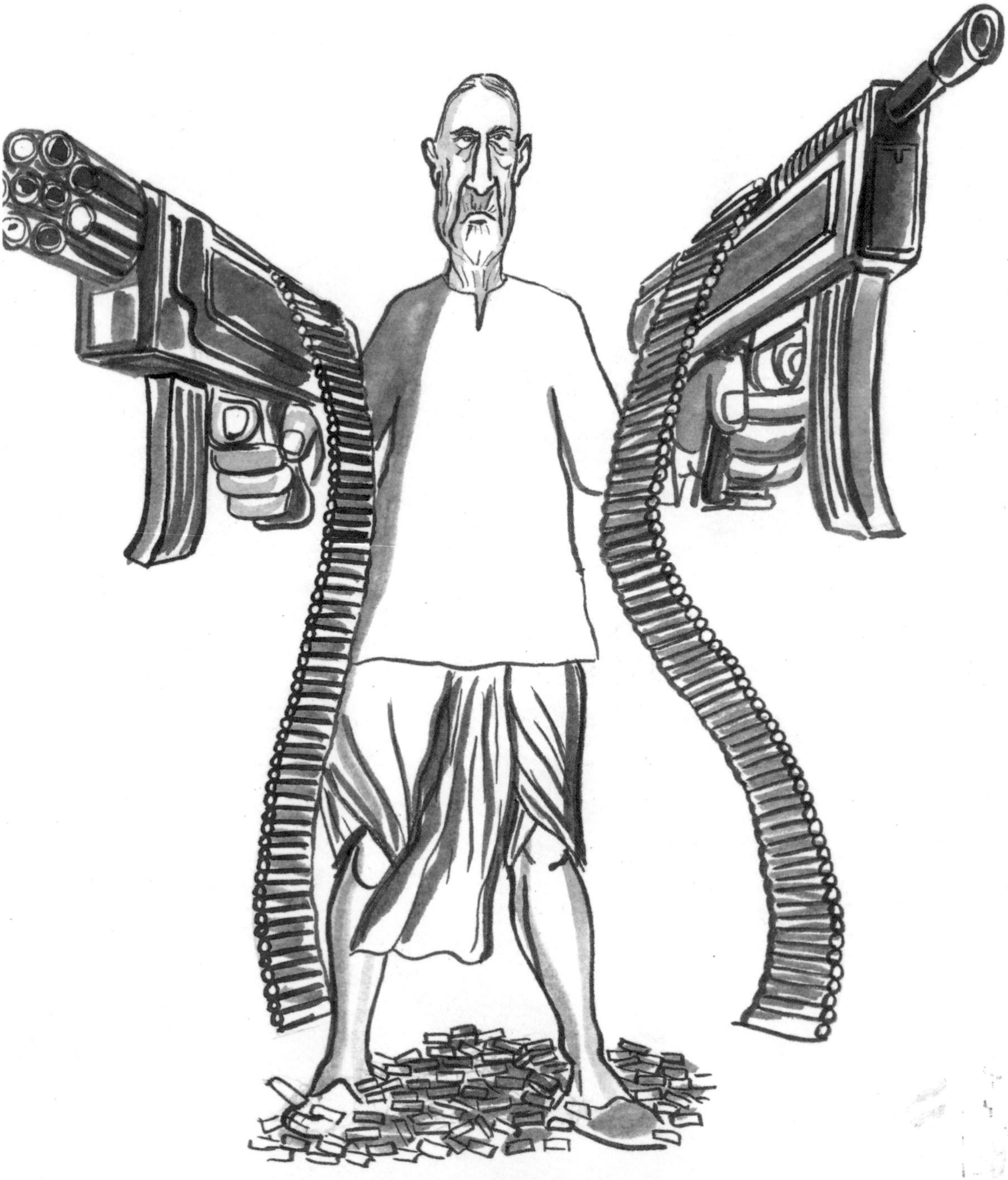

The Jorbagh Circle: That met every Thursday and planned vicious attacks on Jangpura.

Good Morning, Shahpurjat: Naveen Siyani's war transmissions.

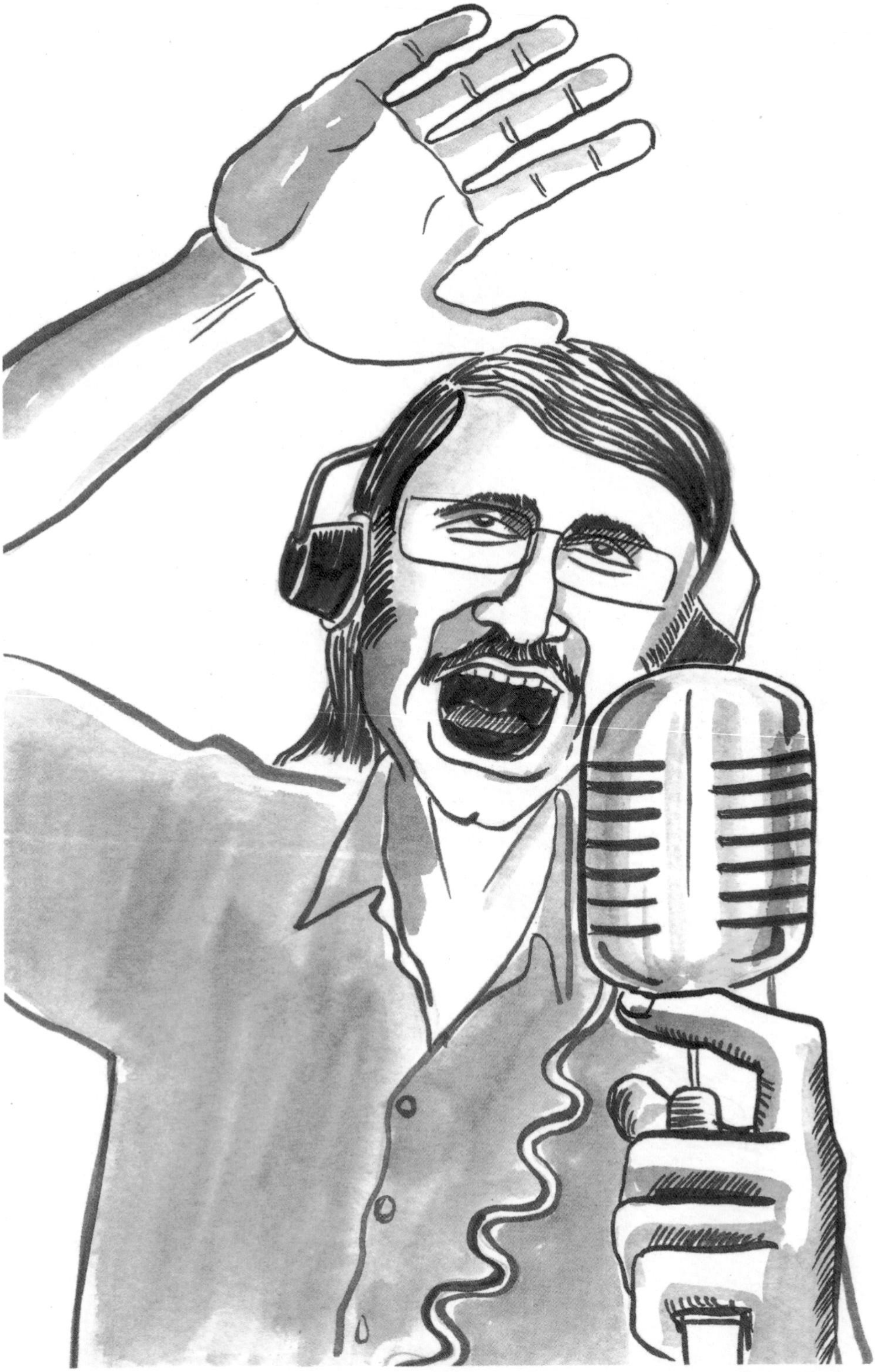

The Green Pagris: The stylish warriors of Shalimar Bagh

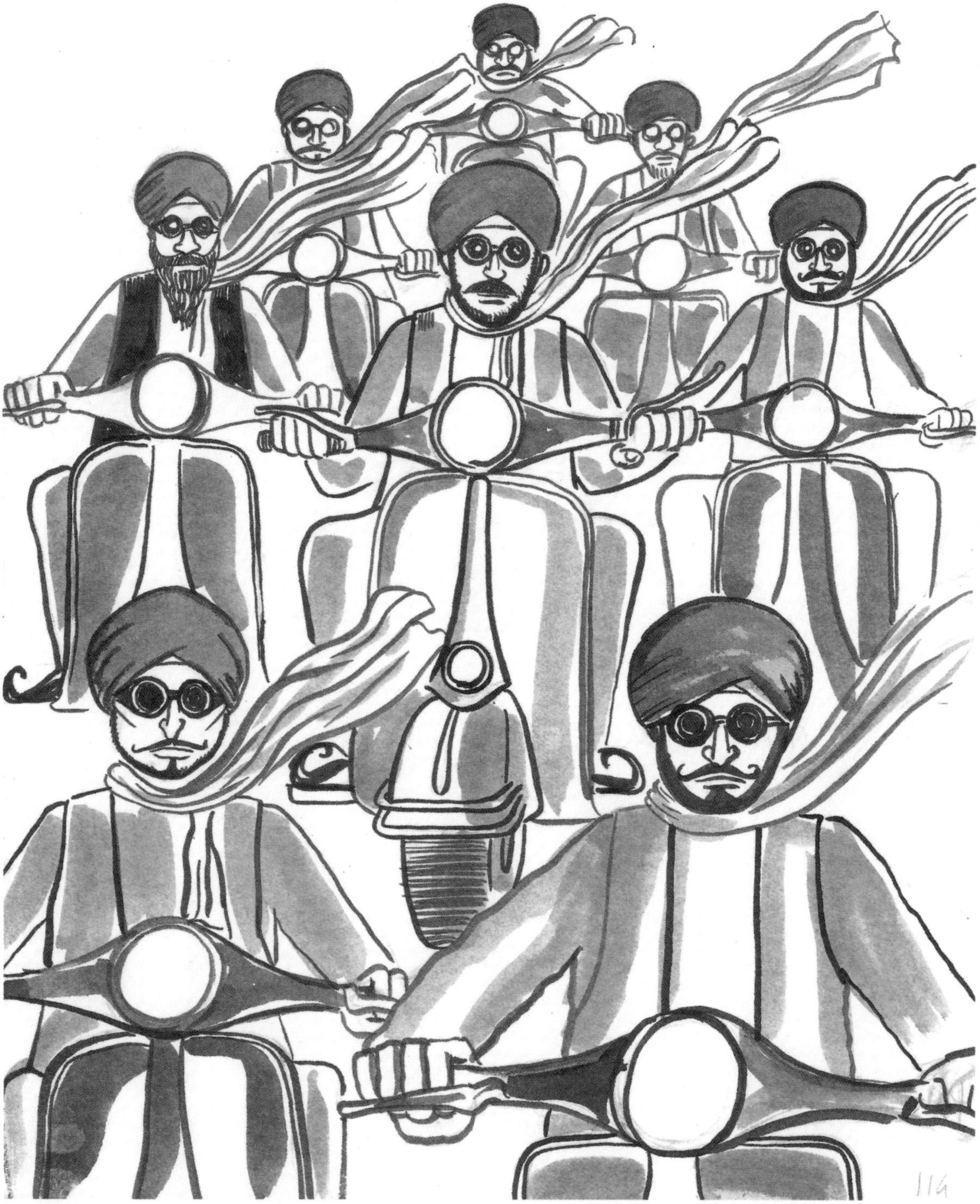

The Dirty Dozen from Alakananda: Men who conducted terrifying nightly raids on Govindpuri.

Full Aluminium Nehru Jacket: *The sack of Sadiq Nagar by South Extension Part II.*

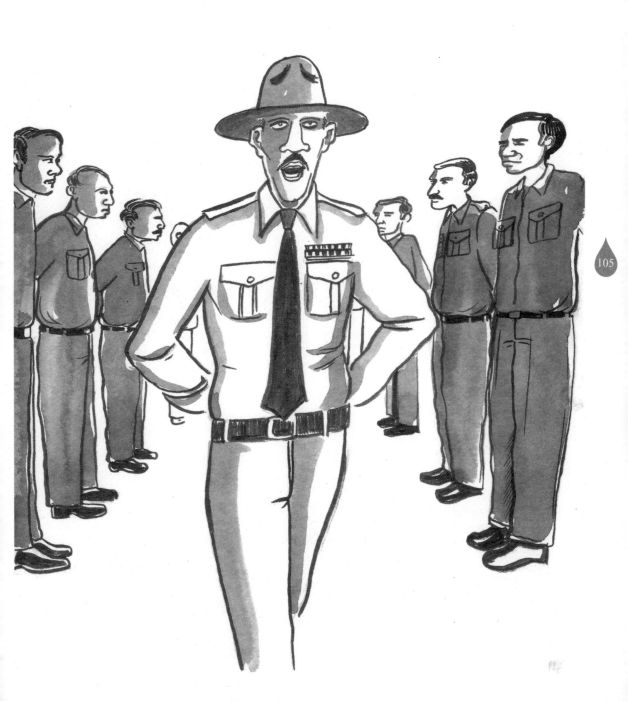

Indraprastha Now.

A quick selfie.
F-5.6

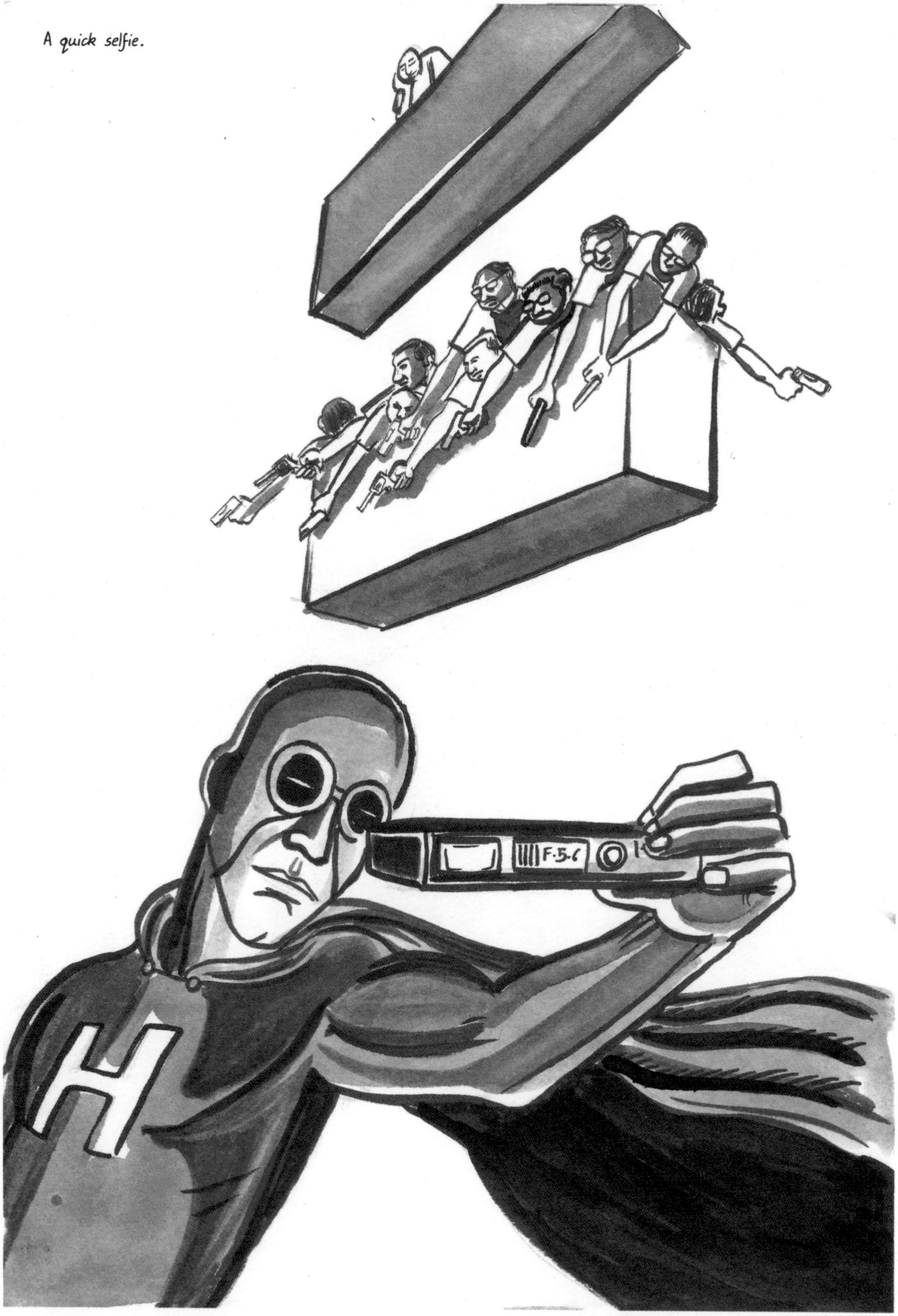

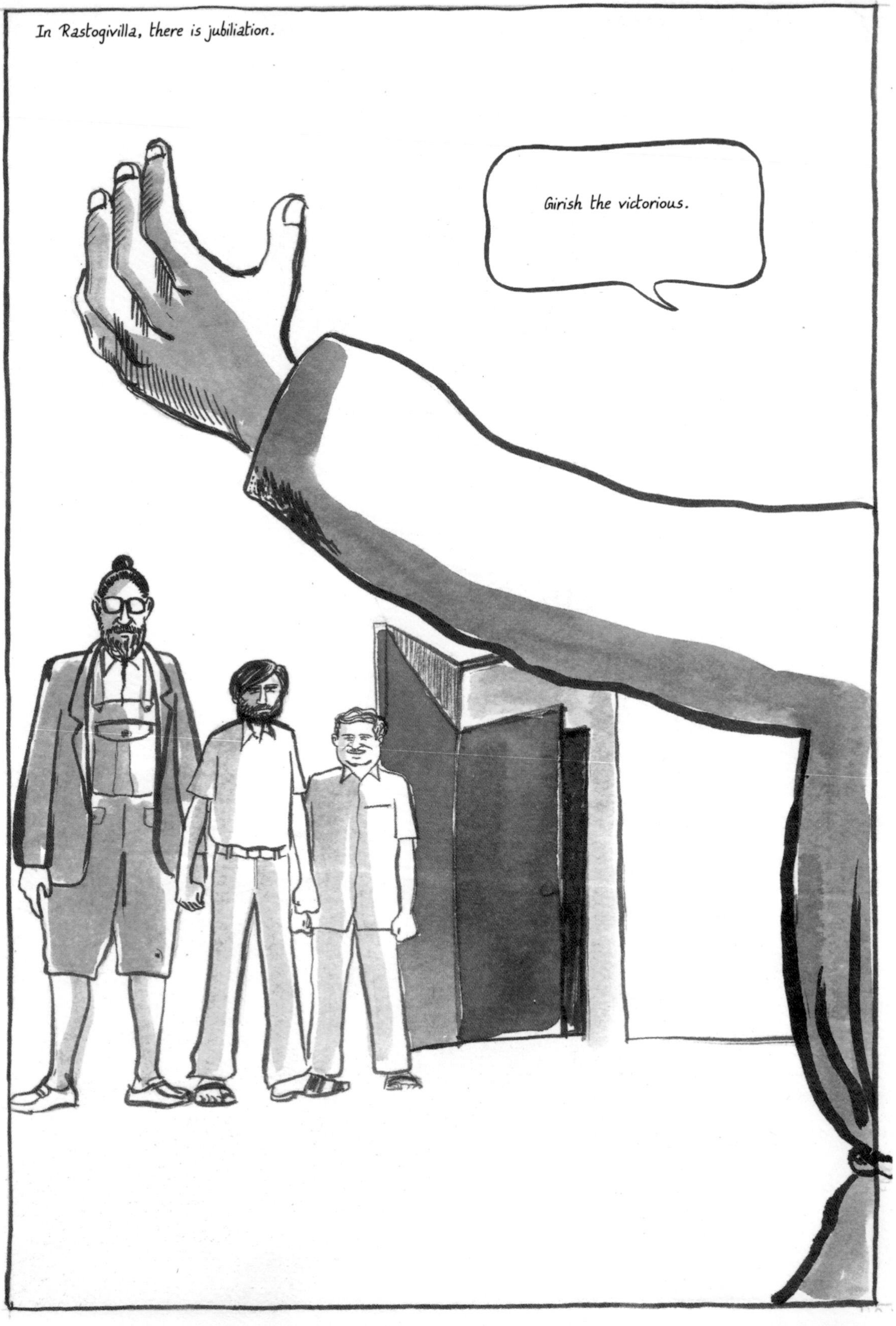
In Rastogivilla, there is jubiliation.
Girish the victorious.

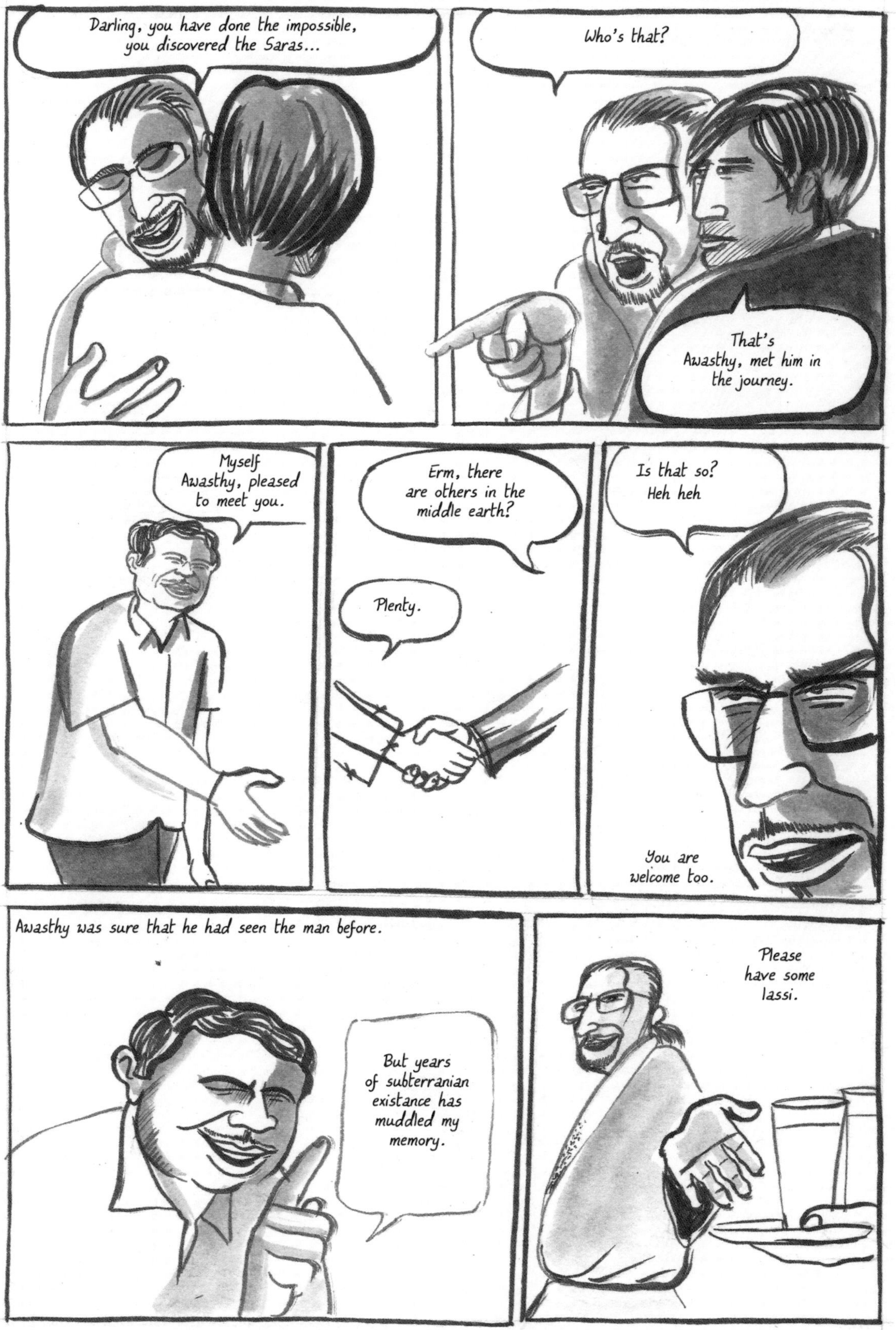
Darling, you have done the impossible, you discovered the Saras...
Who's that?
That's Awasthy, met him in the journey.
Myself Awasthy, pleased to meet you.
Erm, there are others in the middle earth?
Plenty.
Is that so? Heh heh
You are welcome too.
Awasthy was sure that he had seen the man before.
But years of subterranian existance has muddled my memory.
Please have some lassi.

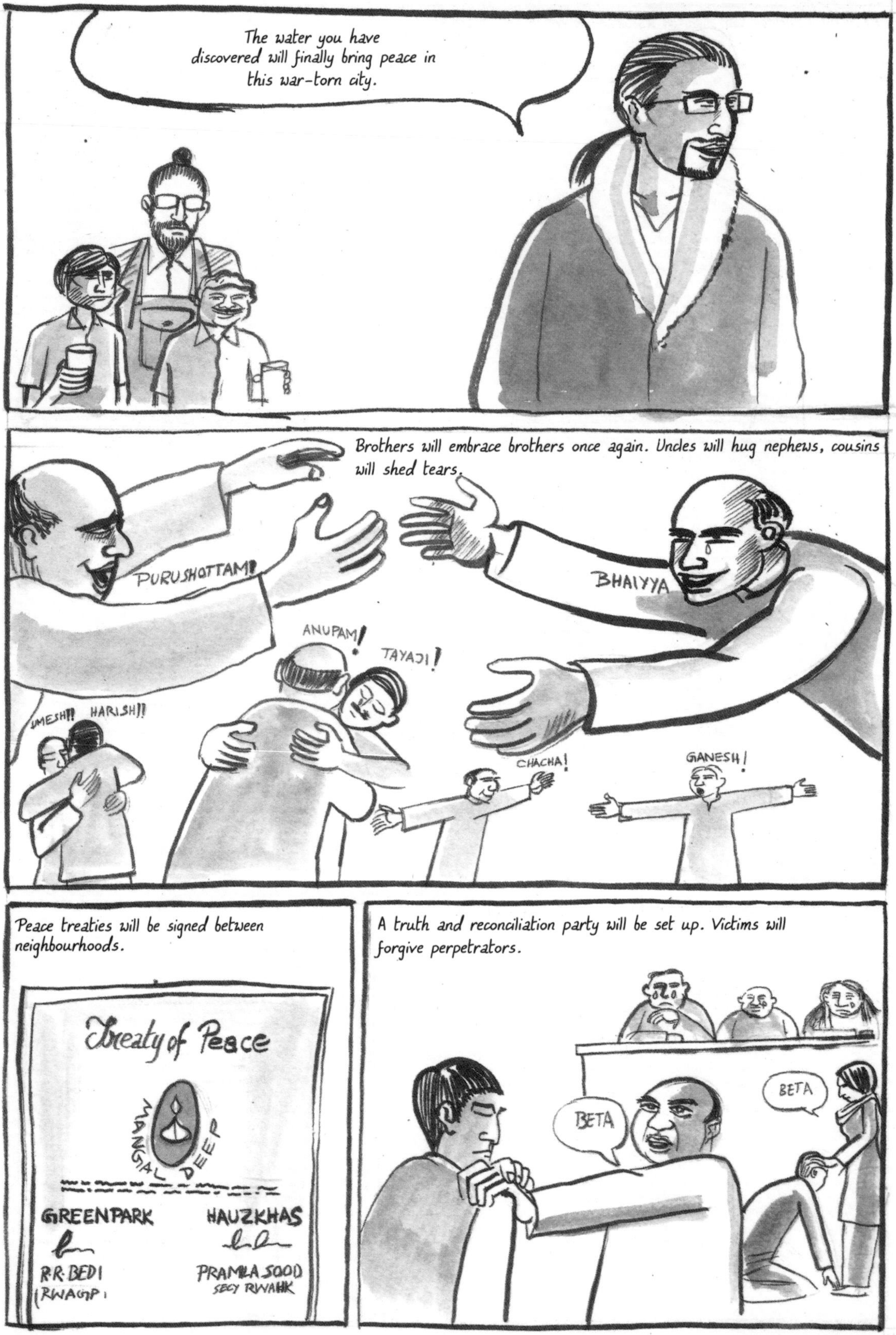

The water you have discovered will finally bring peace in this war-torn city.
Brothers will embrace brothers once again. Uncles will hug nephews, cousins will shed tears.
PURUSHOTTAM!
BHAIYYA
ANUPAM!
TAYAJI!
UMESH!!
HARISH!!
CHACHA!
GANESH!
Peace treaties will be signed between neighbourhoods.
Treaty of Peace
MANGAL DEEP
GREENPARK
HAUZKHAS
R.R. BEDI
(RWAGP
PRAMILA SOOD
SECY RWAHK
A truth and reconciliation party will be set up. Victims will forgive perpetrators.
BETA
BETA

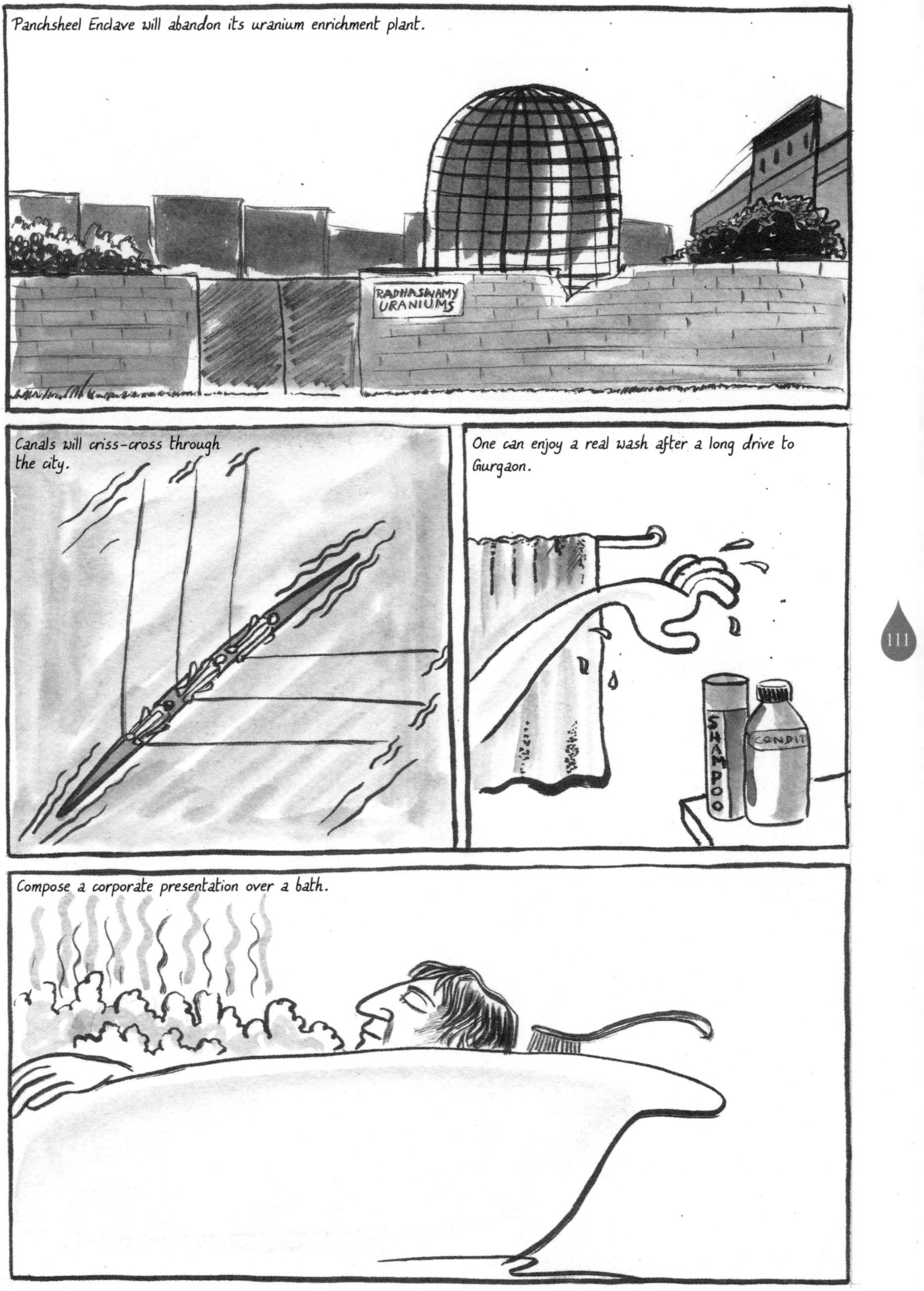
Panchsheel Enclave will abandon its uranium enrichment plant.
RADHASWAMY URANIUMS
Canals will criss-cross through the city.
One can enjoy a real wash after a long drive to Gurgaon.
SHAMPOO
CONDIT
Compose a corporate presentation over a bath.

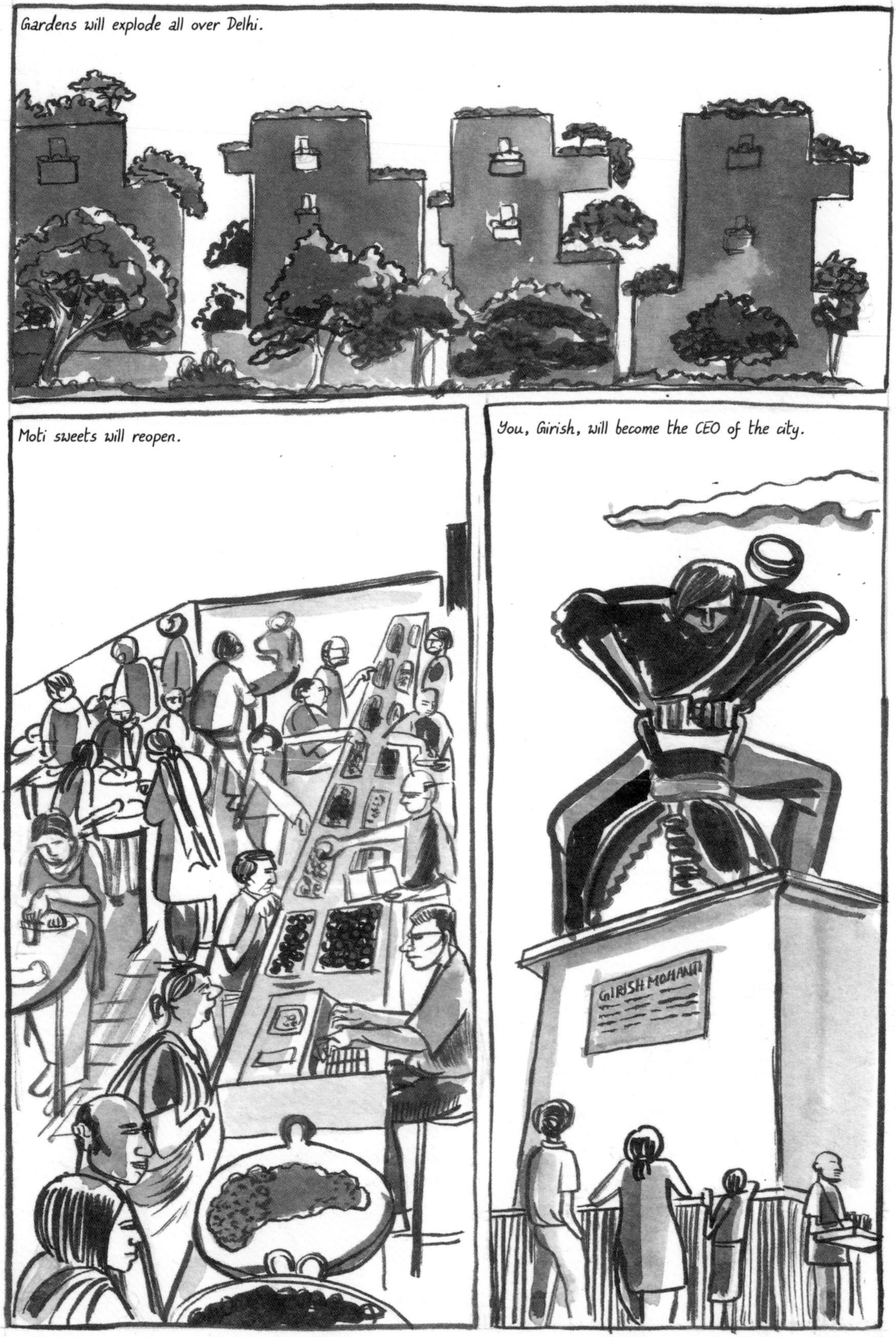
Gardens will explode all over Delhi.
Moti sweets will reopen.
You, Girish, will become the CEO of the city.
GIRISH MOHANTI

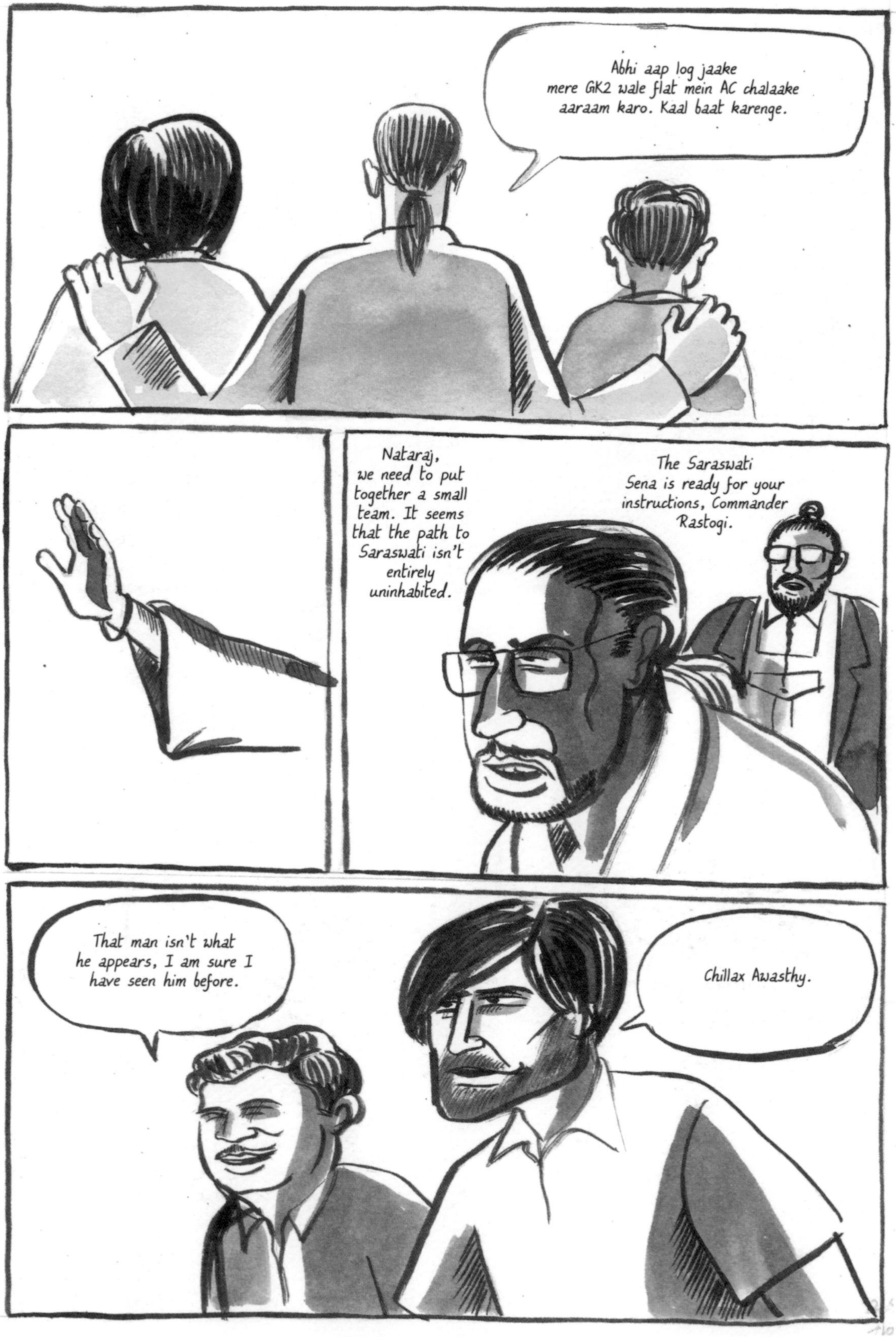
Abhi aap log jaake mere GK2 wale flat mein AC chalaake aaraam karo. Kaal baat karenge.
Nataraj, we need to put together a small team. It seems that the path to Saraswati isn't entirely uninhabited.
The Saraswati Sena is ready for your instructions, Commander Rastogi.
That man isn't what he appears, I am sure I have seen him before.
Chillax Awasthy.

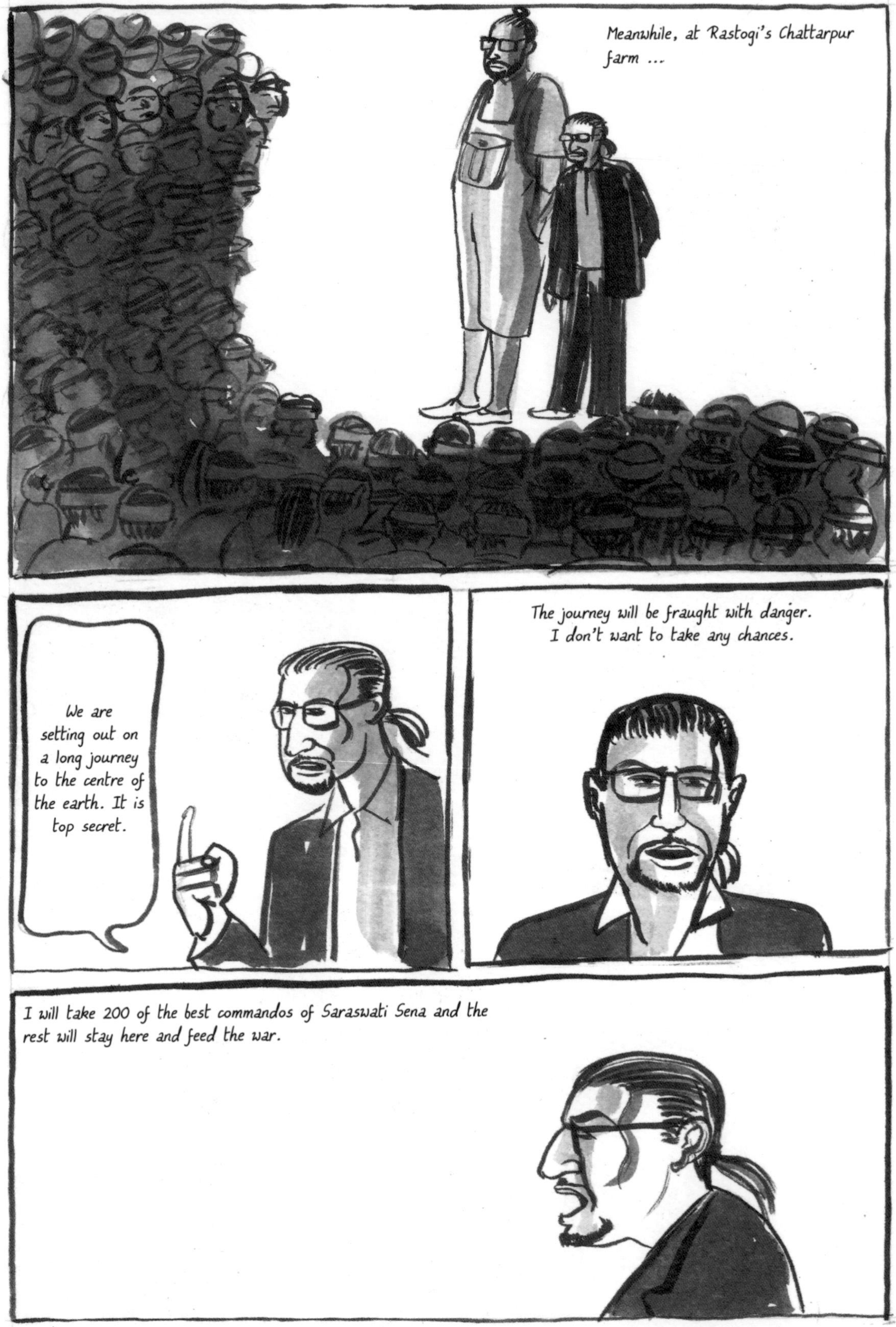
Meanwhile, at Rastogi's Chattarpur farm ...
We are setting out on a long journey to the centre of the earth. It is top secret.
The journey will be fraught with danger. I don't want to take any chances.
I will take 200 of the best commandos of Saraswati Sena and the rest will stay here and feed the war.

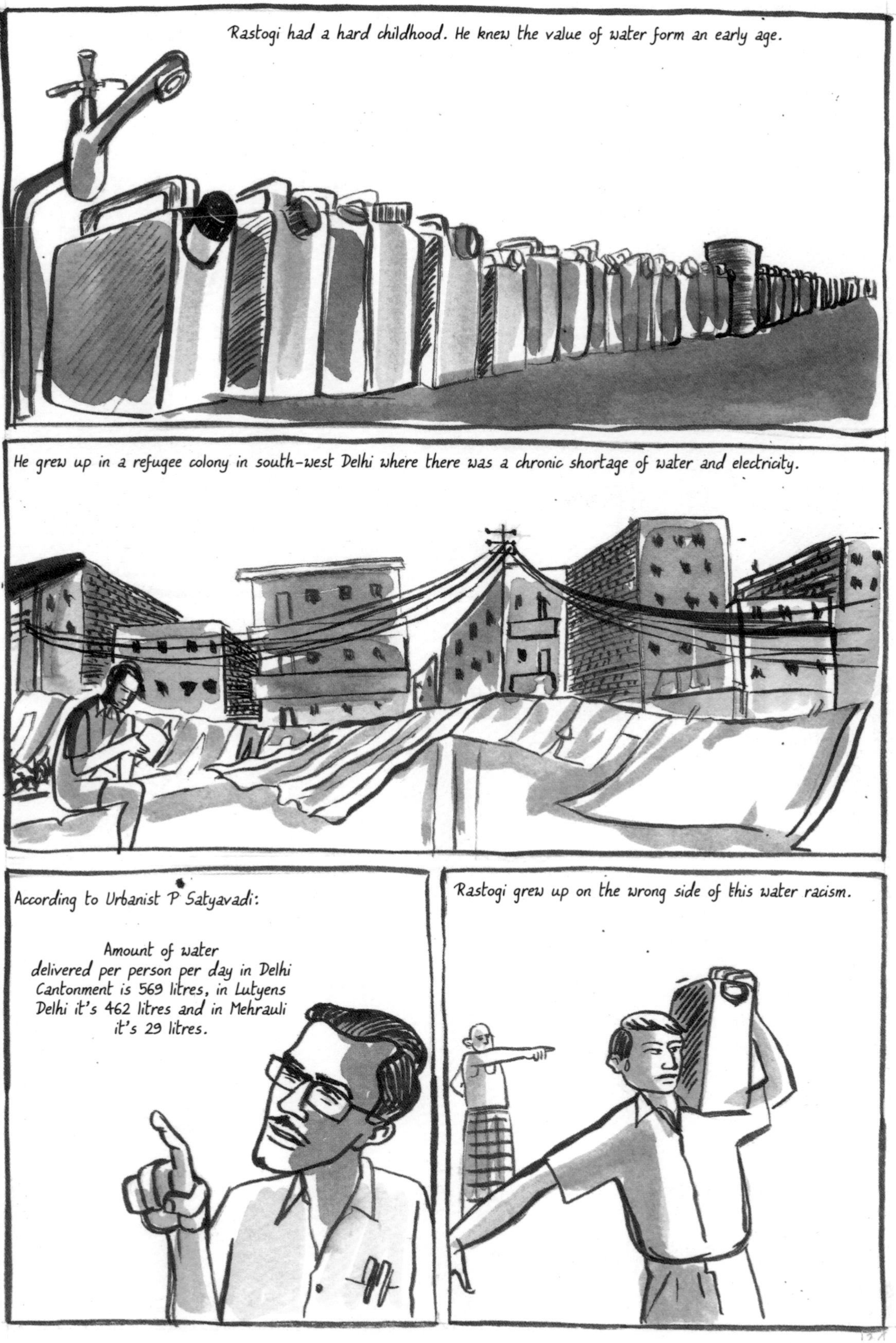
Rastogi had a hard childhood. He knew the value of water form an early age.
He grew up in a refugee colony in south-west Delhi where there was a chronic shortage of water and electricity.
According to Urbanist P Satyavadi:
Amount of water delivered per person per day in Delhi Cantonment is 569 litres, in Lutyens Delhi it's 462 litres and in Mehrauli it's 29 litres.
Rastogi grew up on the wrong side of this water racism.

He was always late for school.

And reached there dripping and odoriferous.

Boys called him ...

KURA

Girls called him ...

KACHRA
TEE HE HE

The maths teacher combined the two and called him ...

K K

Out of frustration, he once threw a stone at a fancy bathroom-ware store in GK2 M-block market.

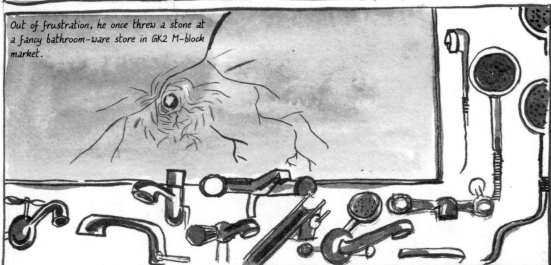

The punishment was disproportionately harsh. He got half a year at a reform school.

This hardened him further.

Once, he almost killed someone. Rastogi was sensitive when it came to water.

Soon people stopped fucking with him.

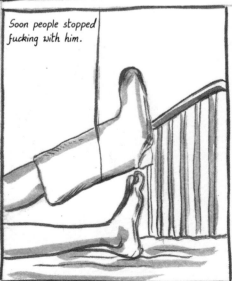

After six months at the reform school he was released. He went back to school, apparently normal.

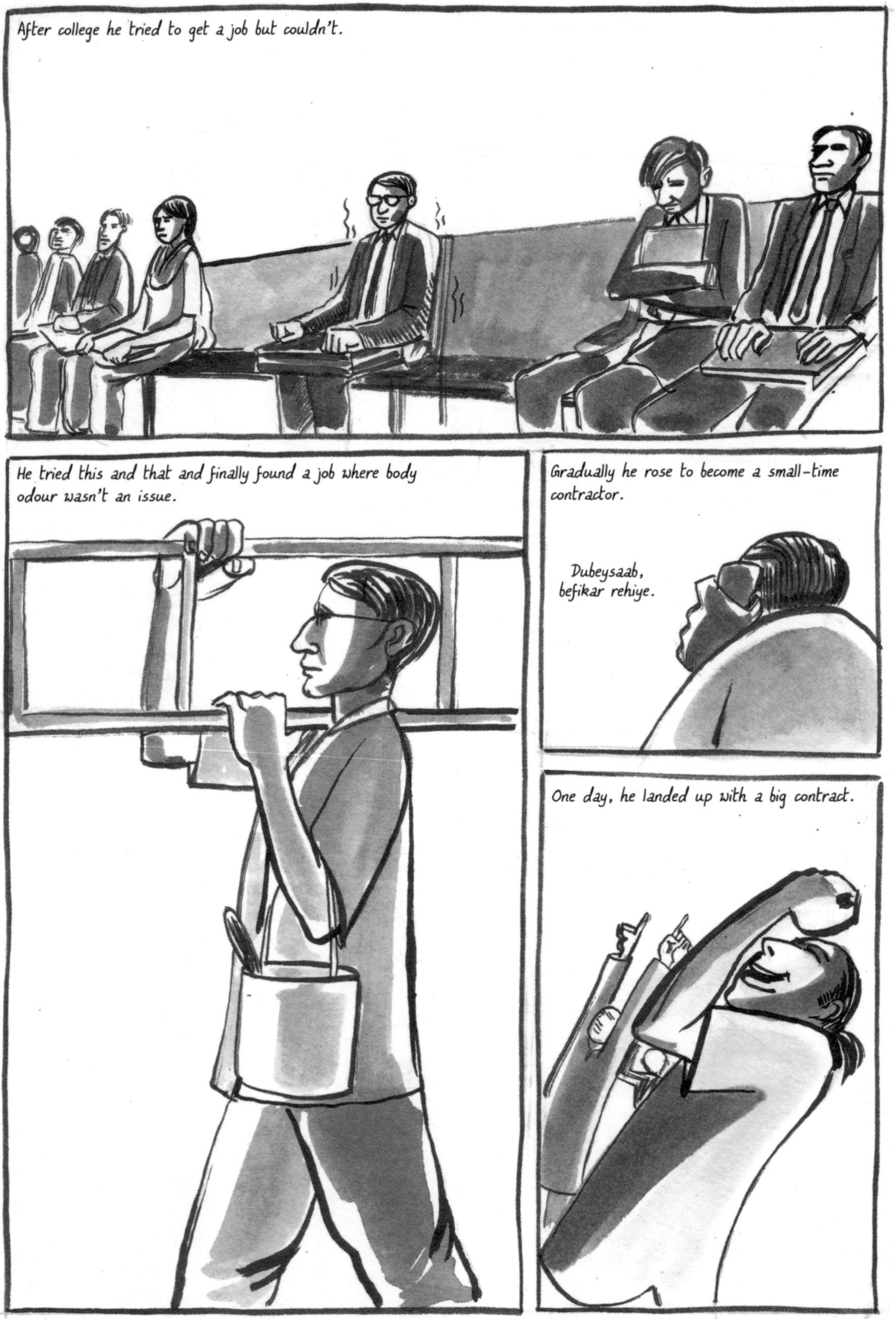
After college he tried to get a job but couldn't.
He tried this and that and finally found a job where body odour wasn't an issue.
Gradually he rose to become a small-time contractor.
Dubeysaab, befikar rehiye.
One day, he landed up with a big contract.

He had two partners. By the end of the year, one of them had been swindled out of his last belongings.

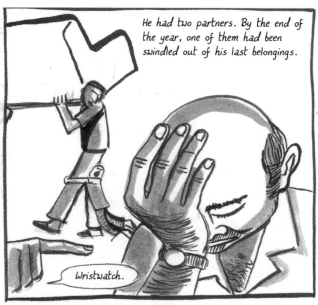

Wristwatch.

The other wasn't so lucky.

He was found dead under mysterious circumstances.

Rastogi grew stronger and stronger. The secret of his success was his skill in spotting loopholes in government rules.

That is how he met Awasthy, the MCD biggy. No wonder neither could remember the other, because both men had made an effort to forget.

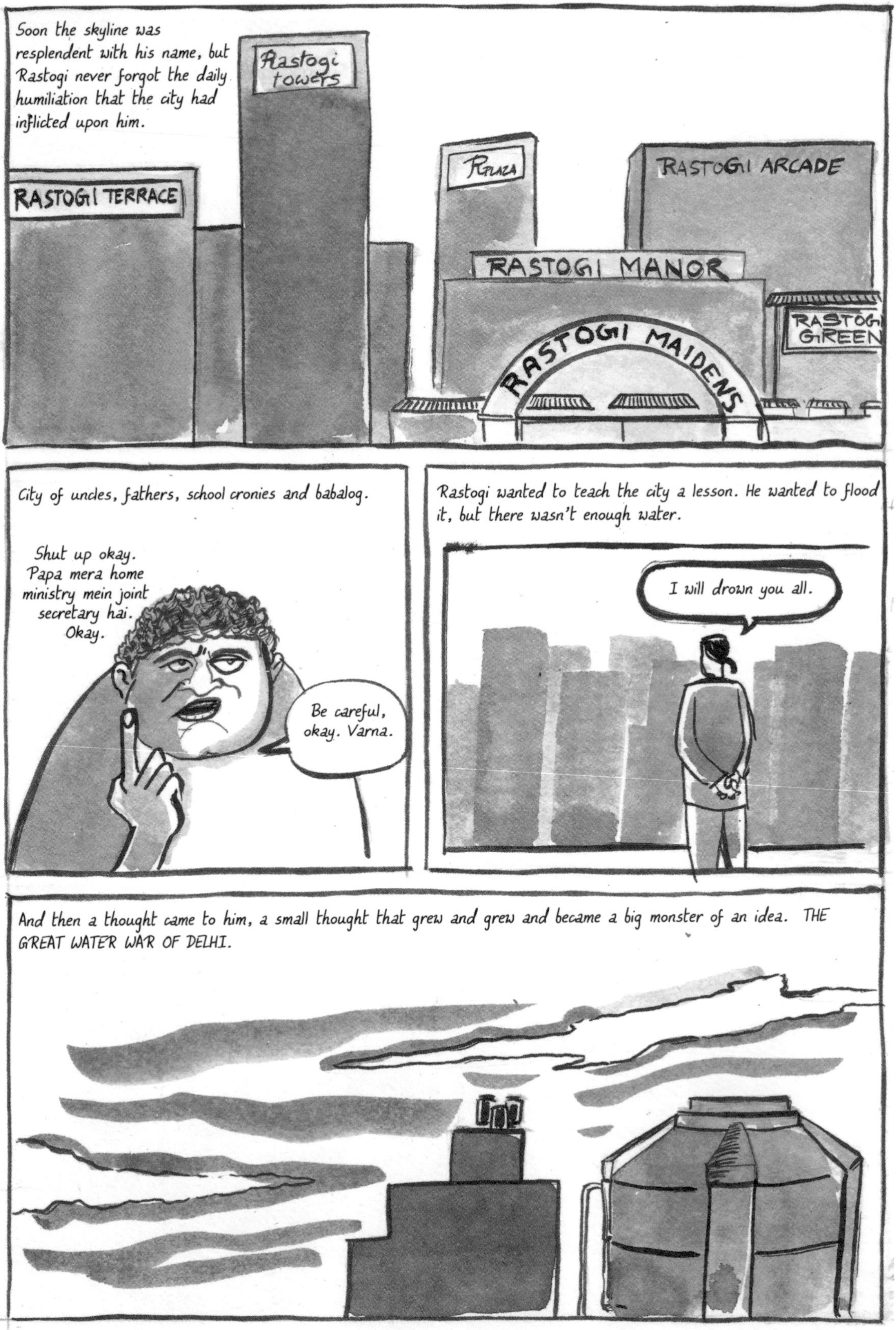
Soon the skyline was resplendent with his name, but Rastogi never forgot the daily humiliation that the city had inflicted upon him.
Rastogi towers
RASTOGI TERRACE
R PLAZA
RASTOGI ARCADE
RASTOGI MANOR
RASTOGI MAIDENS
RASTOGI GREEN
City of uncles, fathers, school cronies and babalog.
Shut up okay. Papa mera home ministry mein joint secretary hai. Okay.
Be careful, okay. Varna.
Rastogi wanted to teach the city a lesson. He wanted to flood it, but there wasn't enough water.
I will drown you all.
And then a thought came to him, a small thought that grew and grew and became a big monster of an idea. THE GREAT WATER WAR OF DELHI.

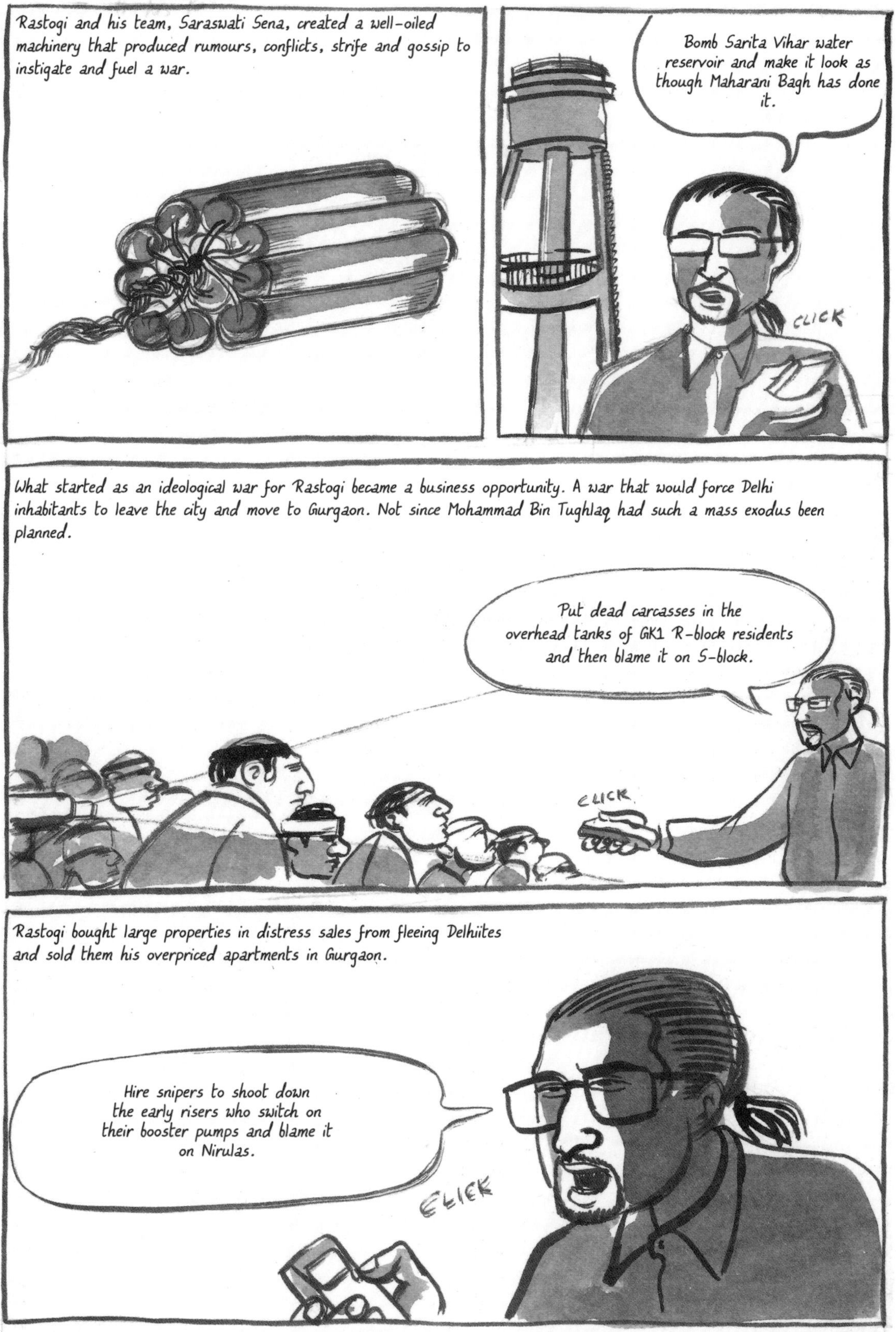
Rastogi and his team, Saraswati Sena, created a well-oiled machinery that produced rumours, conflicts, strife and gossip to instigate and fuel a war.
Bomb Sarita Vihar water reservoir and make it look as though Maharani Bagh has done it.
CLICK
What started as an ideological war for Rastogi became a business opportunity. A war that would force Delhi inhabitants to leave the city and move to Gurgaon. Not since Mohammad Bin Tughlaq had such a mass exodus been planned.
Put dead carcasses in the overhead tanks of GK1 R-block residents and then blame it on S-block.
CLICK
Rastogi bought large properties in distress sales from fleeing Delhiites and sold them his overpriced apartments in Gurgaon.
Hire snipers to shoot down the early risers who switch on their booster pumps and blame it on Nirulas.
CLICK

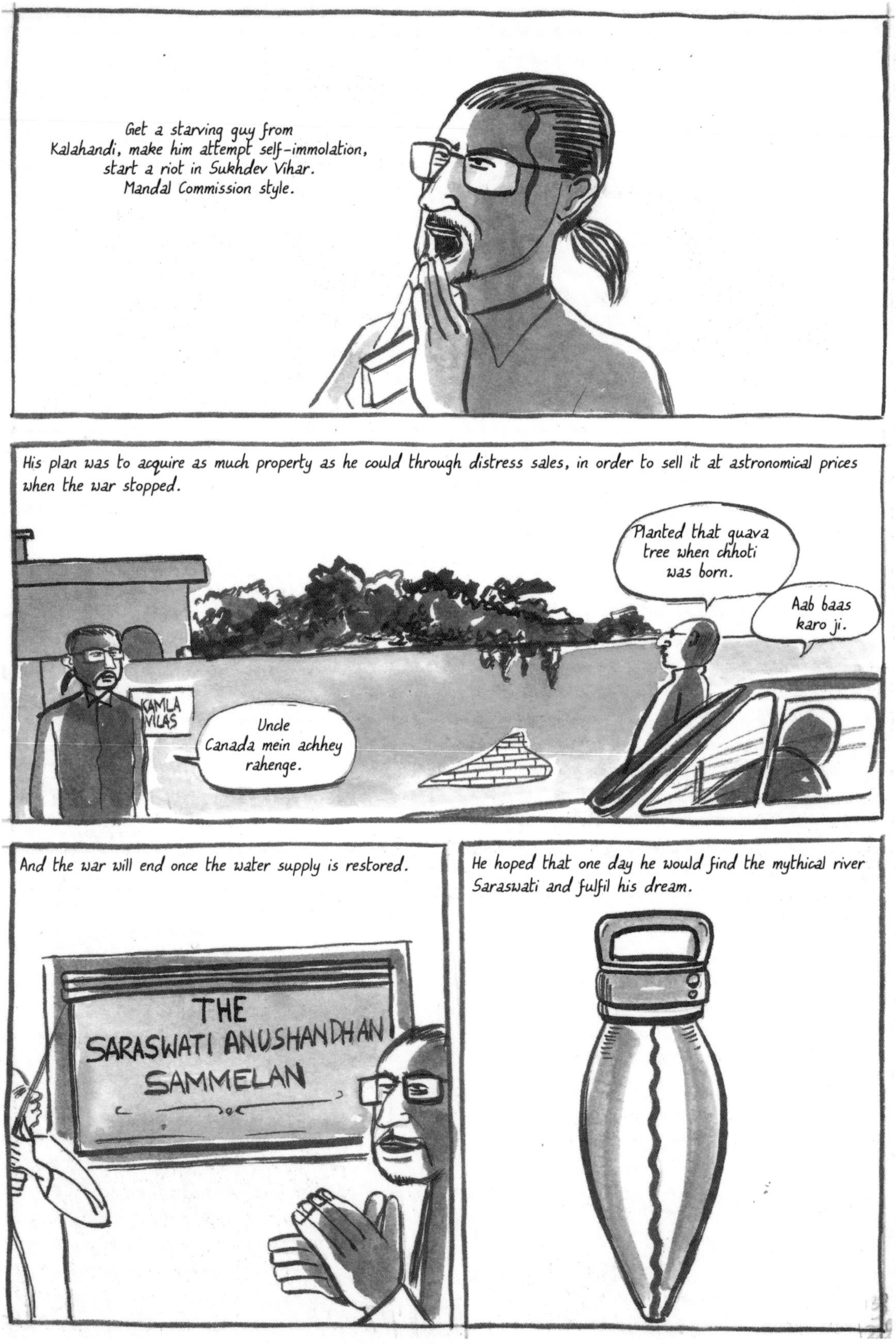
Get a starving guy from Kalahandi, make him attempt self-immolation, start a riot in Sukhdev Vihar. Mandal Commission style.
His plan was to acquire as much property as he could through distress sales, in order to sell it at astronomical prices when the war stopped.
Planted that guava tree when chhoti was born.
Aab baas karo ji.
KAMLA VILAS
Uncle Canada mein achhey rahenge.
And the war will end once the water supply is restored.
THE SARASWATI ANUSHANDHAN SAMMELAN
He hoped that one day he would find the mythical river Saraswati and fulfil his dream.

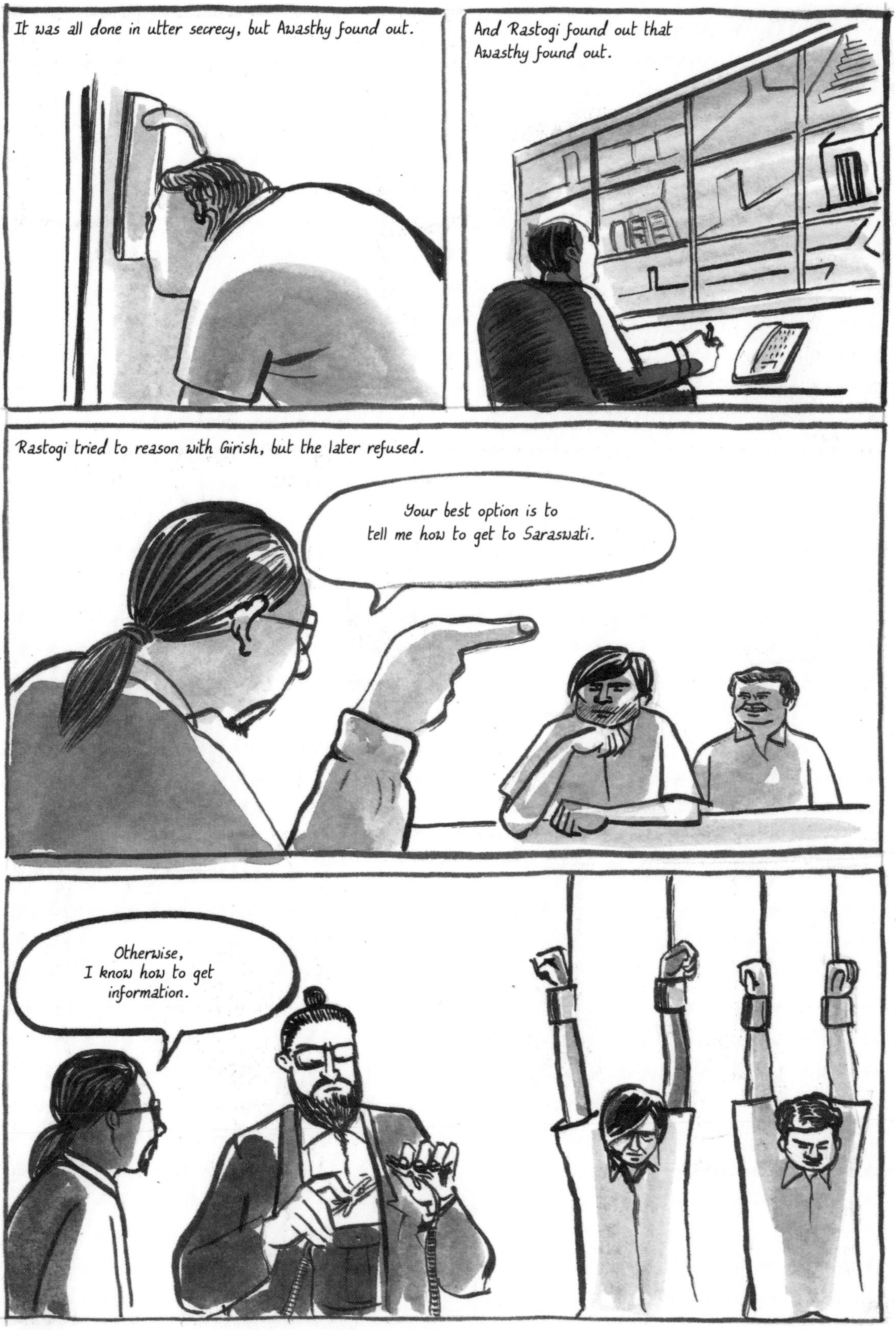

It was all done in utter secrecy, but Awasthy found out.
And Rastogi found out that Awasthy found out.
Rastogi tried to reason with Girish, but the later refused.
Your best option is to tell me how to get to Saraswati.
Otherwise, I know how to get information.

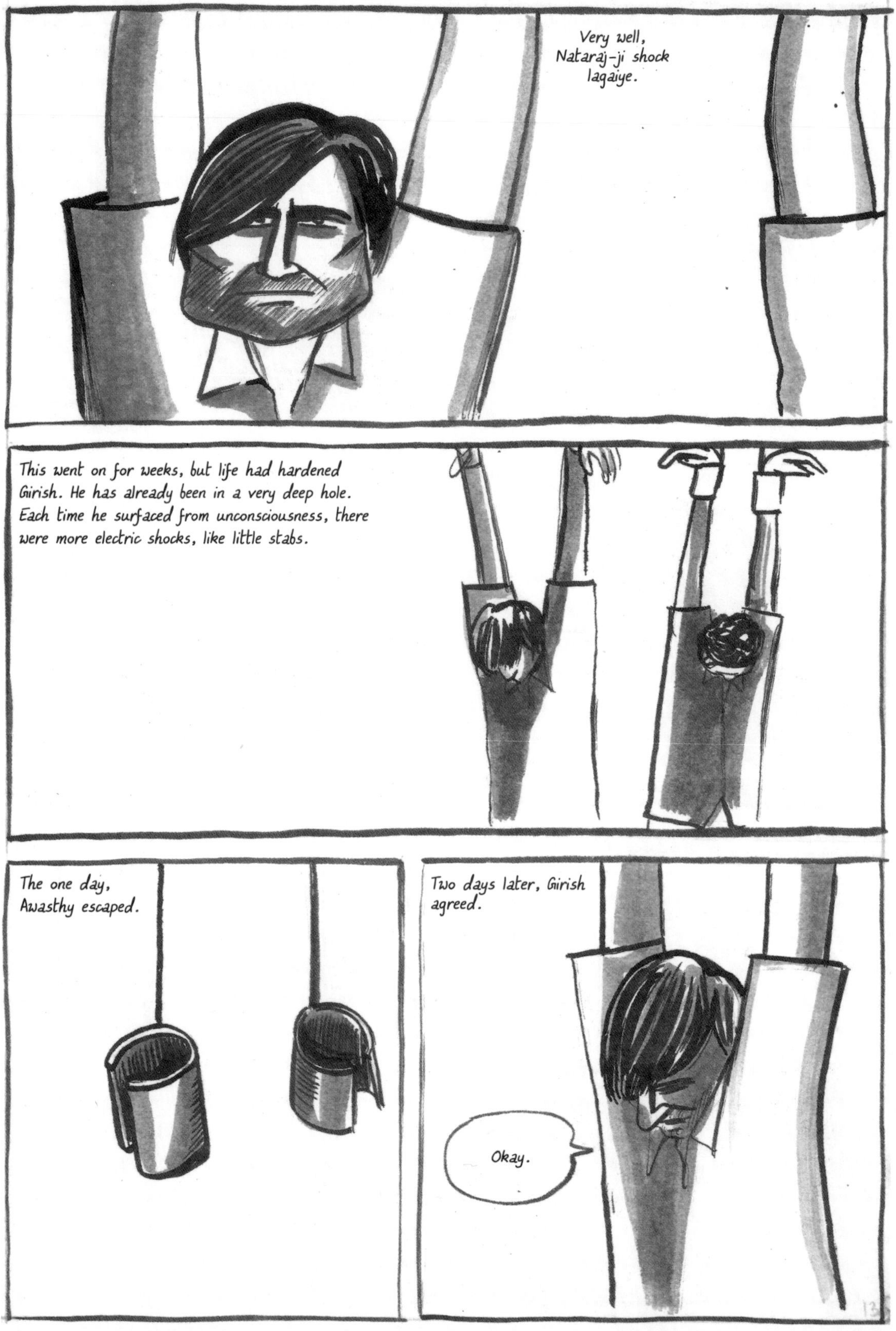
Very well, Nataraj-ji shock lagaiye.
This went on for weeks, but life had hardened Girish. He has already been in a very deep hole. Each time he surfaced from unconsciousness, there were more electric shocks, like little stabs.
The one day, Awasthy escaped.
Two days later, Girish agreed.
Okay.

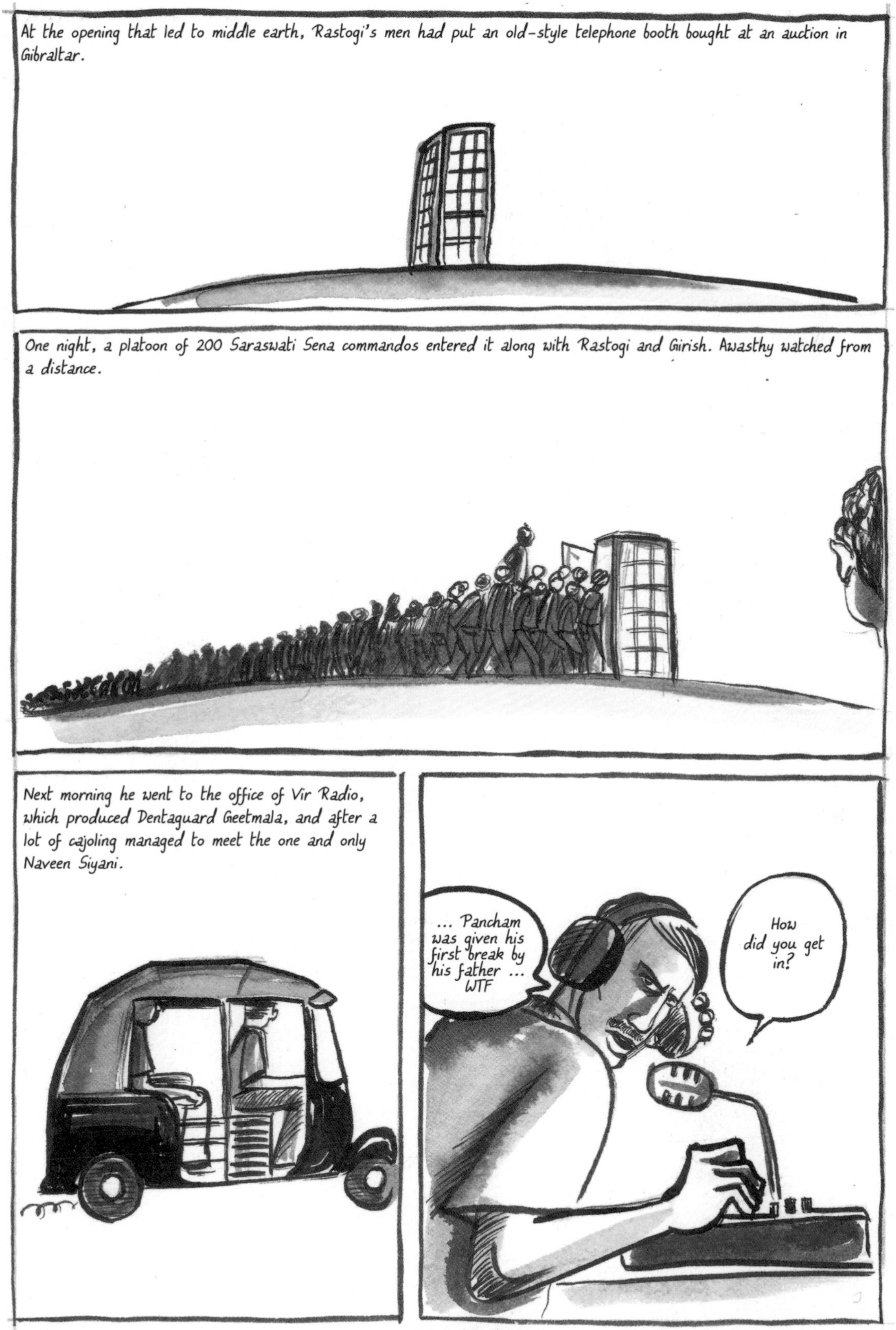
At the opening that led to middle earth, Rastogi's men had put an old-style telephone booth bought at an auction in Gibraltar.
One night, a platoon of 200 Saraswati Sena commandos entered it along with Rastogi and Girish. Awasthy watched from a distance.
Next morning he went to the office of Vir Radio, which produced Dentaguard Geetmala, and after a lot of cajoling managed to meet the one and only Naveen Siyani.
... Pancham was given his first break by his father ... WTF
How did you get in?

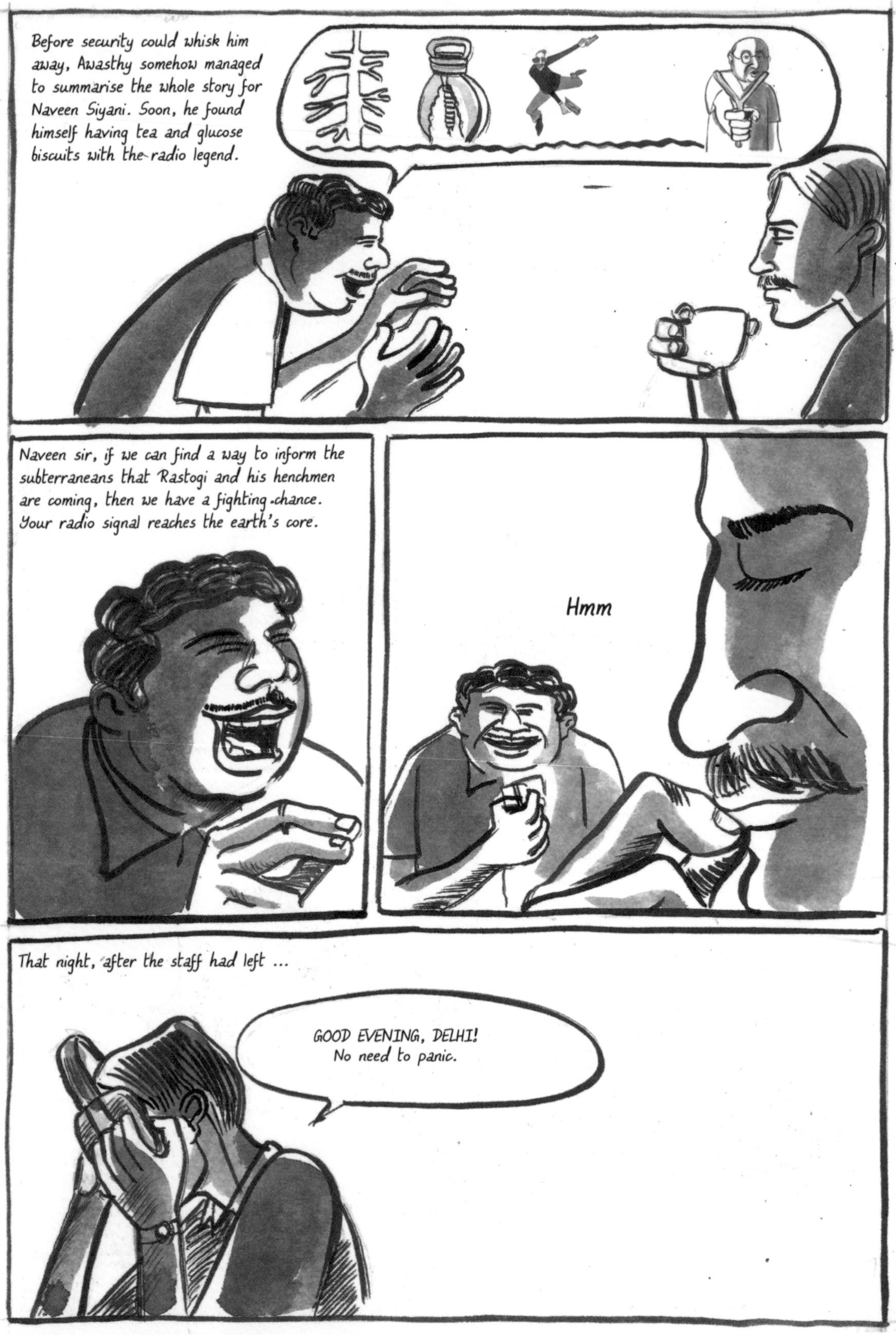
Before security could whisk him away, Awasthy somehow managed to summarise the whole story for Naveen Siyani. Soon, he found himself having tea and glucose biscuits with the radio legend.
Naveen sir, if we can find a way to inform the subterraneans that Rastogi and his henchmen are coming, then we have a fighting chance. Your radio signal reaches the earth's core.
Hmm
That night, after the staff had left ...
GOOD EVENING, DELHI! No need to panic.

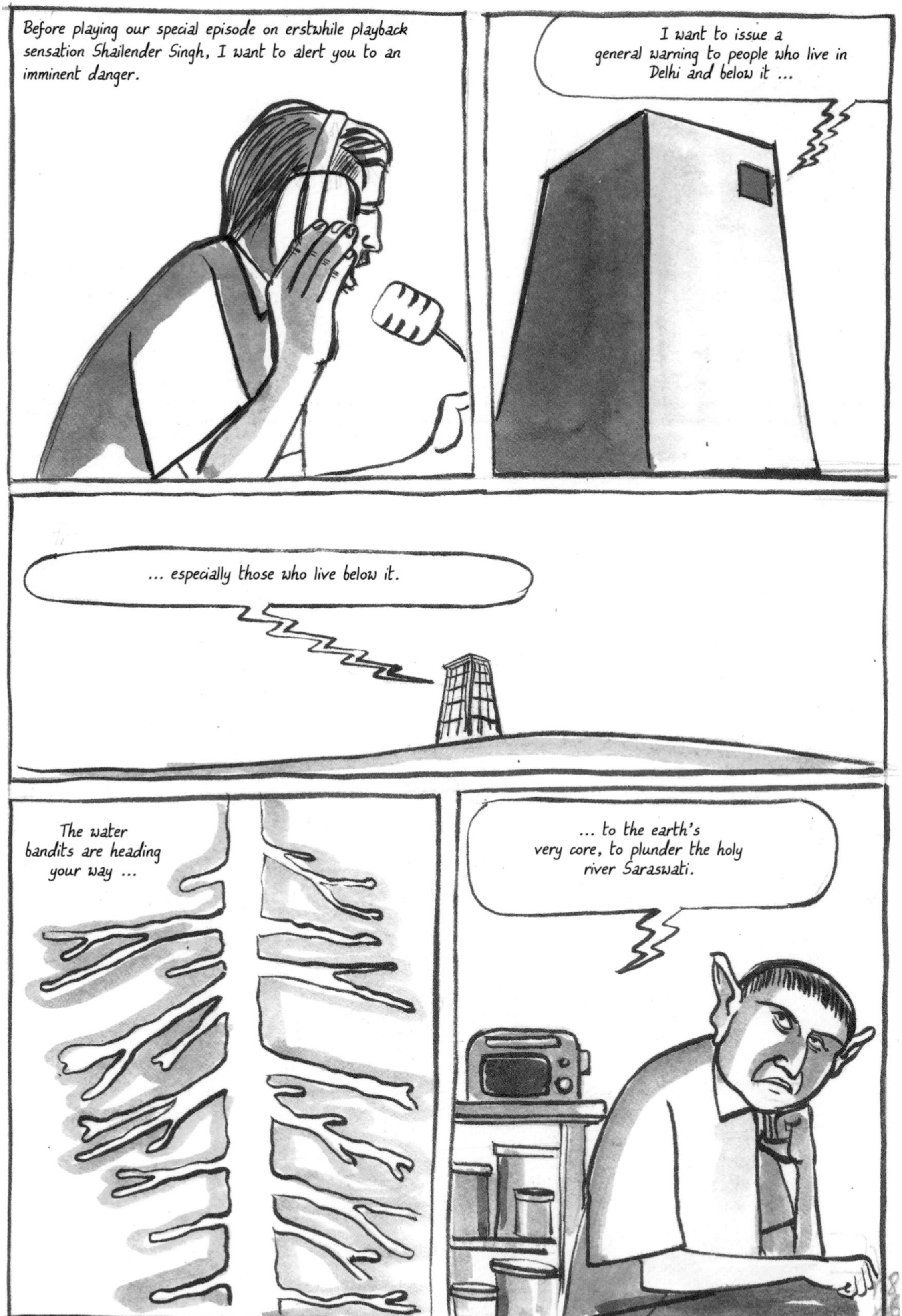
Before playing our special episode on erstwhile playback sensation Shailender Singh, I want to alert you to an imminent danger.
I want to issue a general warning to people who live in Delhi and below it ...
... especially those who live below it.
The water bandits are heading your way ...
... to the earth's very core, to plunder the holy river Saraswati.

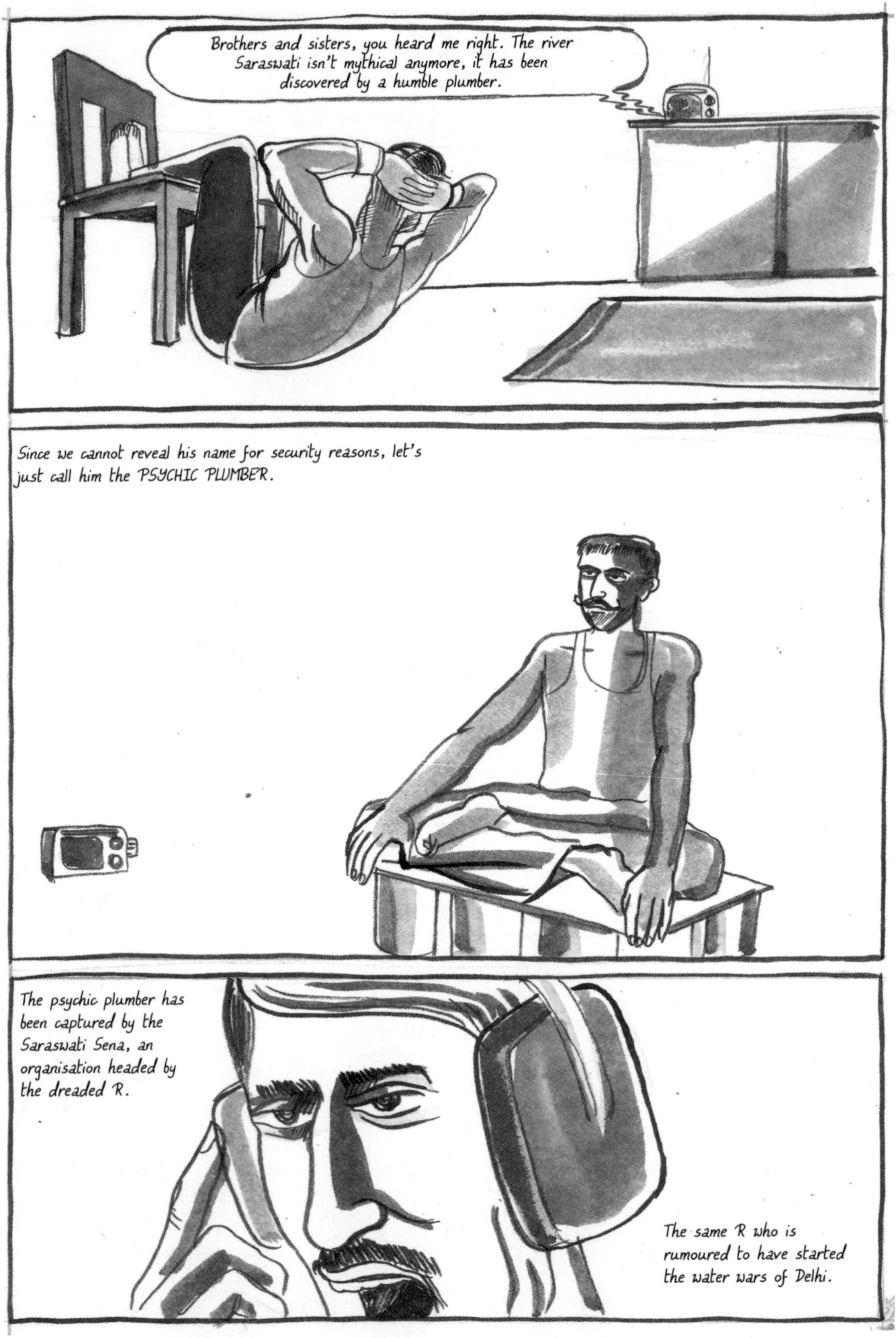
Brothers and sisters, you heard me right. The river Saraswati isn't mythical anymore, it has been discovered by a humble plumber.
Since we cannot reveal his name for security reasons, let's just call him the PSYCHIC PLUMBER.
The psychic plumber has been captured by the Saraswati Sena, an organisation headed by the dreaded R.
The same R who is rumoured to have started the water wars of Delhi.

128

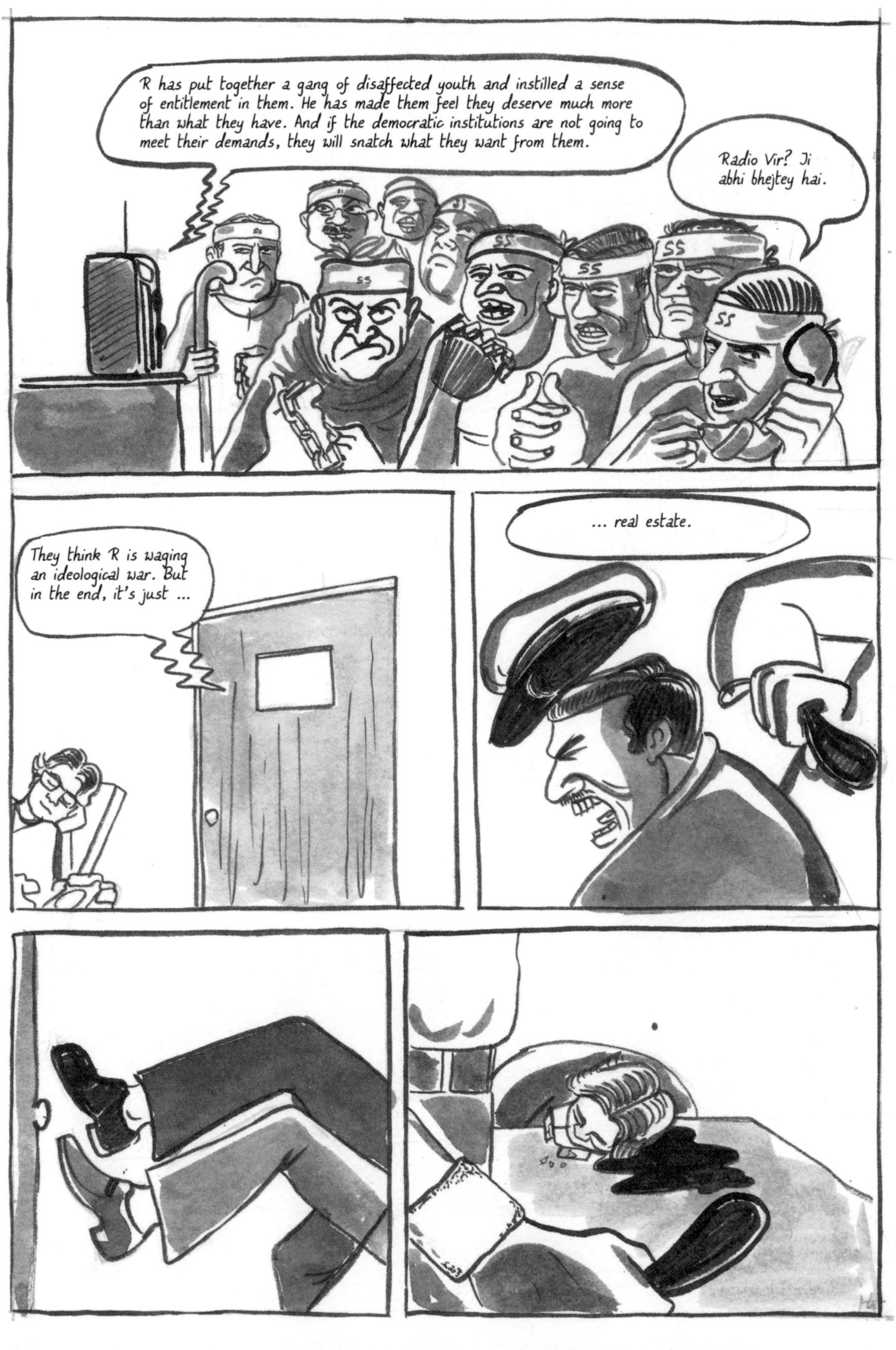
R has put together a gang of disaffected youth and instilled a sense of entitlement in them. He has made them feel they deserve much more than what they have. And if the democratic institutions are not going to meet their demands, they will snatch what they want from them.
Radio Vir? Ji abhi bhejtey hai.
They think R is waging an ideological war. But in the end, it's just ...
... real estate.

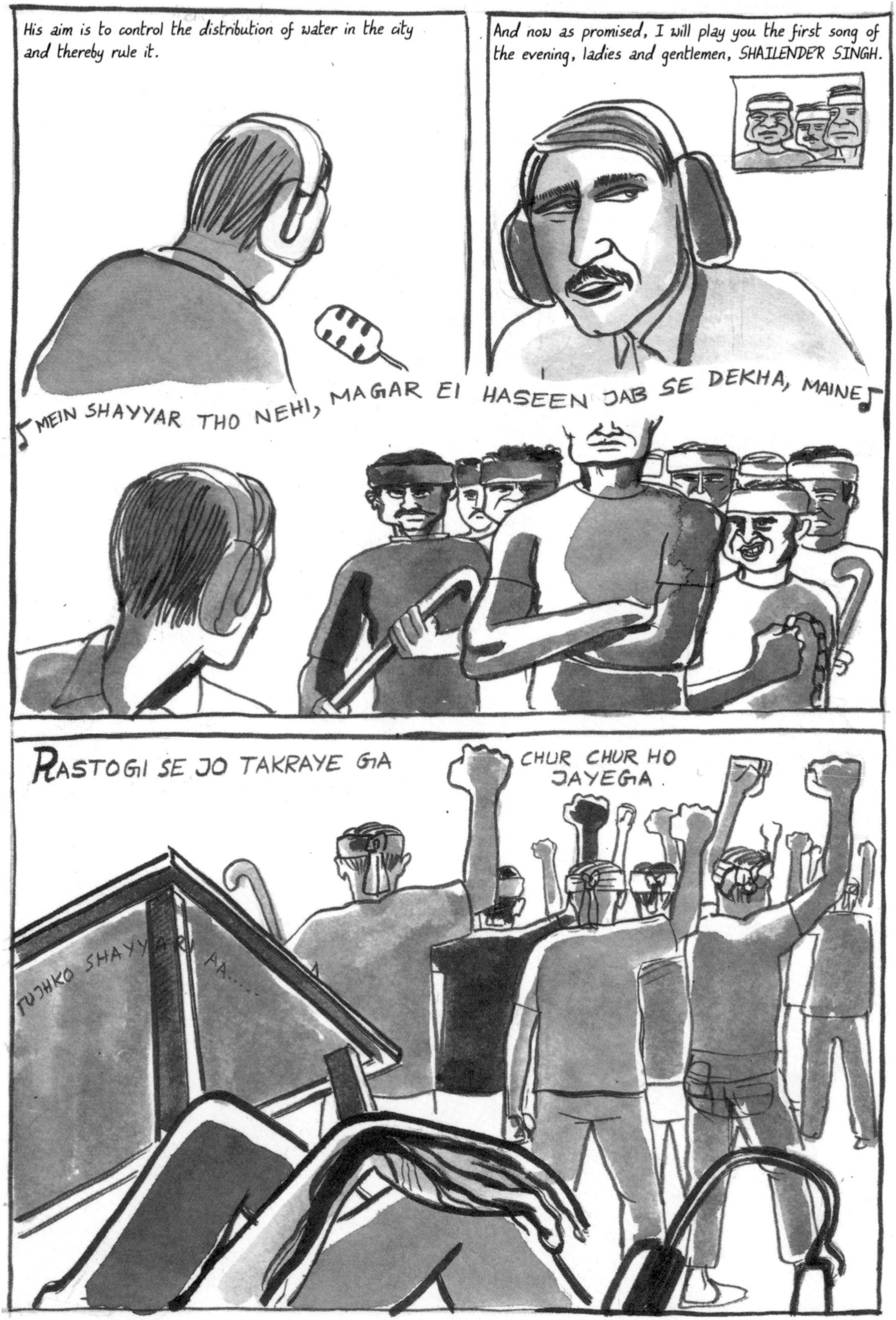
His aim is to control the distribution of water in the city and thereby rule it.
And now as promised, I will play you the first song of the evening, ladies and gentlemen, SHAILENDER SINGH.
MEIN SHAYYAR THO NEHI, MAGAR EI HASEEN JAB SE DEKHA, MAINE
RASTOGI SE JO TAKRAYE GA
CHUR CHUR HO JAYEGA
TUJHKO SHAYYARI AA.....

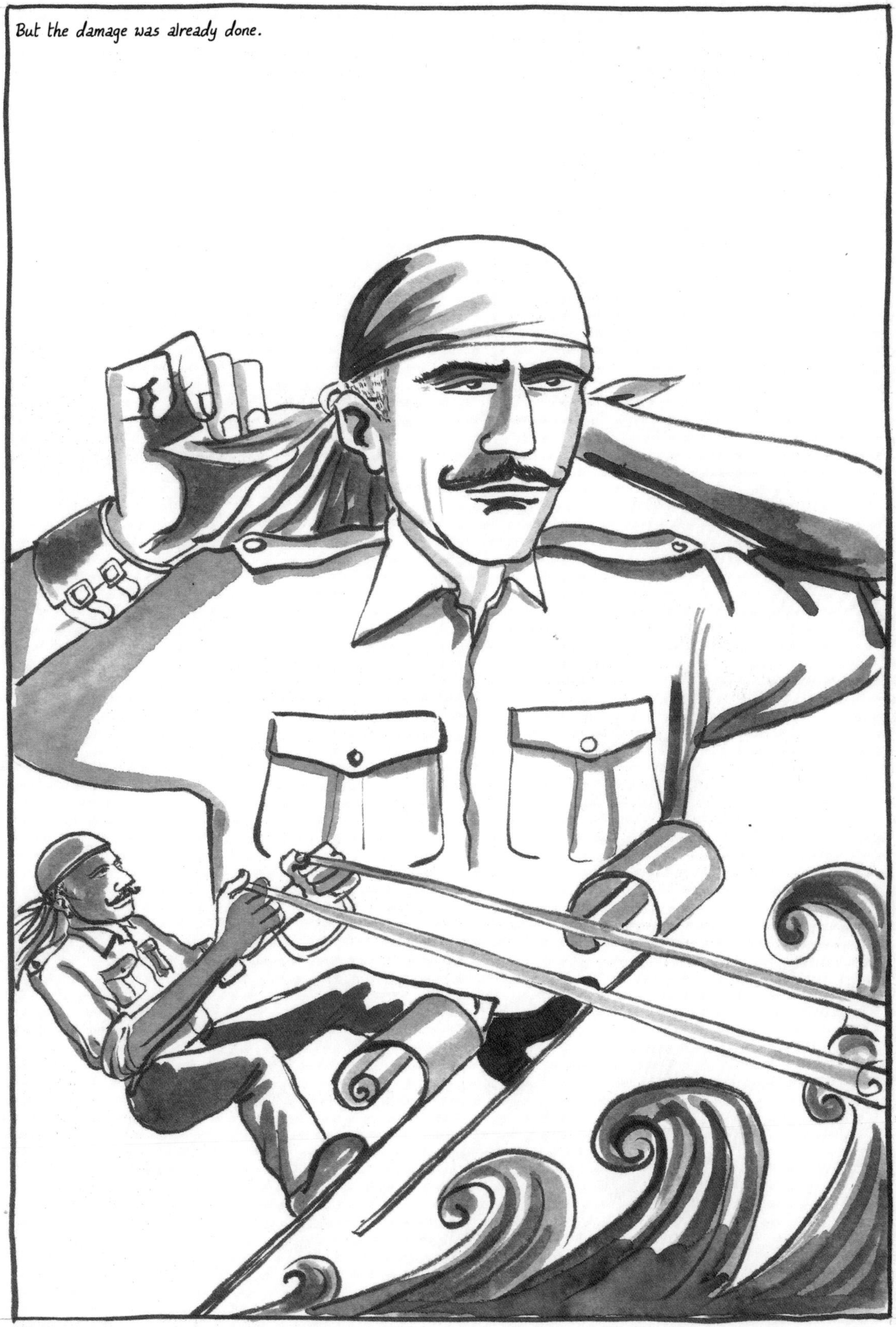
But the damage was already done.

Soon after he heard the radio flash, Col. Gambhir started preparing for battle.

He then went looking for the others ...

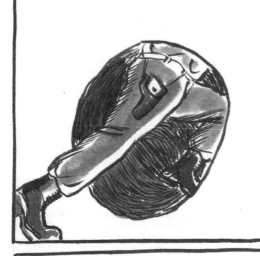

Girish had made a perfect network of tunnels, through which Gambhir moved swiftly.

Occasionally, he made a chalk mark as a cartographic guideline.

As he moved along the quiet corridors, a strategy formed in his mind.

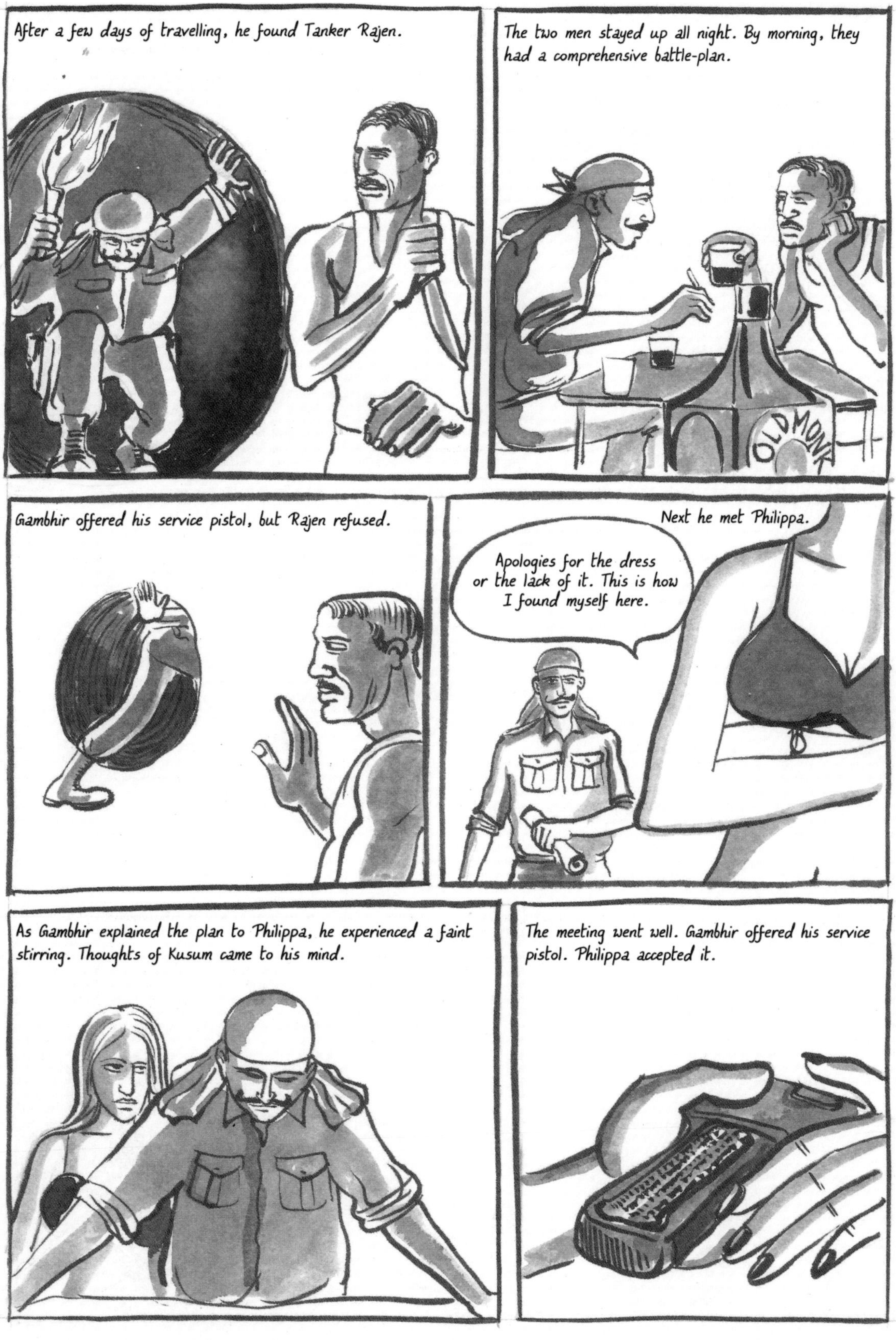
After a few days of travelling, he found Tanker Rajen.
The two men stayed up all night. By morning, they had a comprehensive battle-plan.
OLD MONK
Gambhir offered his service pistol, but Rajen refused.
Next he met Philippa.
Apologies for the dress or the lack of it. This is how I found myself here.
As Gambhir explained the plan to Philippa, he experienced a faint stirring. Thoughts of Kusum came to his mind.
The meeting went well. Gambhir offered his service pistol. Philippa accepted it.

Then Gambhir headed towards Jagat Ram.

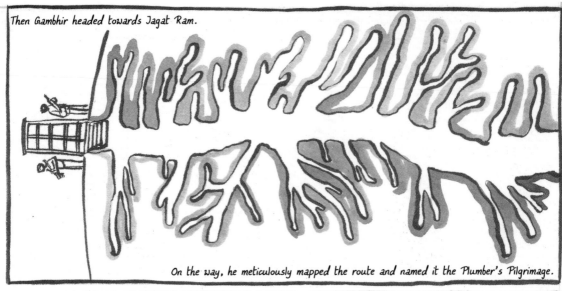

On the way, he meticulously mapped the route and named it the Plumber's Pilgrimage.

Finally, he reached Jagat.

You have to be very silent, Jagat. Wait till they leave your sector. And take them one by one, as many as you can, until you reach the Damodaran Point.

Then rush to the western bank of the Saraswati and rendezvous at Chettri Ghat.

And lie low.

I'm good at that.

And that's your weapon.

The Saraswati Sena progressed steadily ...

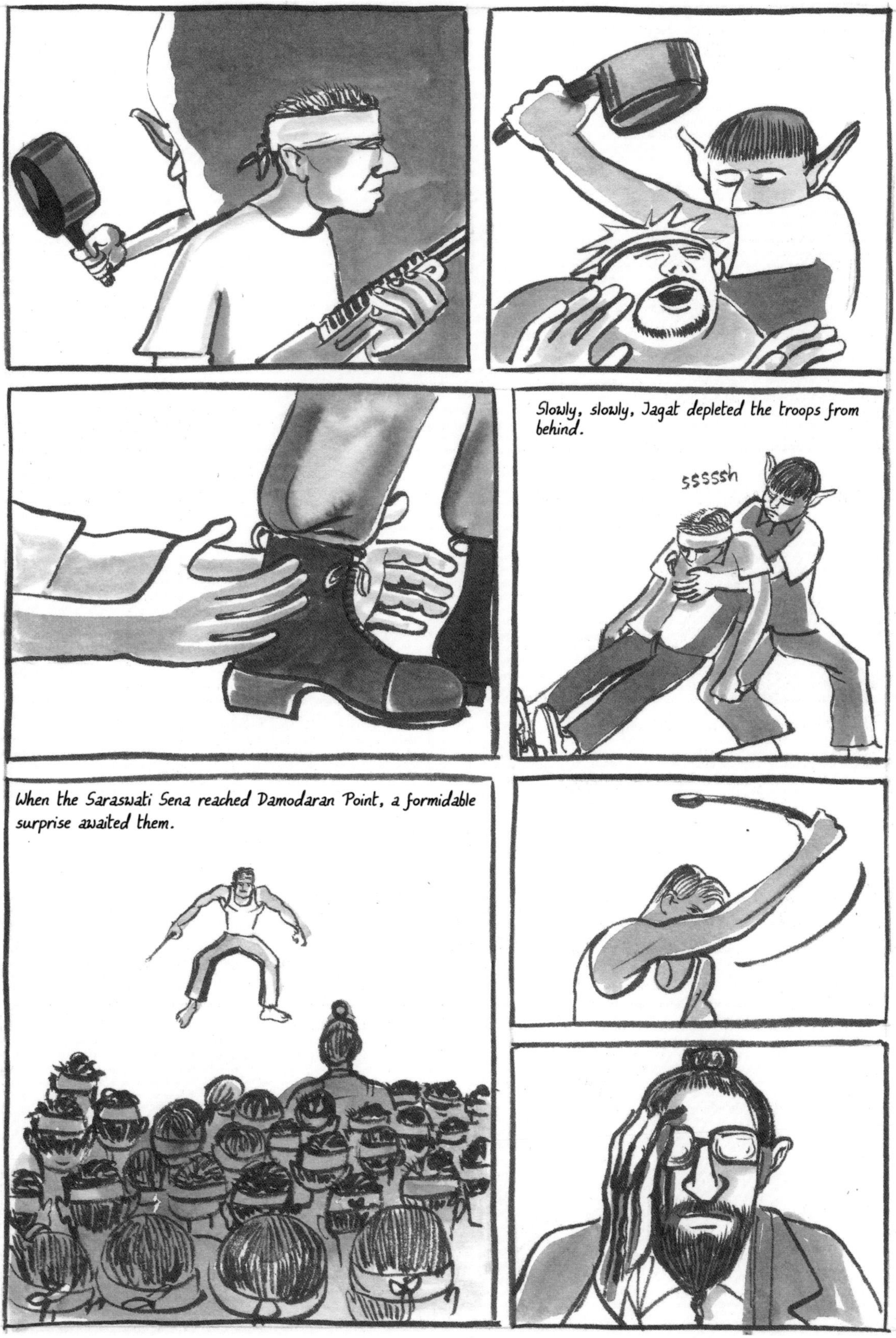

Slowly, slowly, Jagat depleted the troops from behind.
ssssssh
When the Saraswati Sena reached Damodaran Point, a formidable surprise awaited them.

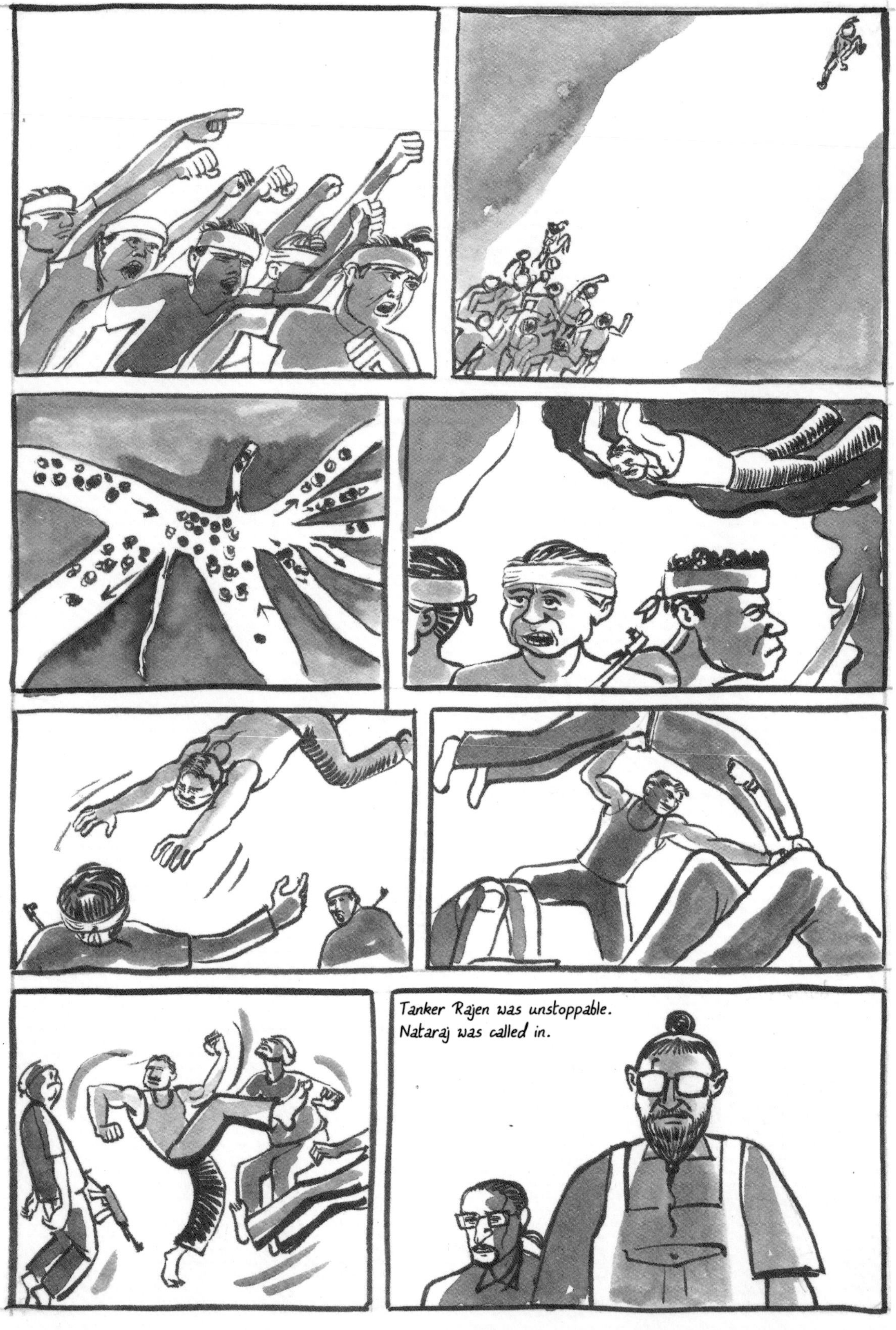
Tanker Rajen was unstoppable.
Nataraj was called in.

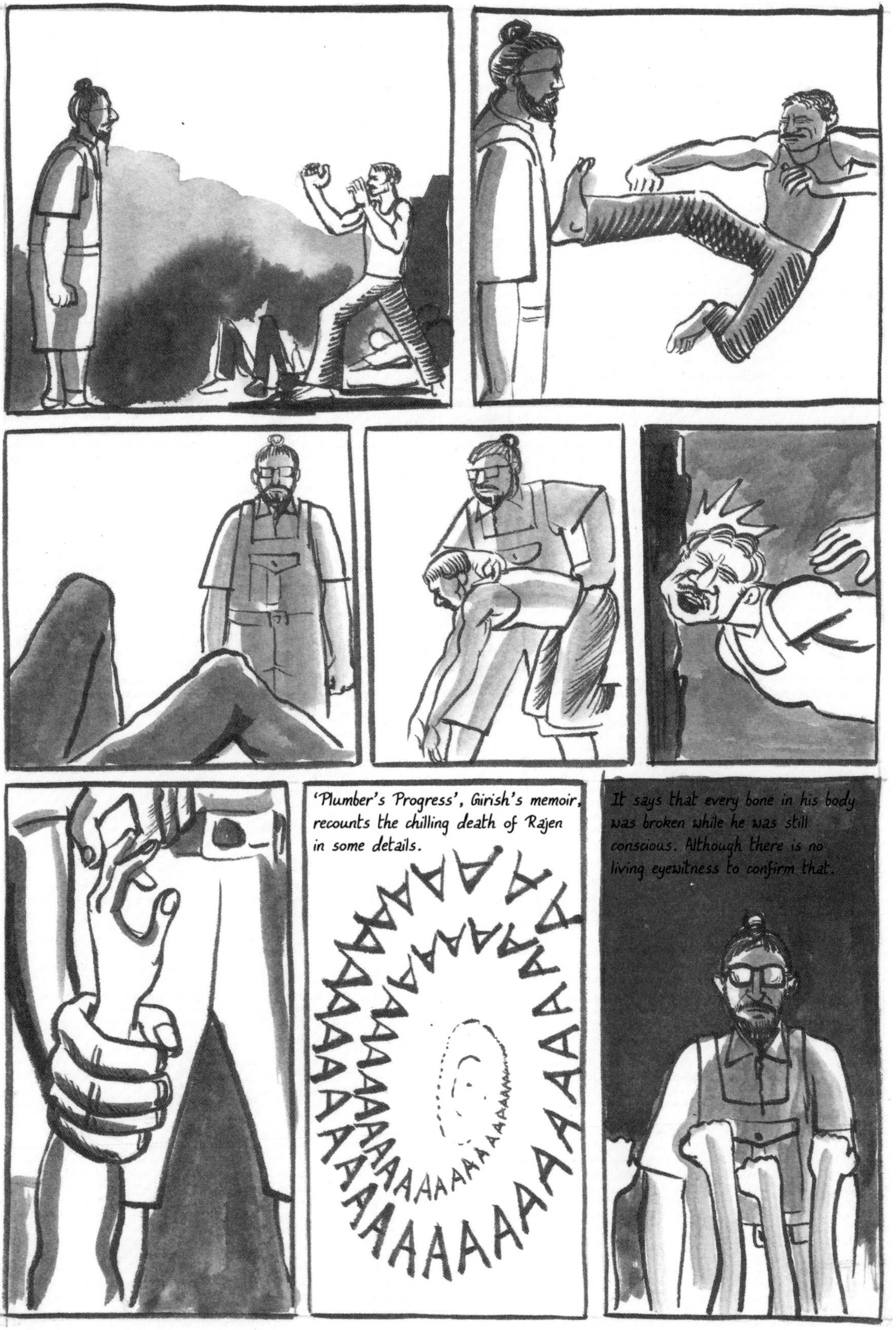
'Plumber's Progress', Girish's memoir, recounts the chilling death of Rajen in some details.
It says that every bone in his body was broken while he was still conscious. Although there is no living eyewitness to confirm that.

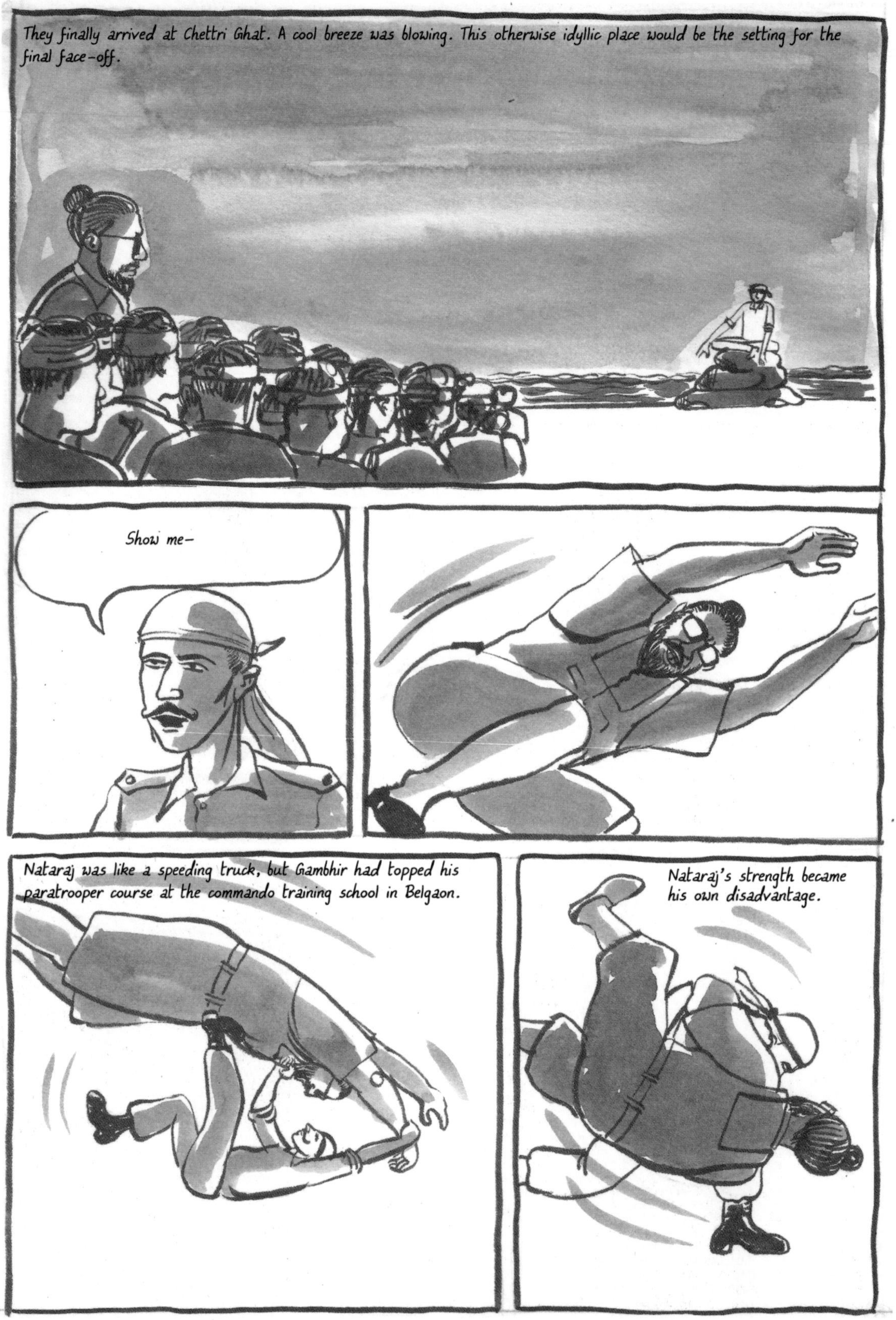
They finally arrived at Chettri Ghat. A cool breeze was blowing. This otherwise idyllic place would be the setting for the final face-off.
Show me-
Nataraj was like a speeding truck, but Gambhir had topped his paratrooper course at the commando training school in Belgaon.
Nataraj's strength became his own disadvantage.

138

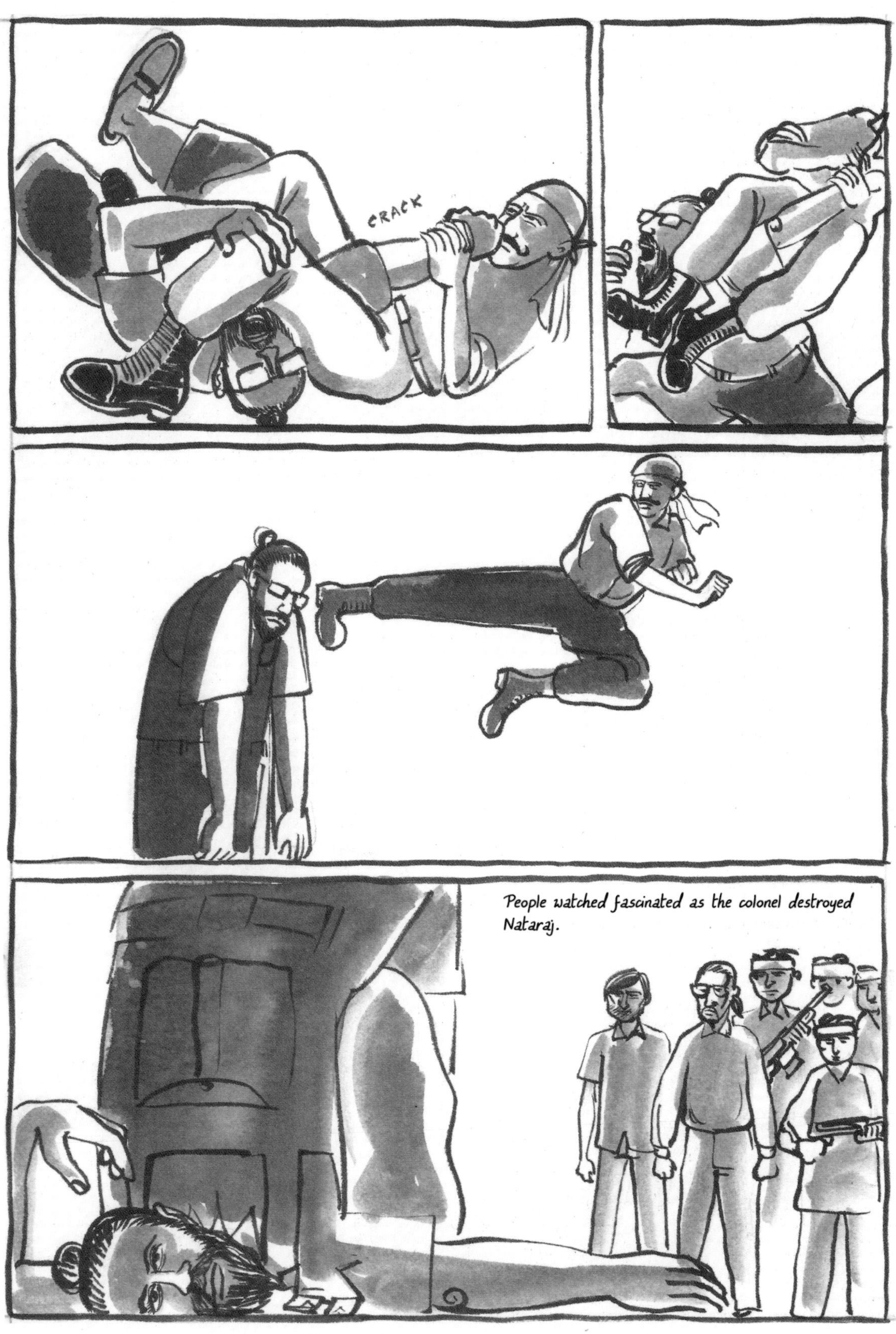
CRACK
People watched fascinated as the colonel destroyed Nataraj.

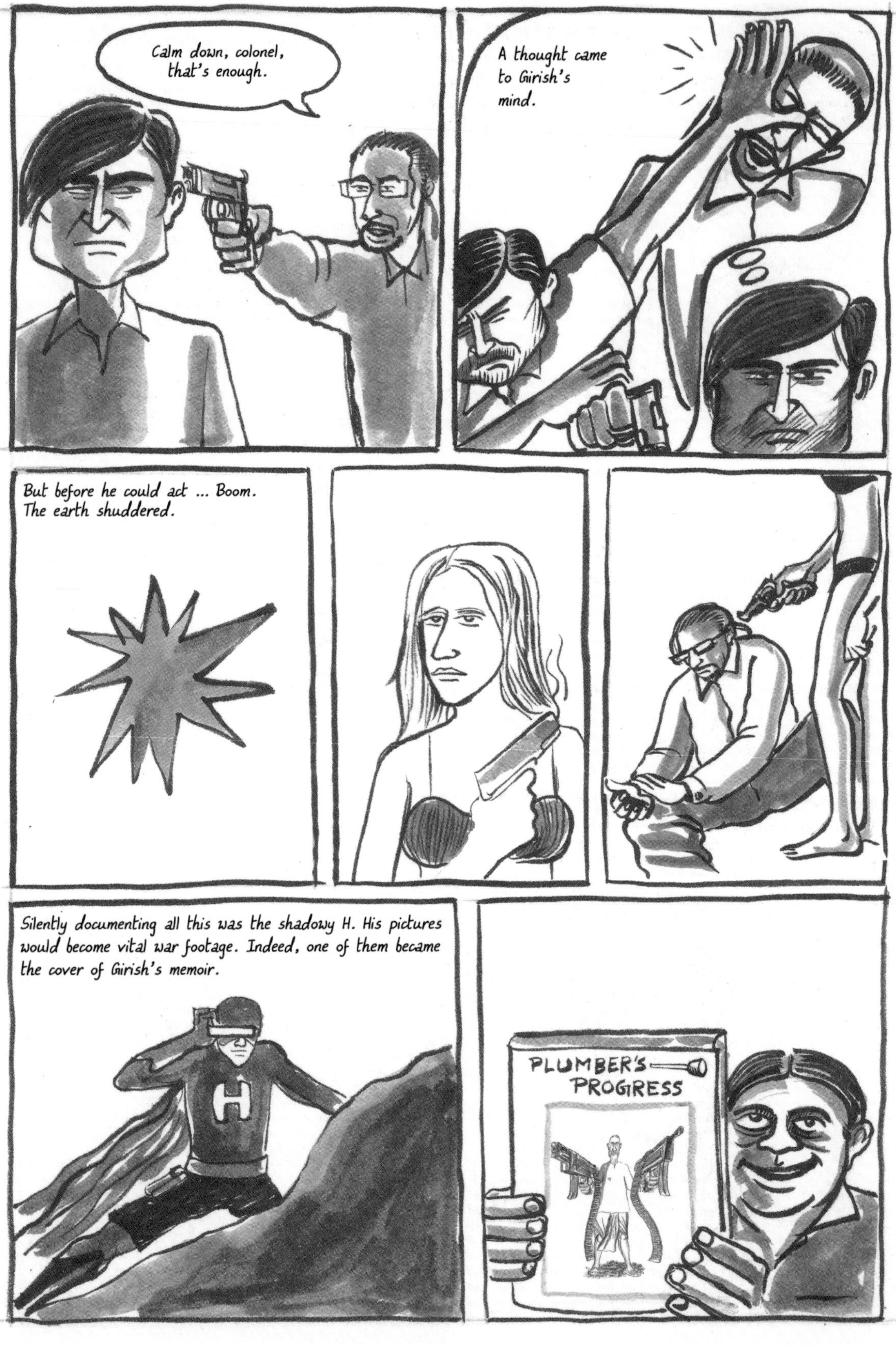
Calm down, colonel, that's enough.
A thought came to Girish's mind.
But before he could act ... Boom. The earth shuddered.
Silently documenting all this was the shadowy H. His pictures would become vital war footage. Indeed, one of them became the cover of Girish's memoir.
PLUMBER'S PROGRESS

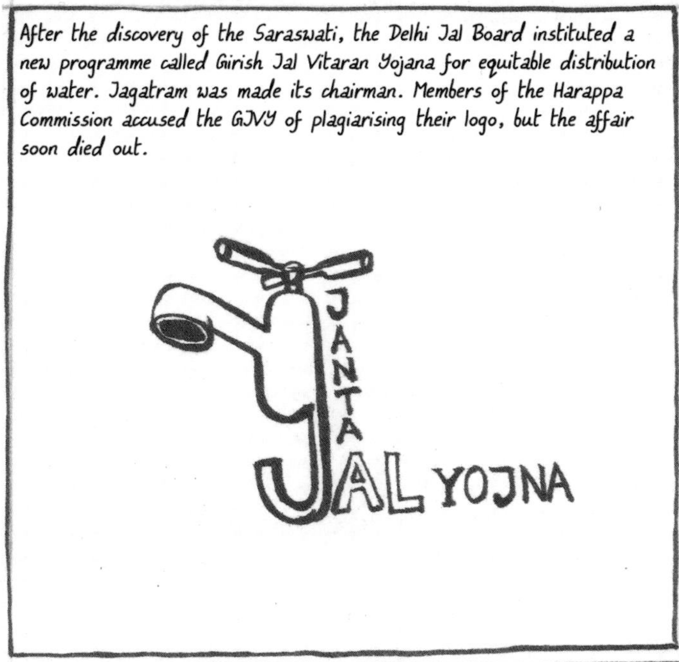
After the discovery of the Saraswati, the Delhi Jal Board instituted a new programme called Girish Jal Vitaran Yojana for equitable distribution of water. Jagatram was made its chairman. Members of the Harappa Commission accused the GJVY of plagiarising their logo, but the affair soon died out.
JANTA
JAL YOJNA

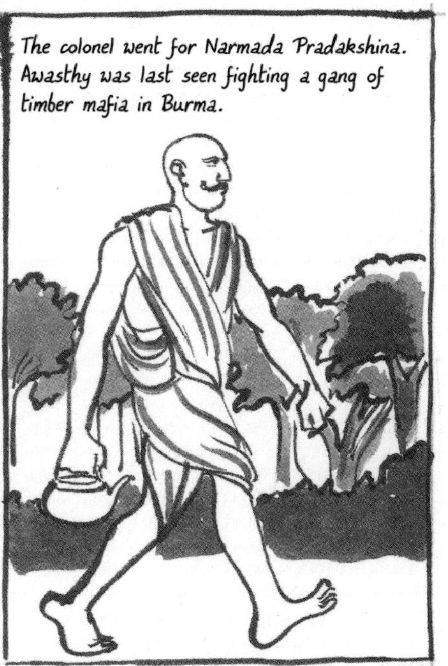
The colonel went for Narmada Pradakshina. Awasthy was last seen fighting a gang of timber mafia in Burma.

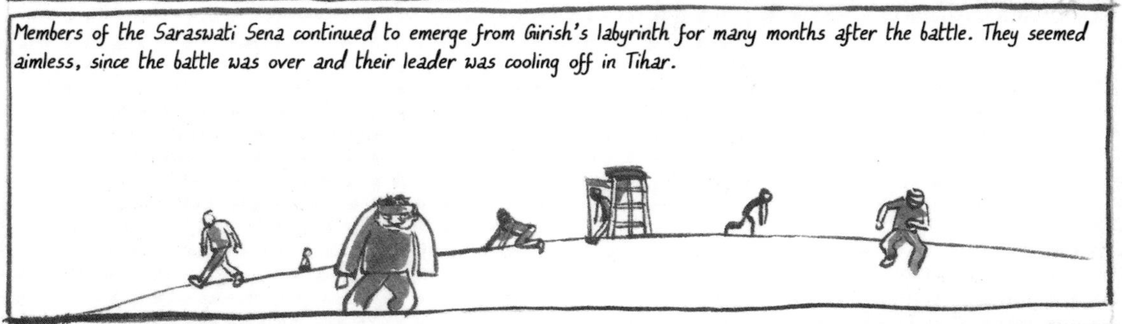
Members of the Saraswati Sena continued to emerge from Girish's labyrinth for many months after the battle. They seemed aimless, since the battle was over and their leader was cooling off in Tihar.

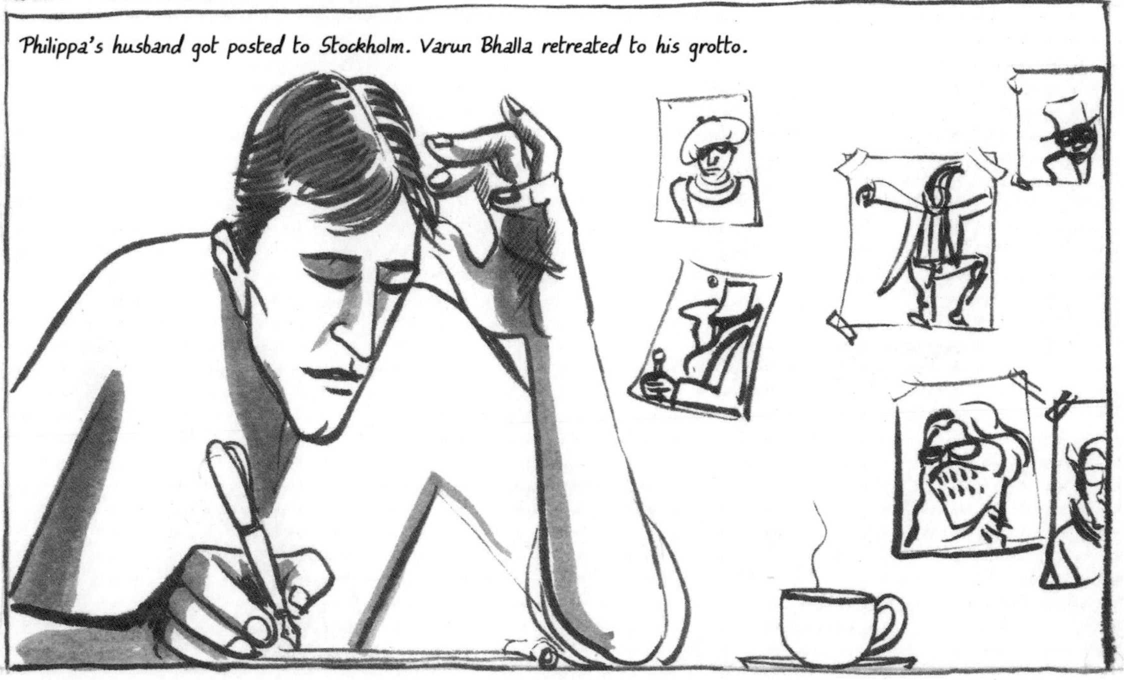
Philippa's husband got posted to Stockholm. Varun Bhalla retreated to his grotto.

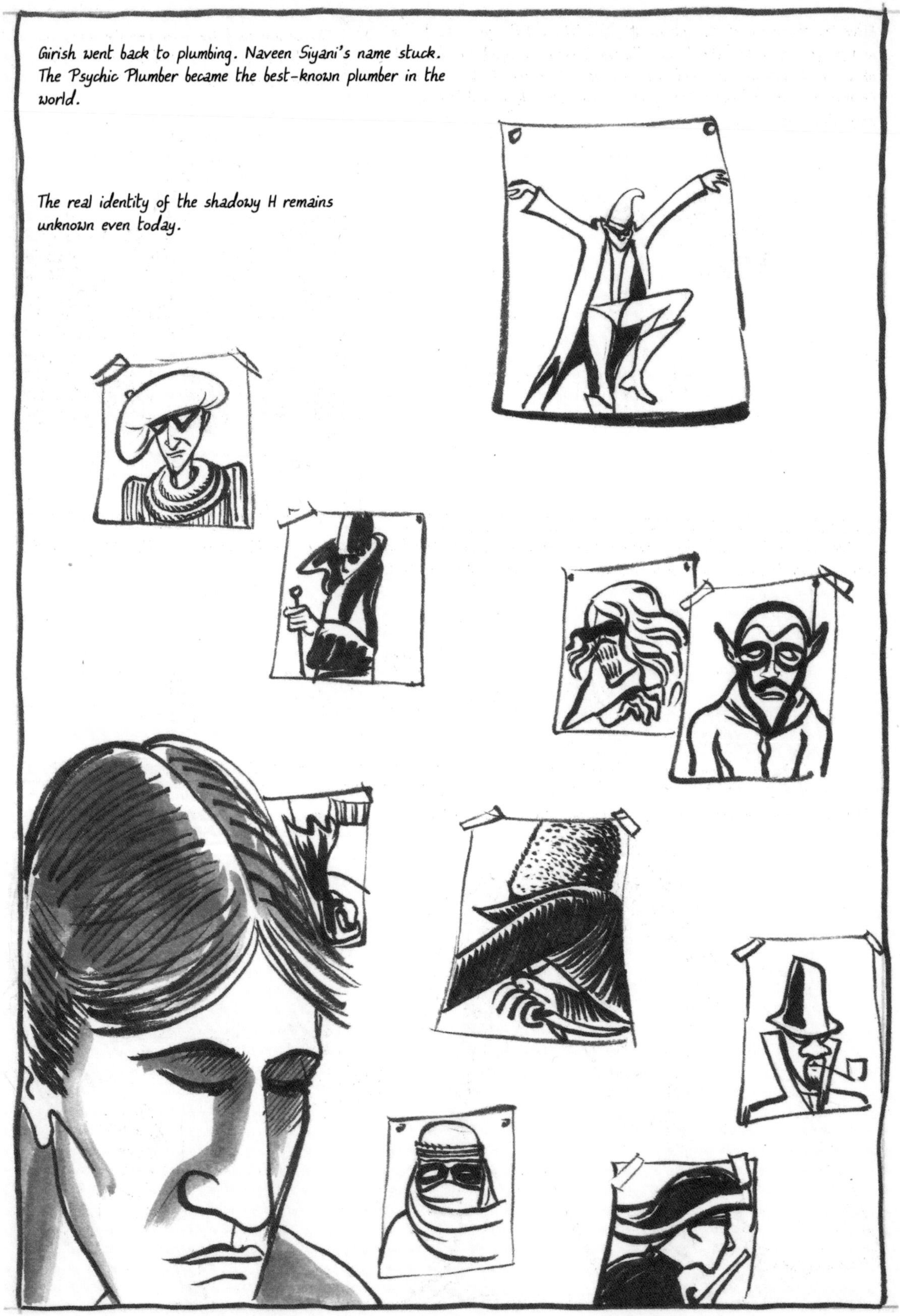
Girish went back to plumbing. Naveen Siyani's name stuck. The Psychic Plumber became the best-known plumber in the world.
The real identity of the shadowy H remains unknown even today.